DESTROYER

Story: Robert Kirkman
Art: Cory Walker
Colors: Val Staples
Letters: VC's Rus Wooton
Assistant Editor: Sebastian Girner
Editor: Axel Alonso

Collection Editor & Designer: Cory Levine
Assistant Editors: Alex Starbuck & John Denning
Editors, Special Projects: Jennifer Grünwald & Mark D. Beazley
Senior Editor, Special Projects: Jeff Youngquist
Senior Vice President of Sales: David Gabriel

Editor in Chief: Joe Quesada
Publisher: Dan Buckley
Executive Producer: Alan Fine

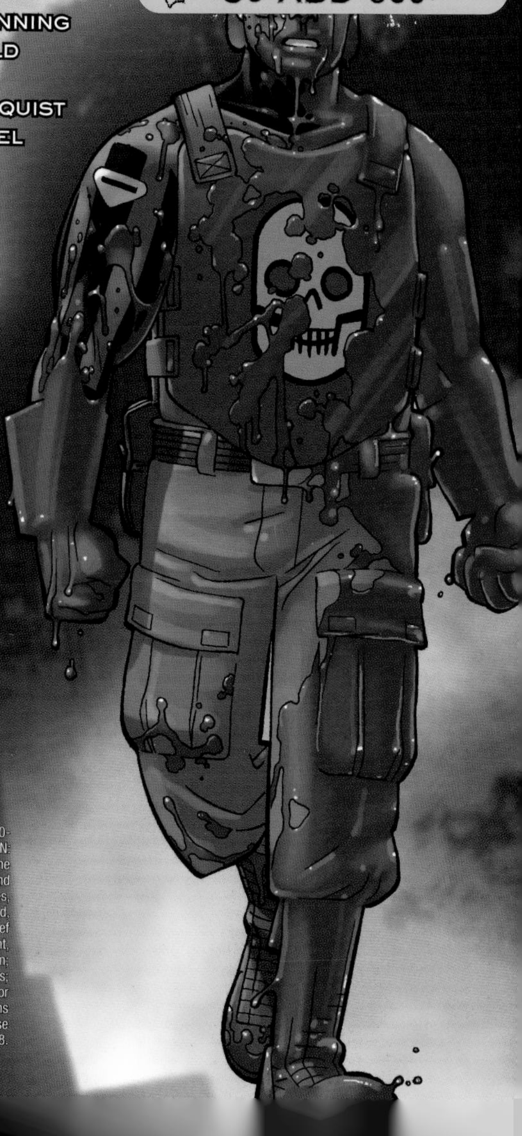

ESTROYER. Contains material originally published in magazine form as DESTROYER #1-5. First printing 2009. ISBN# 978-0-851-4246-1. Published by MARVEL PUBLISHING, INC., a subsidiary of MARVEL ENTERTAINMENT, INC. OFFICE OF PUBLICATION: 17 5th Avenue, New York, NY 10016. $24.99 per copy in the .S. (GST #R127032852); Canadian Agreement #40668537. **Printed in the U.S.A.** ALAN FINE, EVP - Office Of The Chief xecutive Marvel Entertainment, Inc. & CMO Marvel Characters B.V.; DAN BUCKLEY, Chief Executive Officer and Publisher - Print, nimation & Digital Media; JIM SOKOLOWSKI, Chief Operating Officer; DAVID GABRIEL, SVP of Publishing Sales & Circulation; AVID BOGART, SVP of Business Affairs & Talent Management; MICHAEL PASCIULLO, VP Merchandising & Communications; M O'KEEFE, VP of Operations & Logistics; DAN CARR, Executive Director of Publishing Technology; JUSTIN F. GABRIE, Director Publishing & Editorial Operations; SUSAN CRESPI, Editorial Operations Manager; ALEX MORALES, Publishing Operations anager; STAN LEE, Chairman Emeritus. For information regarding advertising in Marvel Comics or on Marvel.com, please ontact Mitch Dane, Advertising Director, at mdane@marvel.com. For Marvel subscription inquiries, please call 800-217-9158. **anufactured between 9/28/09 and 10/28/09 by WORLD COLOR PRESS INC., VERSAILLES, KY, USA.**

)987654321

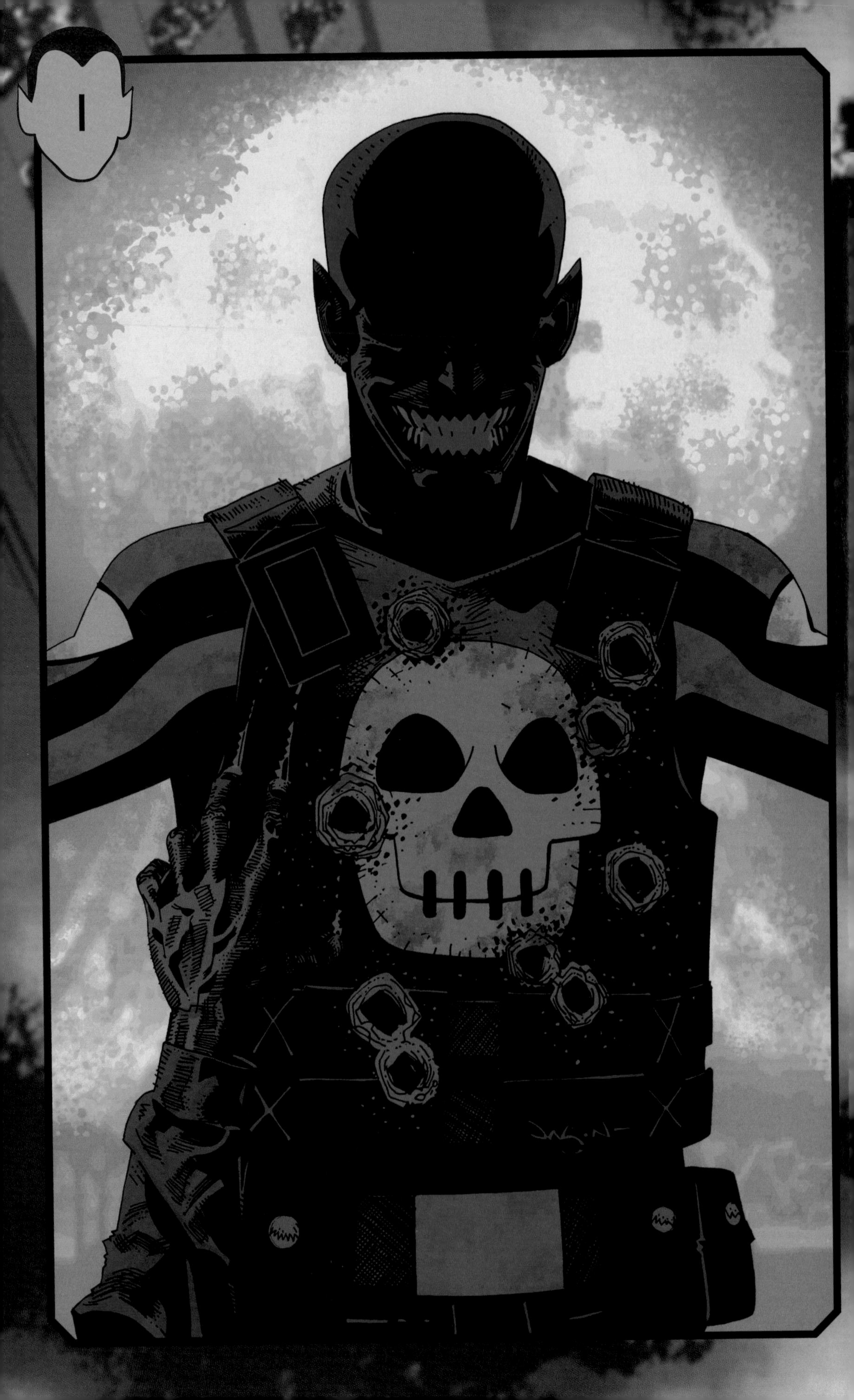

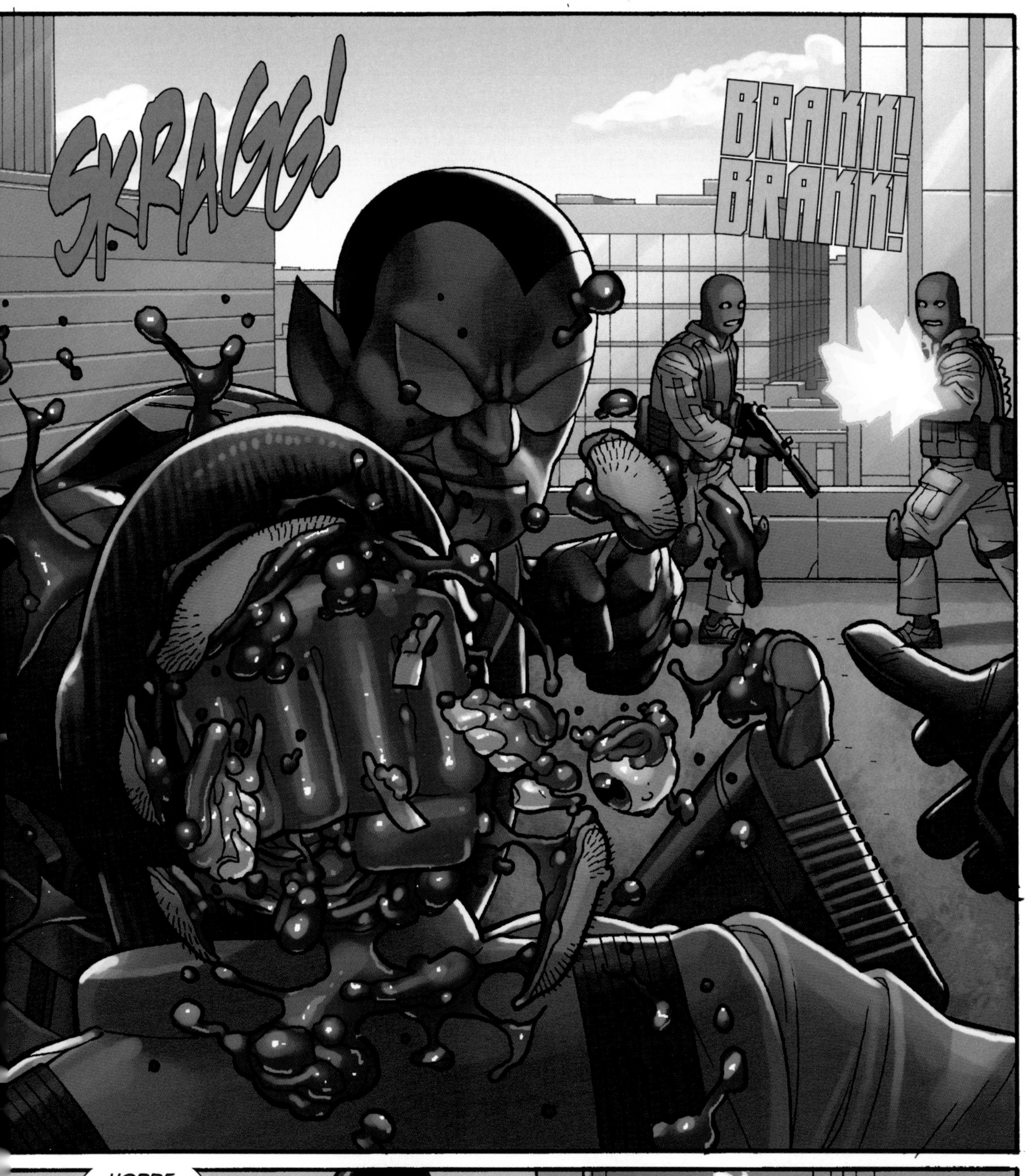
SKRAGG!
BRAKK! BRAKK!

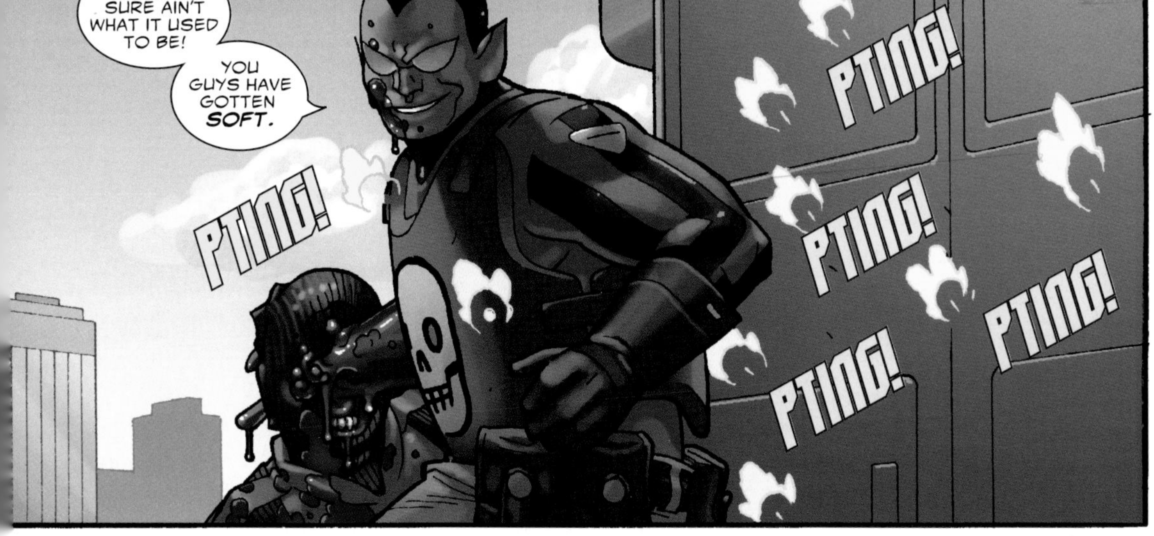
HORDE SURE AIN'T WHAT IT USED TO BE!
YOU GUYS HAVE GOTTEN SOFT.
PTING!
PTING!
PTING!
PTING!
PTING!

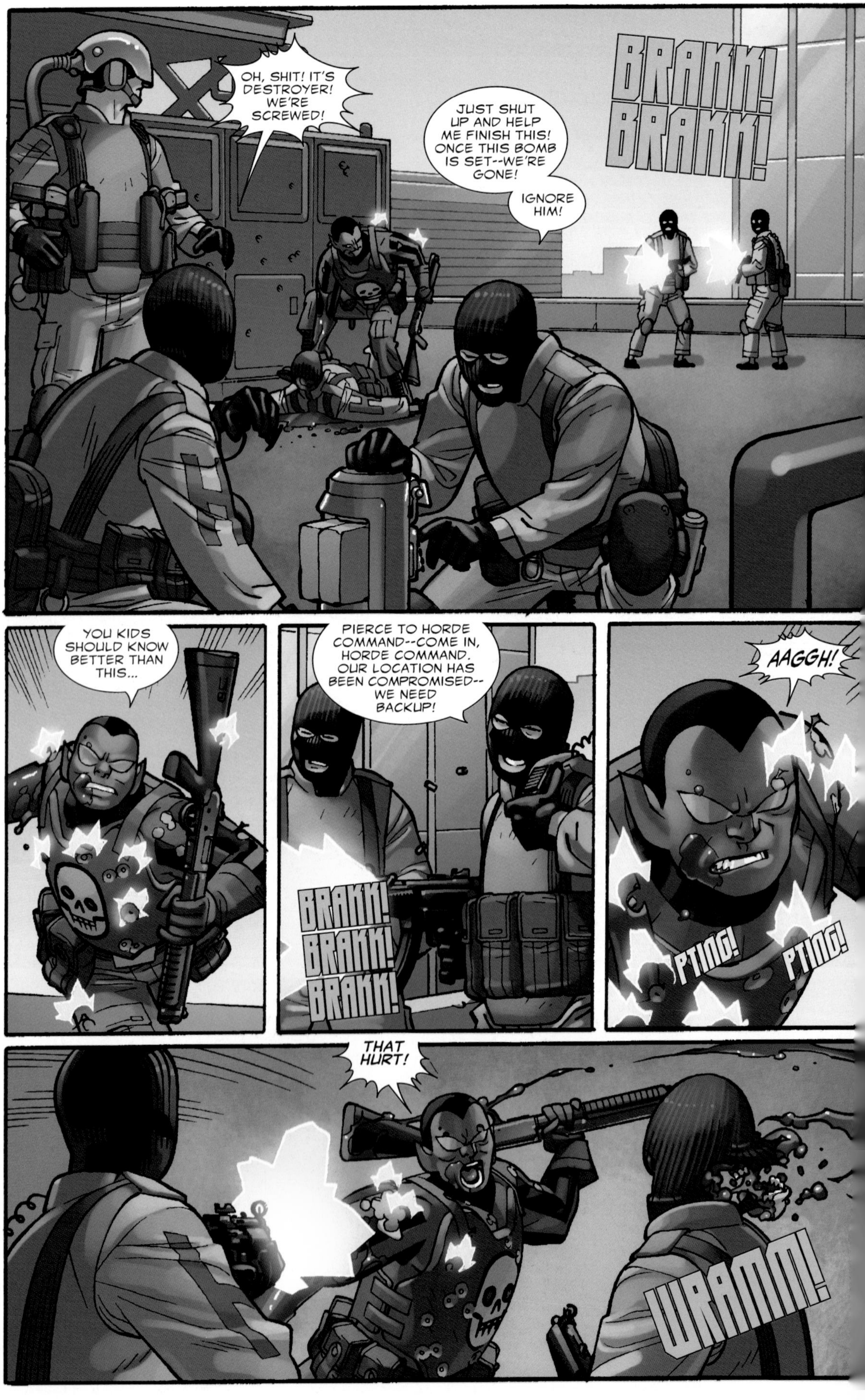
OH, SHIT! IT'S DESTROYER! WE'RE SCREWED!
JUST SHUT UP AND HELP ME FINISH THIS! ONCE THIS BOMB IS SET--WE'RE GONE!
IGNORE HIM!
BRAKK! BRAKK!
YOU KIDS SHOULD KNOW BETTER THAN THIS...
PIERCE TO HORDE COMMAND--COME IN, HORDE COMMAND. OUR LOCATION HAS BEEN COMPROMISED--WE NEED BACKUP!
BRAKK! BRAKK! BRAKK!
AAGGH!
PTING! PTING!
THAT HURT!
WRAMM!

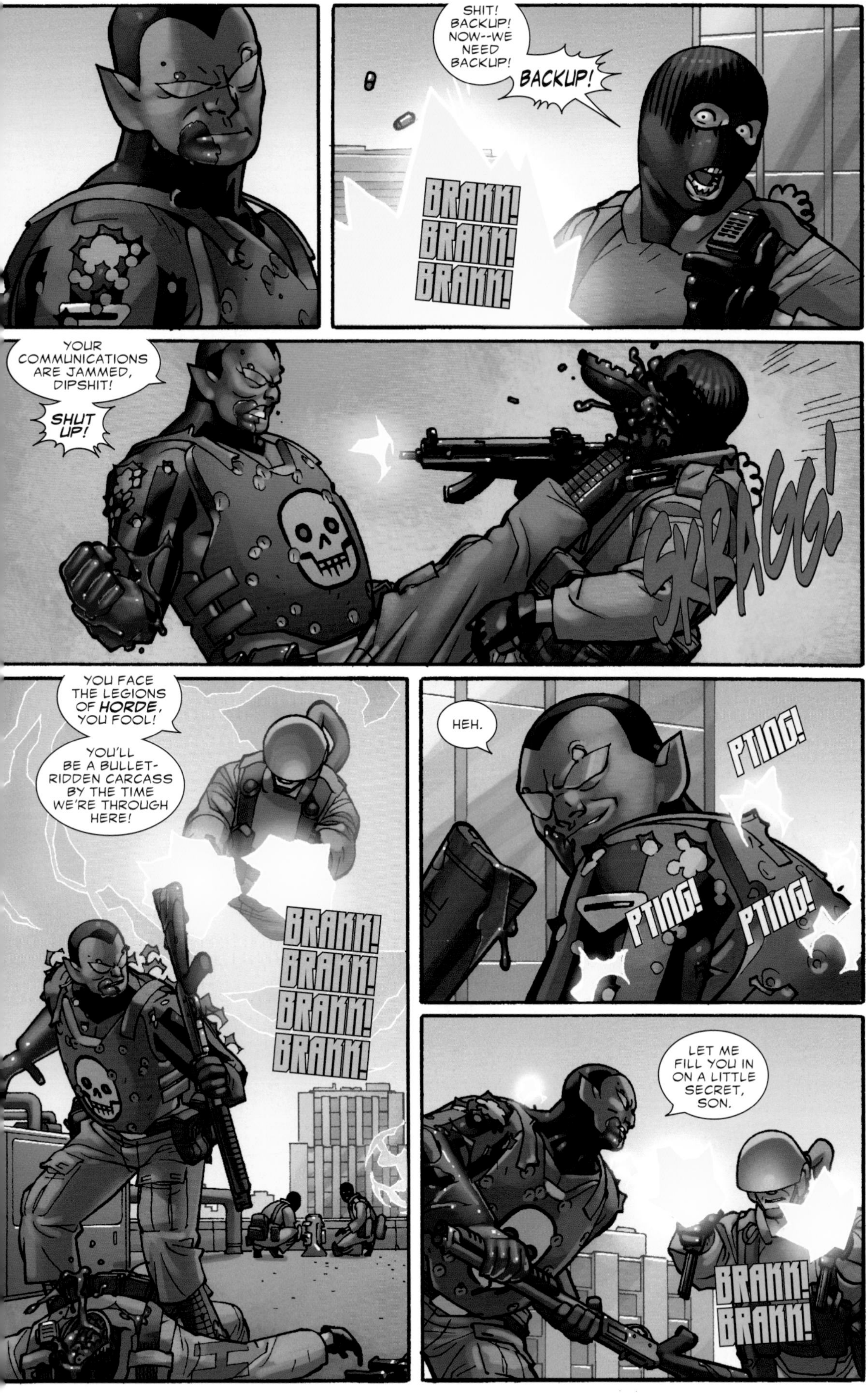
SHIT! BACKUP! NOW--WE NEED BACKUP!
BACKUP!
BRAKK! BRAKK! BRAKK!
YOUR COMMUNICATIONS ARE JAMMED, DIPSHIT!
SHUT UP!
SKRAGG!
YOU FACE THE LEGIONS OF HORDE, YOU FOOL!
YOU'LL BE A BULLET-RIDDEN CARCASS BY THE TIME WE'RE THROUGH HERE!
BRAKK! BRAKK! BRAKK! BRAKK!
HEH.
PTING!
PTING!
PTING!
LET ME FILL YOU IN ON A LITTLE SECRET, SON.
BRAKK! BRAKK!

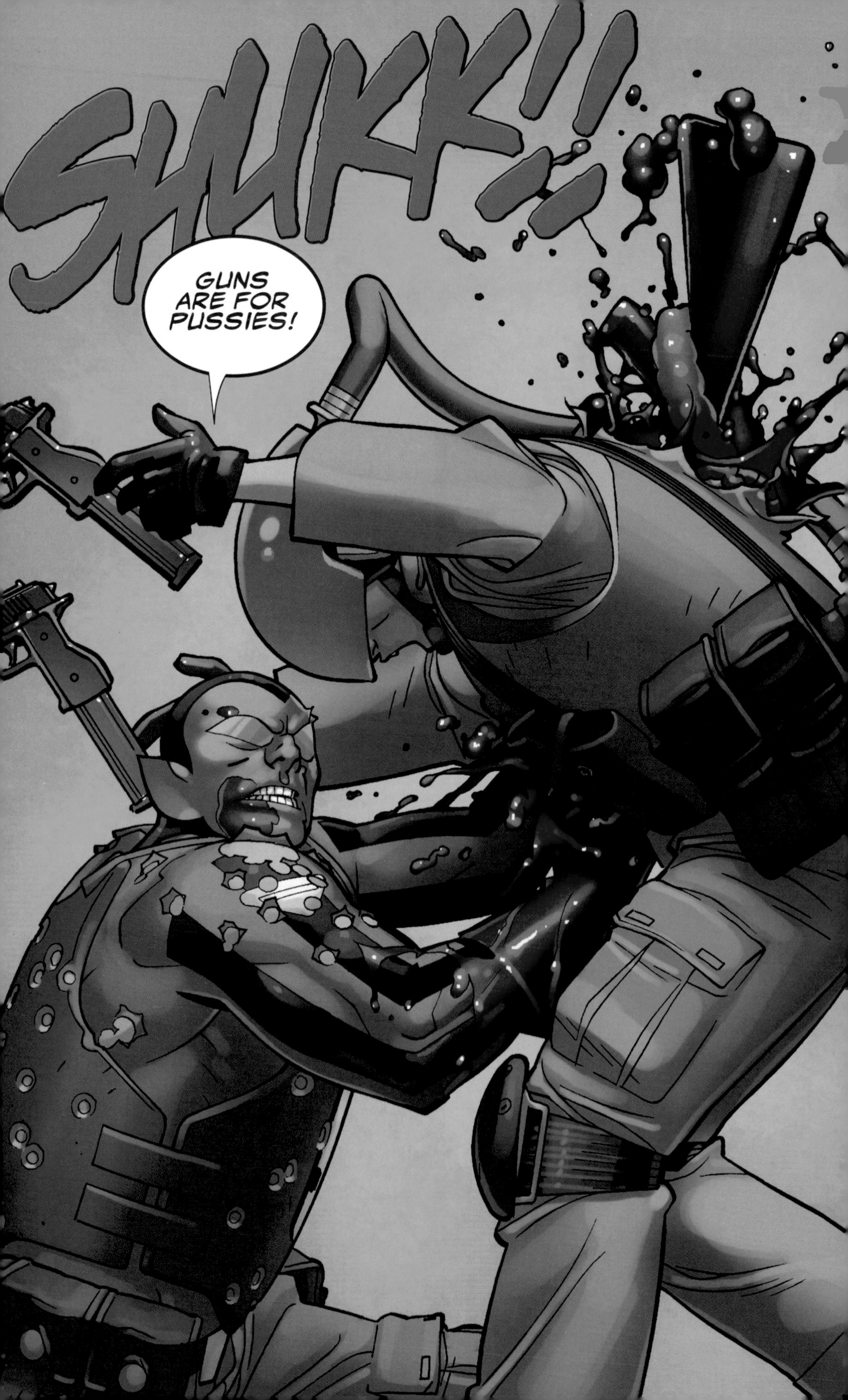
SHUKK!!
GUNS ARE FOR PUSSIES!

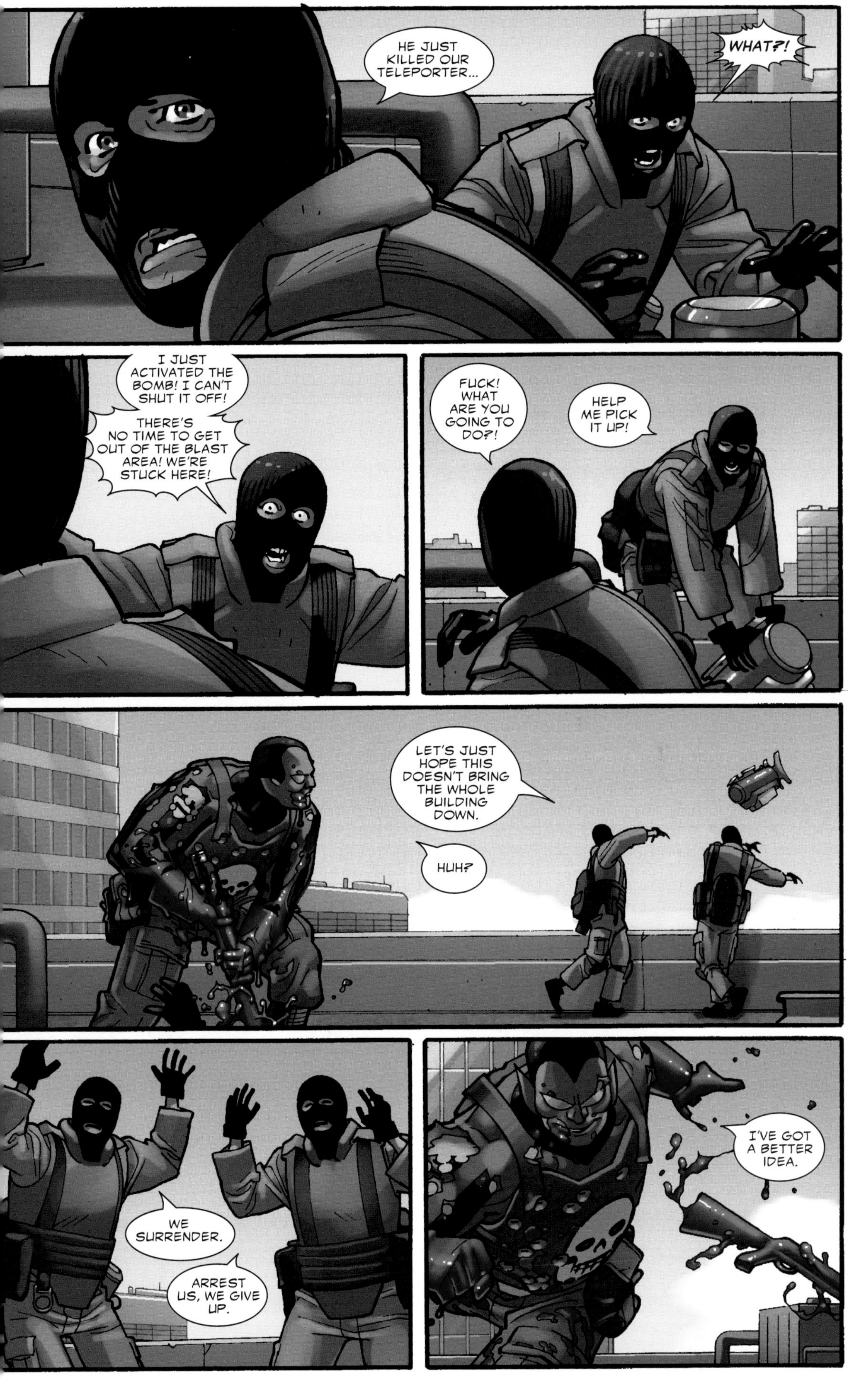
HE JUST KILLED OUR TELEPORTER...
WHAT?!
I JUST ACTIVATED THE BOMB! I CAN'T SHUT IT OFF!
THERE'S NO TIME TO GET OUT OF THE BLAST AREA! WE'RE STUCK HERE!
FUCK! WHAT ARE YOU GOING TO DO?!
HELP ME PICK IT UP!
LET'S JUST HOPE THIS DOESN'T BRING THE WHOLE BUILDING DOWN.
HUH?
WE SURRENDER.
ARREST US, WE GIVE UP.
I'VE GOT A BETTER IDEA.

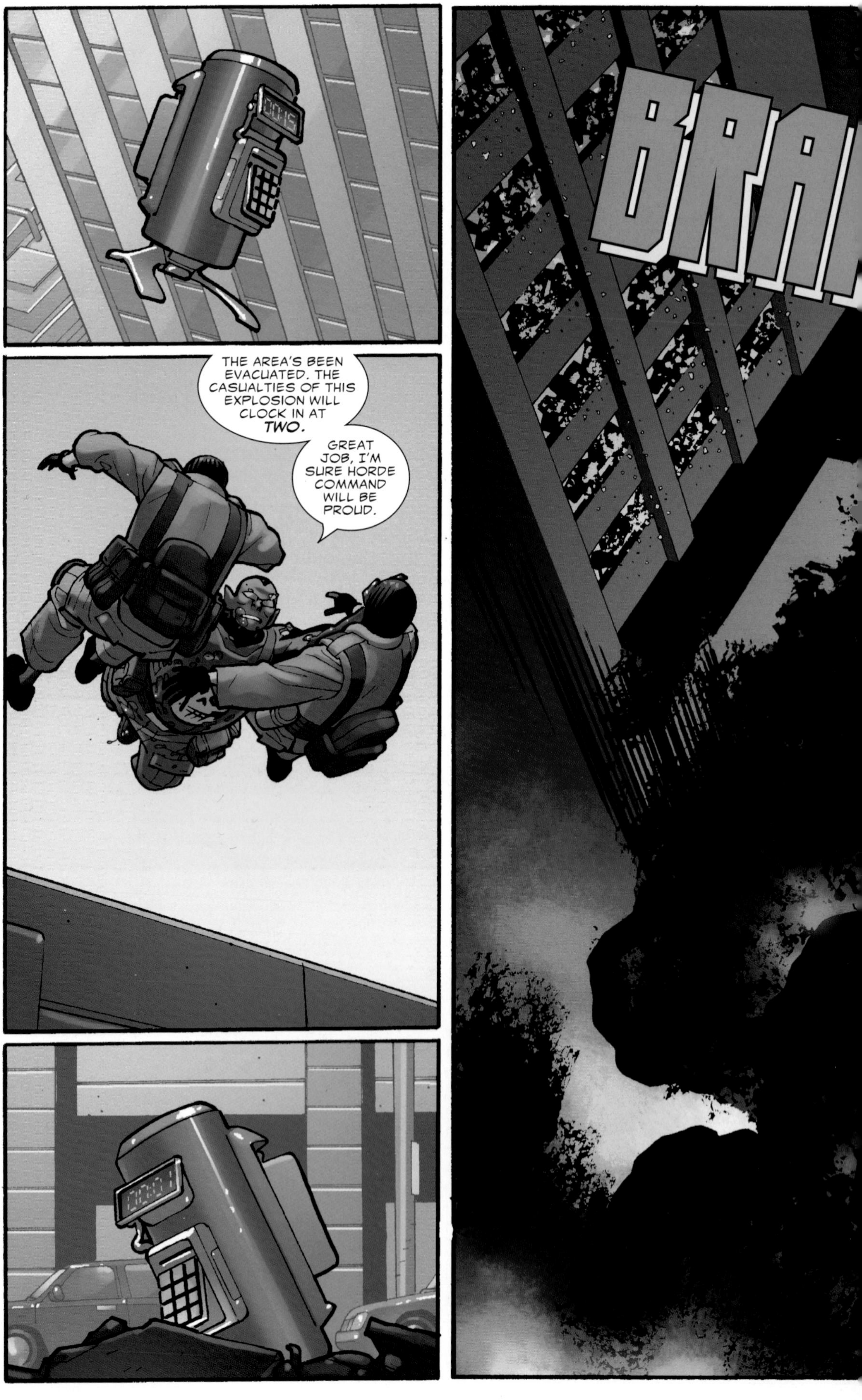
00:15
THE AREA'S BEEN EVACUATED. THE CASUALTIES OF THIS EXPLOSION WILL CLOCK IN AT TWO.
GREAT JOB, I'M SURE HORDE COMMAND WILL BE PROUD.
BRA

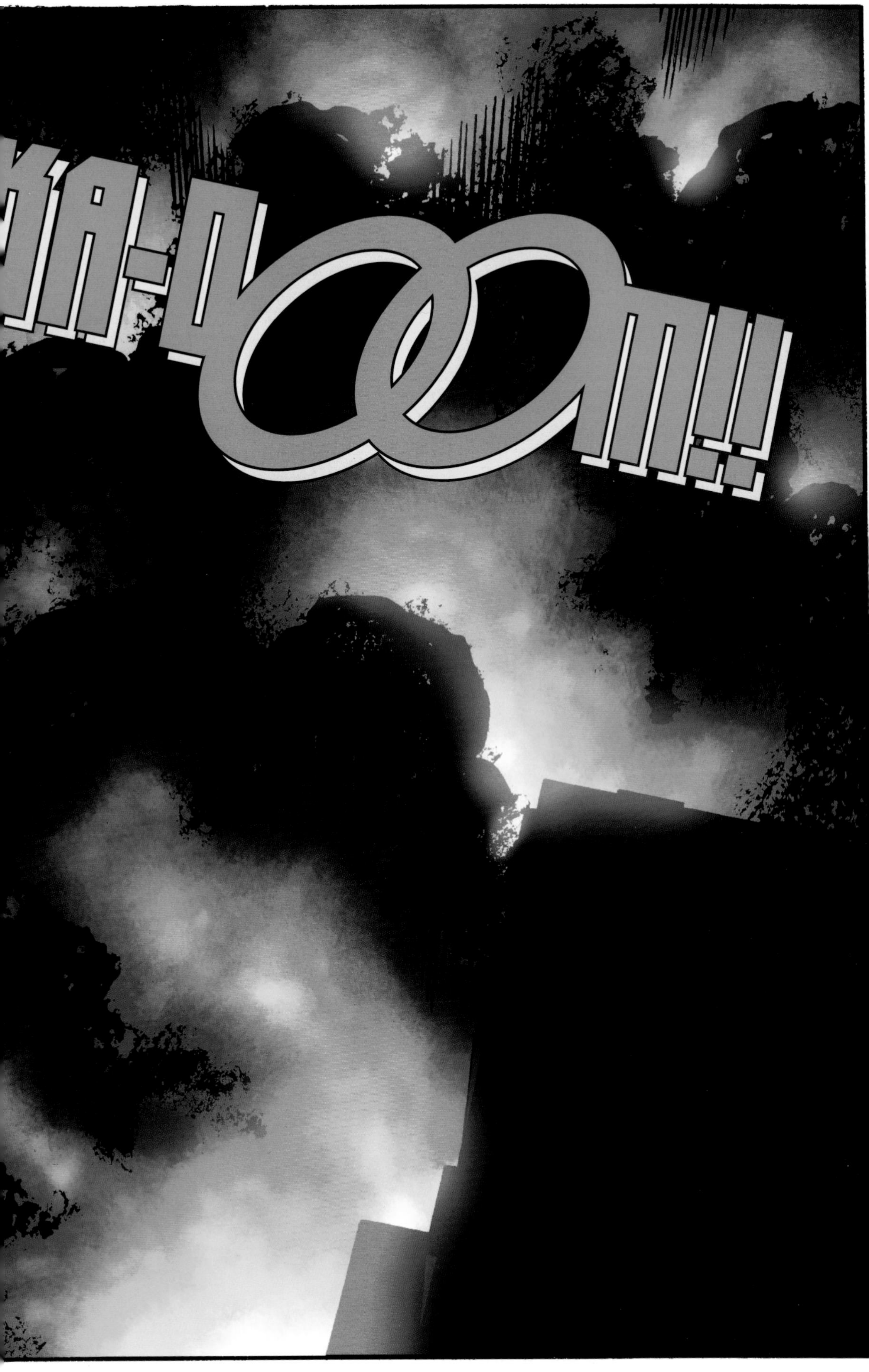
KA-DOOM!!

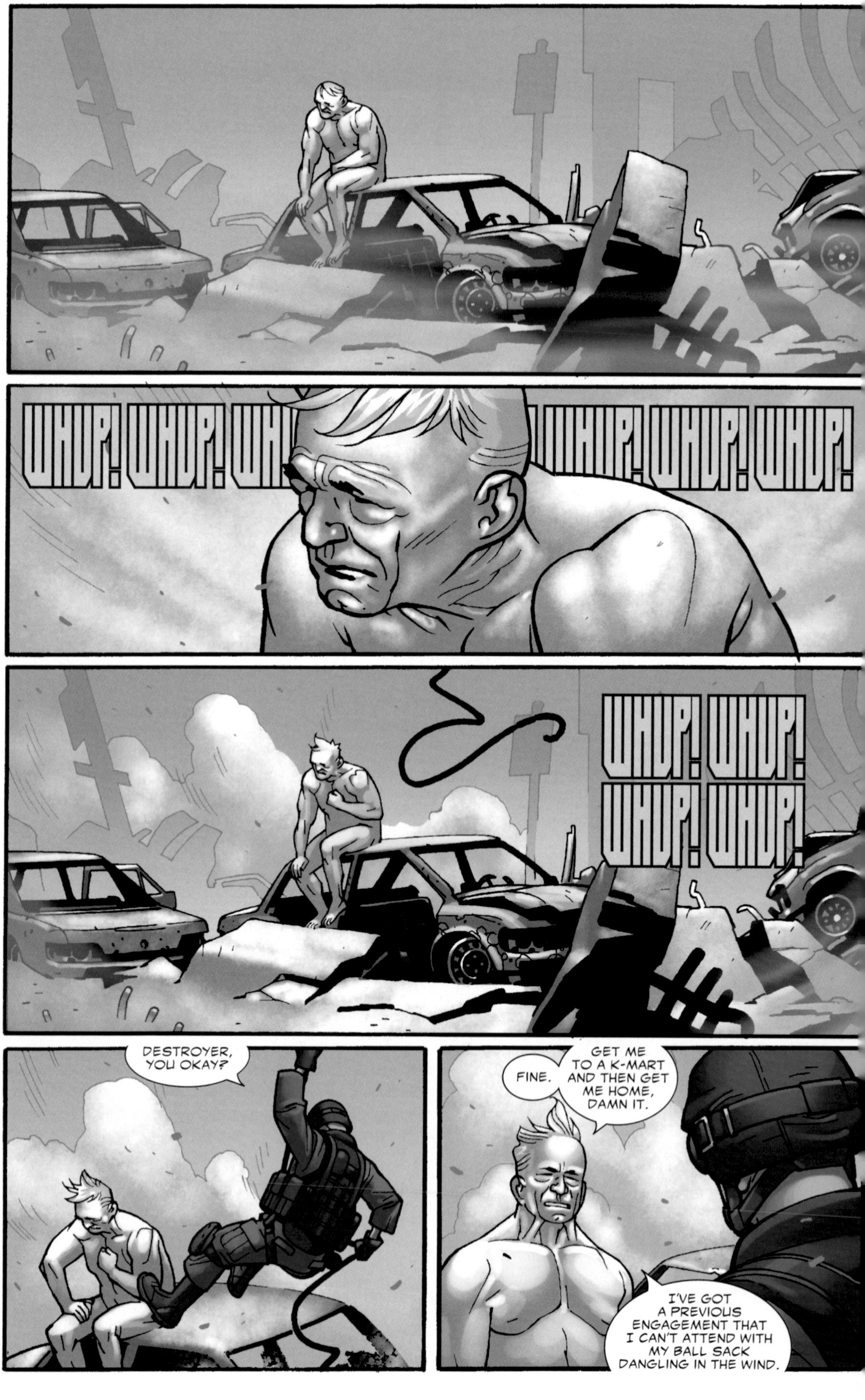
WHUP! WHUP! WHUP! WHUP! WHUP! WHUP!
WHUP! WHUP! WHUP! WHUP!
DESTROYER, YOU OKAY?
FINE.
GET ME TO A K-MART AND THEN GET ME HOME, DAMN IT.
I'VE GOT A PREVIOUS ENGAGEMENT THAT I CAN'T ATTEND WITH MY BALL SACK DANGLING IN THE WIND.

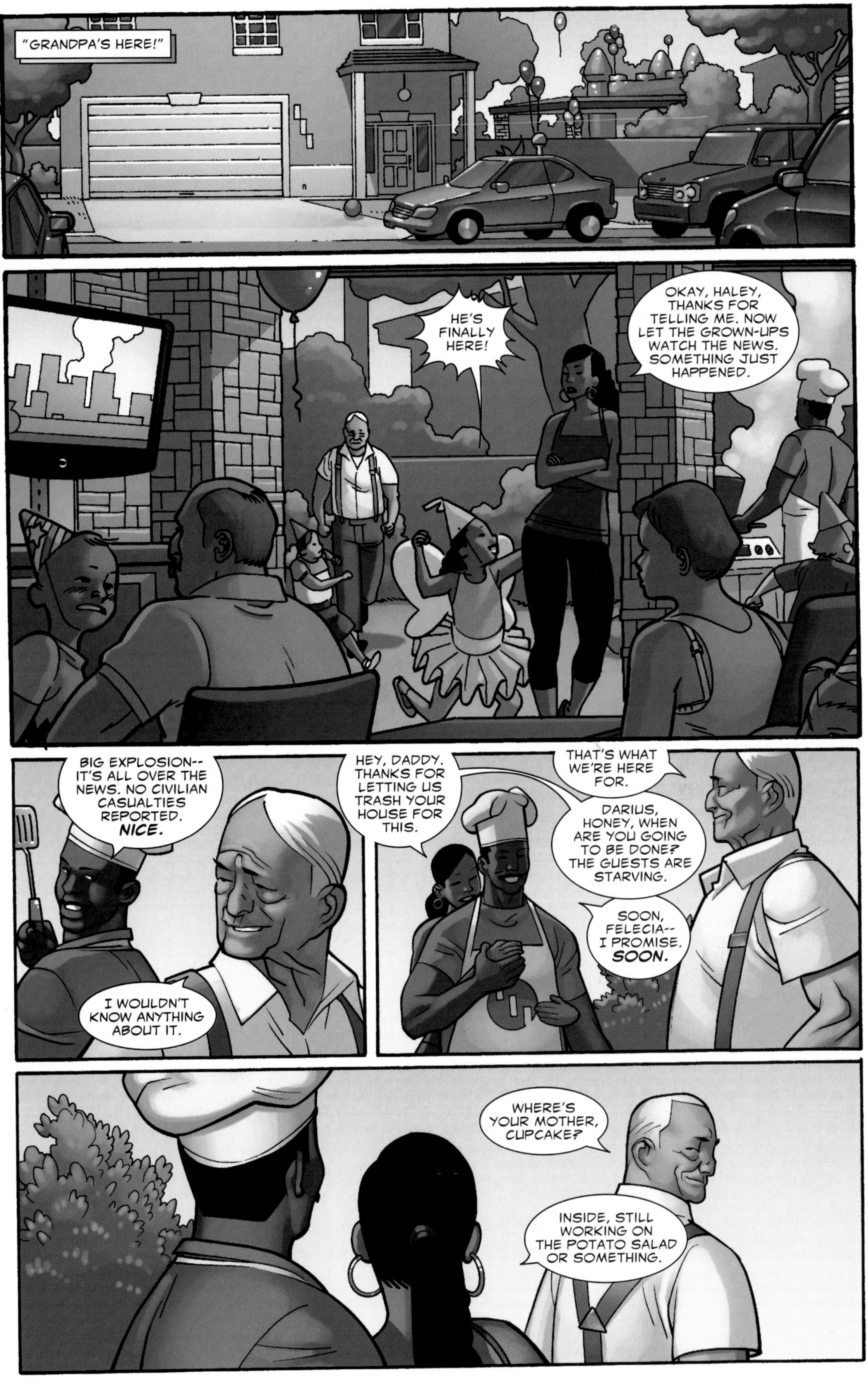
"GRANDPA'S HERE!"
HE'S FINALLY HERE!
OKAY, HALEY, THANKS FOR TELLING ME. NOW LET THE GROWN-UPS WATCH THE NEWS. SOMETHING JUST HAPPENED.
BIG EXPLOSION-- IT'S ALL OVER THE NEWS. NO CIVILIAN CASUALTIES REPORTED. **NICE.**
I WOULDN'T KNOW ANYTHING ABOUT IT.
HEY, DADDY. THANKS FOR LETTING US TRASH YOUR HOUSE FOR THIS.
THAT'S WHAT WE'RE HERE FOR.
DARIUS, HONEY, WHEN ARE YOU GOING TO BE DONE? THE GUESTS ARE STARVING.
SOON, FELECIA-- I PROMISE. **SOON.**
WHERE'S YOUR MOTHER, CUPCAKE?
INSIDE, STILL WORKING ON THE POTATO SALAD OR SOMETHING.

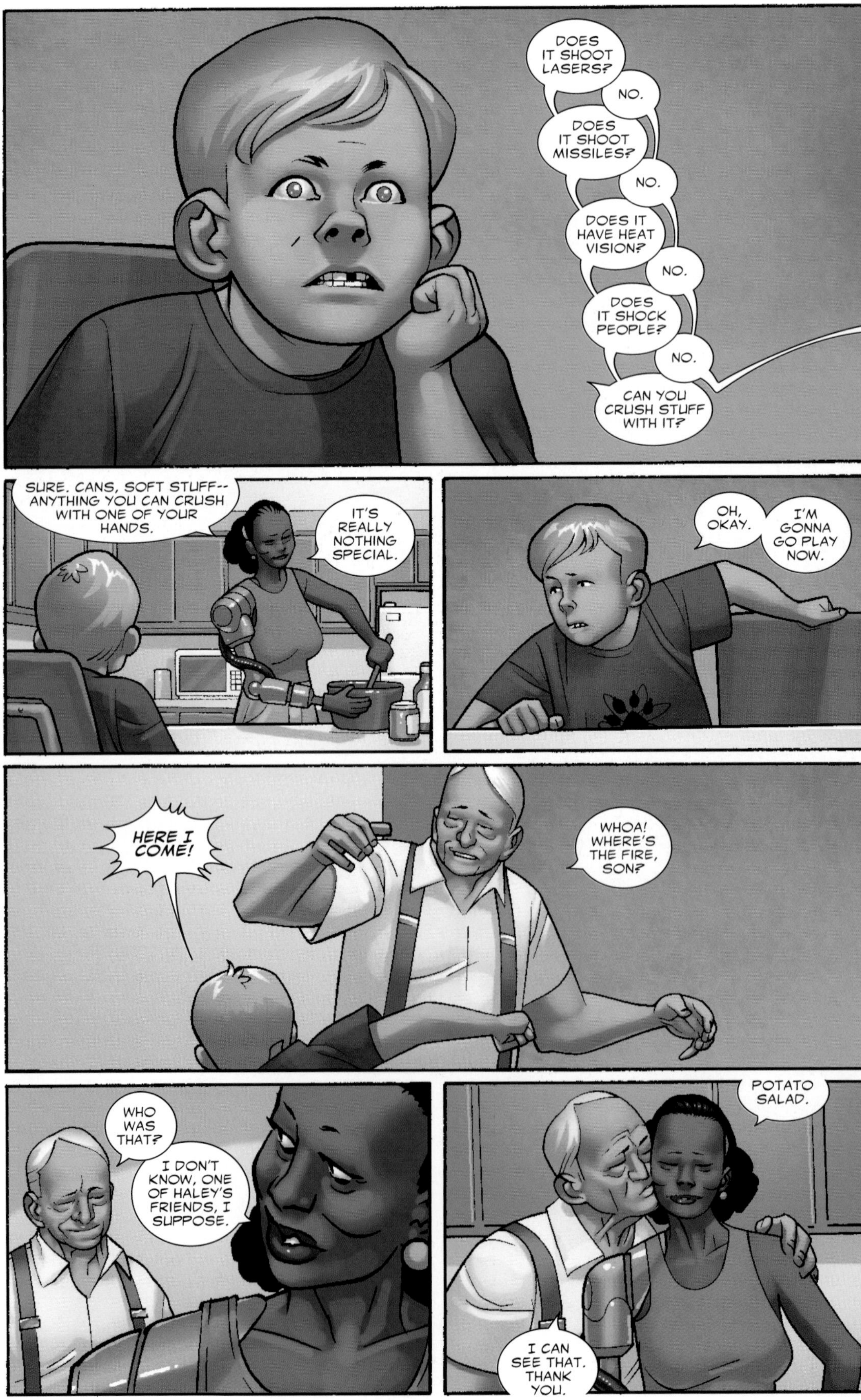
DOES IT SHOOT LASERS?
NO.
DOES IT SHOOT MISSILES?
NO.
DOES IT HAVE HEAT VISION?
NO.
DOES IT SHOCK PEOPLE?
NO.
CAN YOU CRUSH STUFF WITH IT?
SURE. CANS, SOFT STUFF-- ANYTHING YOU CAN CRUSH WITH ONE OF YOUR HANDS.
IT'S REALLY NOTHING SPECIAL.
OH, OKAY.
I'M GONNA GO PLAY NOW.
HERE I COME!
WHOA! WHERE'S THE FIRE, SON?
WHO WAS THAT?
I DON'T KNOW, ONE OF HALEY'S FRIENDS, I SUPPOSE.
POTATO SALAD.
I CAN SEE THAT. THANK YOU.

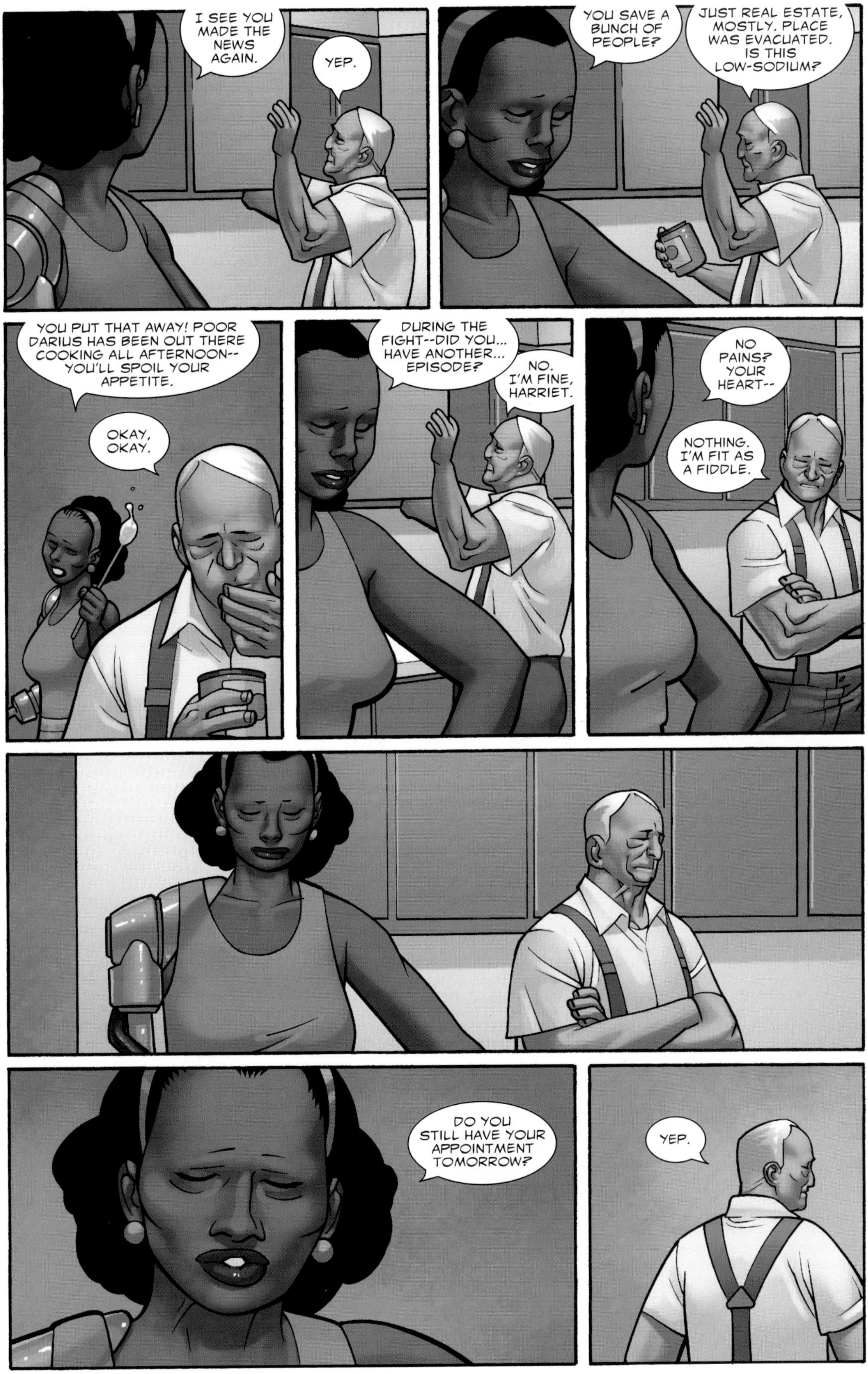
I SEE YOU MADE THE NEWS AGAIN.
YEP.
YOU SAVE A BUNCH OF PEOPLE?
JUST REAL ESTATE, MOSTLY. PLACE WAS EVACUATED. IS THIS LOW-SODIUM?
YOU PUT THAT AWAY! POOR DARIUS HAS BEEN OUT THERE COOKING ALL AFTERNOON--YOU'LL SPOIL YOUR APPETITE.
OKAY, OKAY.
DURING THE FIGHT--DID YOU... HAVE ANOTHER... EPISODE?
NO. I'M FINE, HARRIET.
NO PAINS? YOUR HEART--
NOTHING. I'M FIT AS A FIDDLE.
DO YOU STILL HAVE YOUR APPOINTMENT TOMORROW?
YEP.

"YOU'RE *DYING*."

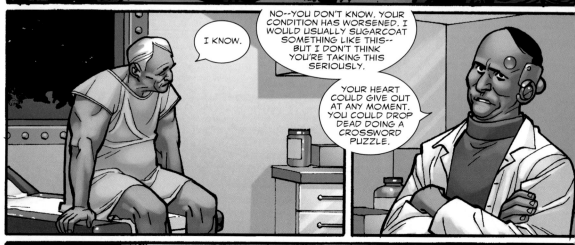

I KNOW.

NO--YOU DON'T KNOW. YOUR CONDITION HAS WORSENED. I WOULD USUALLY SUGARCOAT SOMETHING LIKE THIS-- BUT I DON'T THINK YOU'RE TAKING THIS SERIOUSLY.

YOUR HEART COULD GIVE OUT AT ANY MOMENT. YOU COULD DROP DEAD DOING A CROSSWORD PUZZLE.

LUCKY FOR ME, I DON'T TOUCH THE THINGS.

I KNOW-- YOU'RE TOO BUSY JUMPING OUT OF HELICOPTERS AND BOUNCING BULLETS OFF YOUR SKULL. YOU'VE GOT TO *STOP THIS*, KEENE.

YOU HAVE TO *RETIRE*.

YOU KNOW I CAN'T DO THAT.

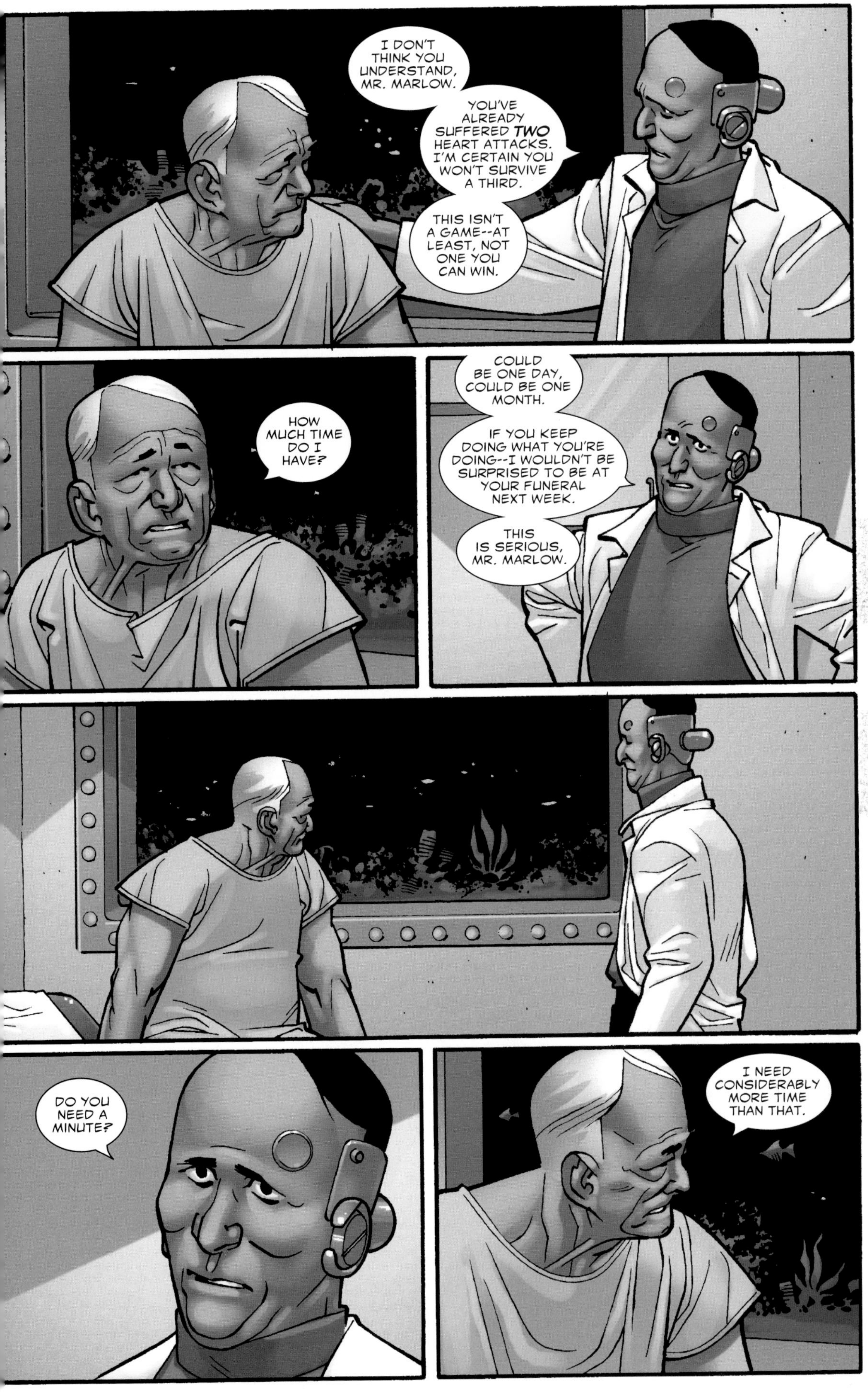
I DON'T THINK YOU UNDERSTAND, MR. MARLOW.
YOU'VE ALREADY SUFFERED **TWO** HEART ATTACKS. I'M CERTAIN YOU WON'T SURVIVE A THIRD.
THIS ISN'T A GAME--AT LEAST, NOT ONE YOU CAN WIN.
HOW MUCH TIME DO I HAVE?
COULD BE ONE DAY, COULD BE ONE MONTH.
IF YOU KEEP DOING WHAT YOU'RE DOING--I WOULDN'T BE SURPRISED TO BE AT YOUR FUNERAL NEXT WEEK.
THIS IS SERIOUS, MR. MARLOW.
DO YOU NEED A MINUTE?
I NEED CONSIDERABLY MORE TIME THAN THAT.

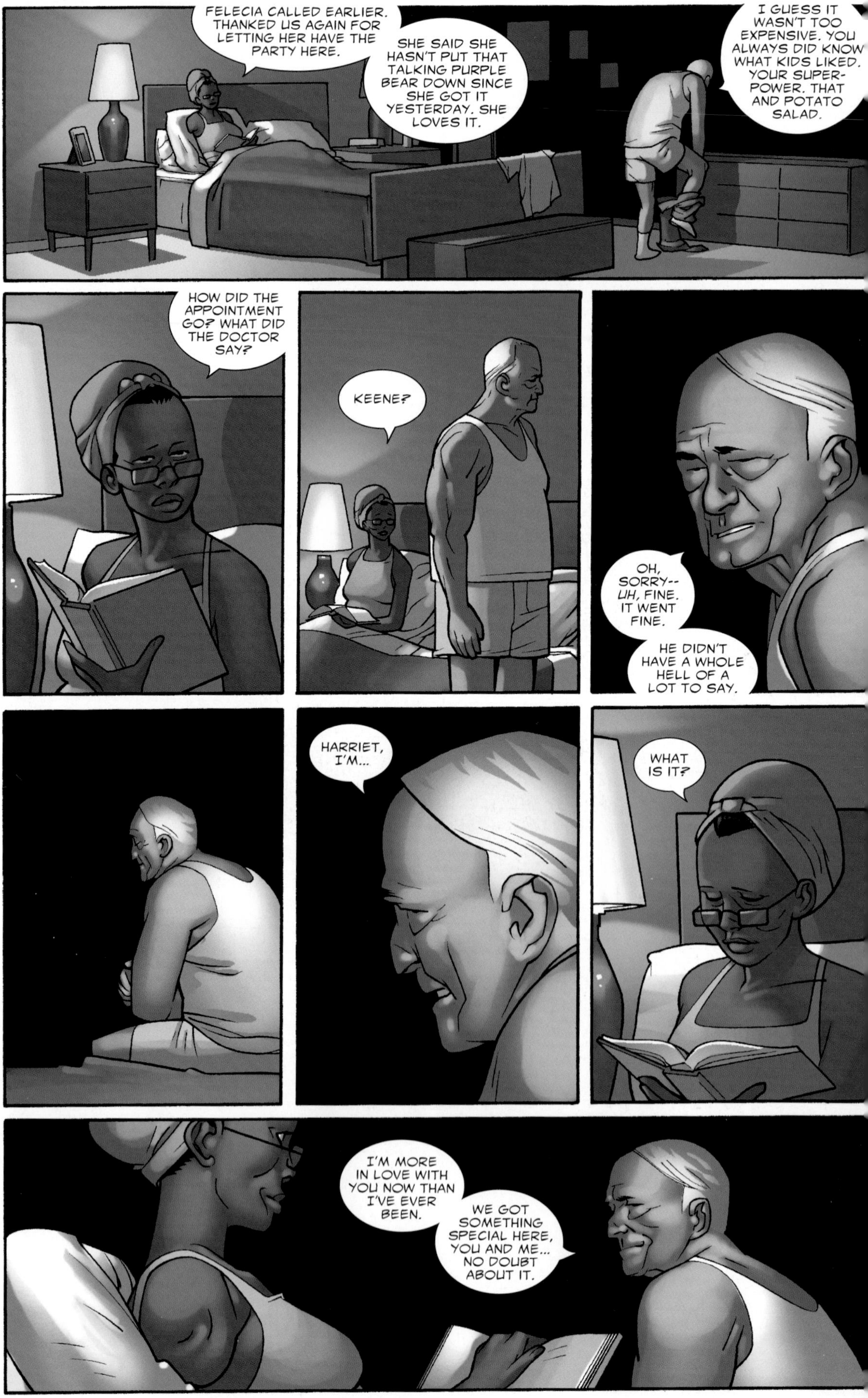
FELECIA CALLED EARLIER. THANKED US AGAIN FOR LETTING HER HAVE THE PARTY HERE.
SHE SAID SHE HASN'T PUT THAT TALKING PURPLE BEAR DOWN SINCE SHE GOT IT YESTERDAY. SHE LOVES IT.
I GUESS IT WASN'T TOO EXPENSIVE. YOU ALWAYS DID KNOW WHAT KIDS LIKED. YOUR SUPER-POWER. THAT AND POTATO SALAD.
HOW DID THE APPOINTMENT GO? WHAT DID THE DOCTOR SAY?
KEENE?
OH, SORRY-- UH, FINE. IT WENT FINE.
HE DIDN'T HAVE A WHOLE HELL OF A LOT TO SAY.
HARRIET, I'M...
WHAT IS IT?
I'M MORE IN LOVE WITH YOU NOW THAN I'VE EVER BEEN.
WE GOT SOMETHING SPECIAL HERE, YOU AND ME... NO DOUBT ABOUT IT.

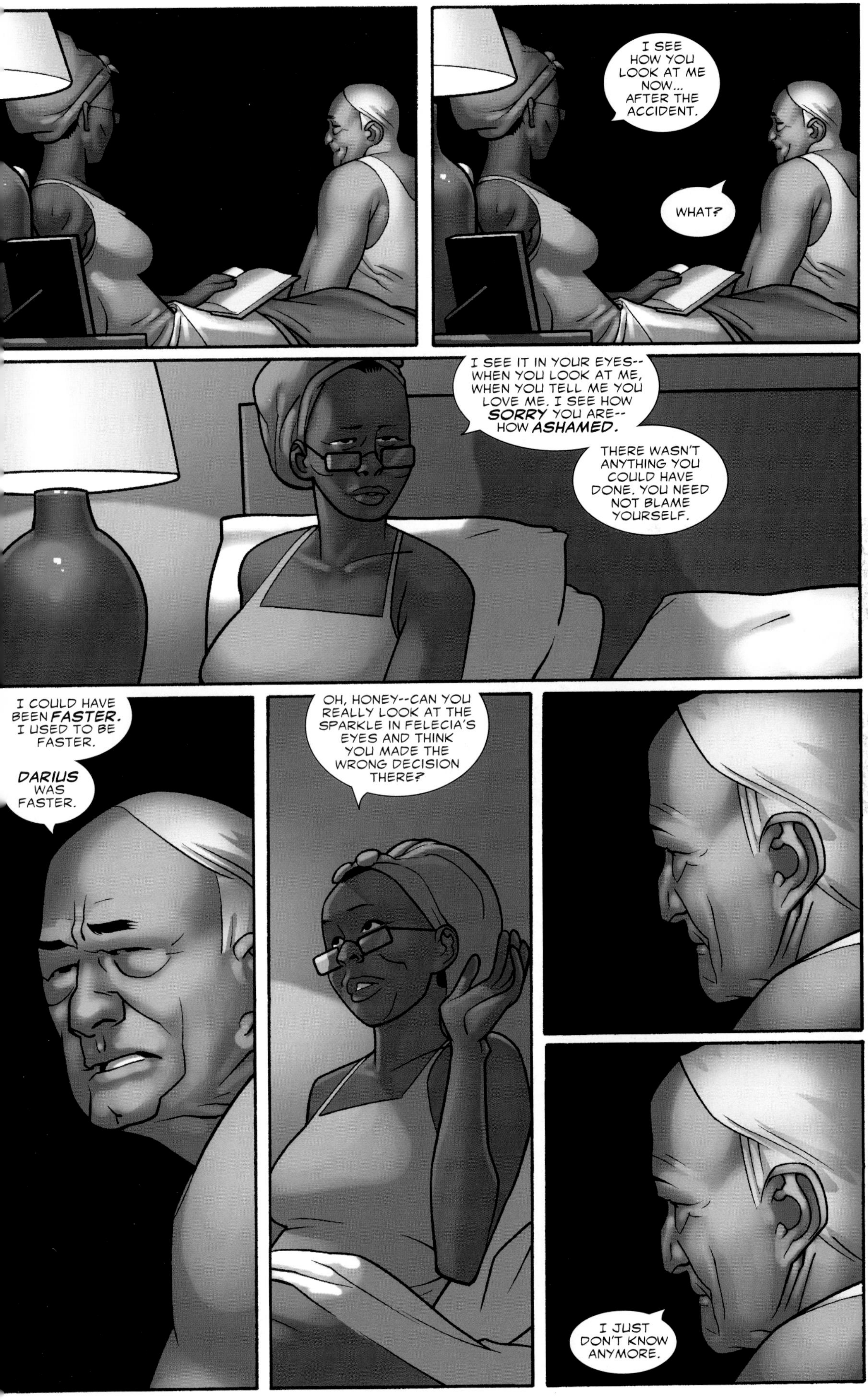
I SEE HOW YOU LOOK AT ME NOW... AFTER THE ACCIDENT.
WHAT?
I SEE IT IN YOUR EYES-- WHEN YOU LOOK AT ME, WHEN YOU TELL ME YOU LOVE ME. I SEE HOW SORRY YOU ARE-- HOW ASHAMED.
THERE WASN'T ANYTHING YOU COULD HAVE DONE. YOU NEED NOT BLAME YOURSELF.
I COULD HAVE BEEN FASTER. I USED TO BE FASTER.
DARIUS WAS FASTER.
OH, HONEY--CAN YOU REALLY LOOK AT THE SPARKLE IN FELECIA'S EYES AND THINK YOU MADE THE WRONG DECISION THERE?
I JUST DON'T KNOW ANYMORE.

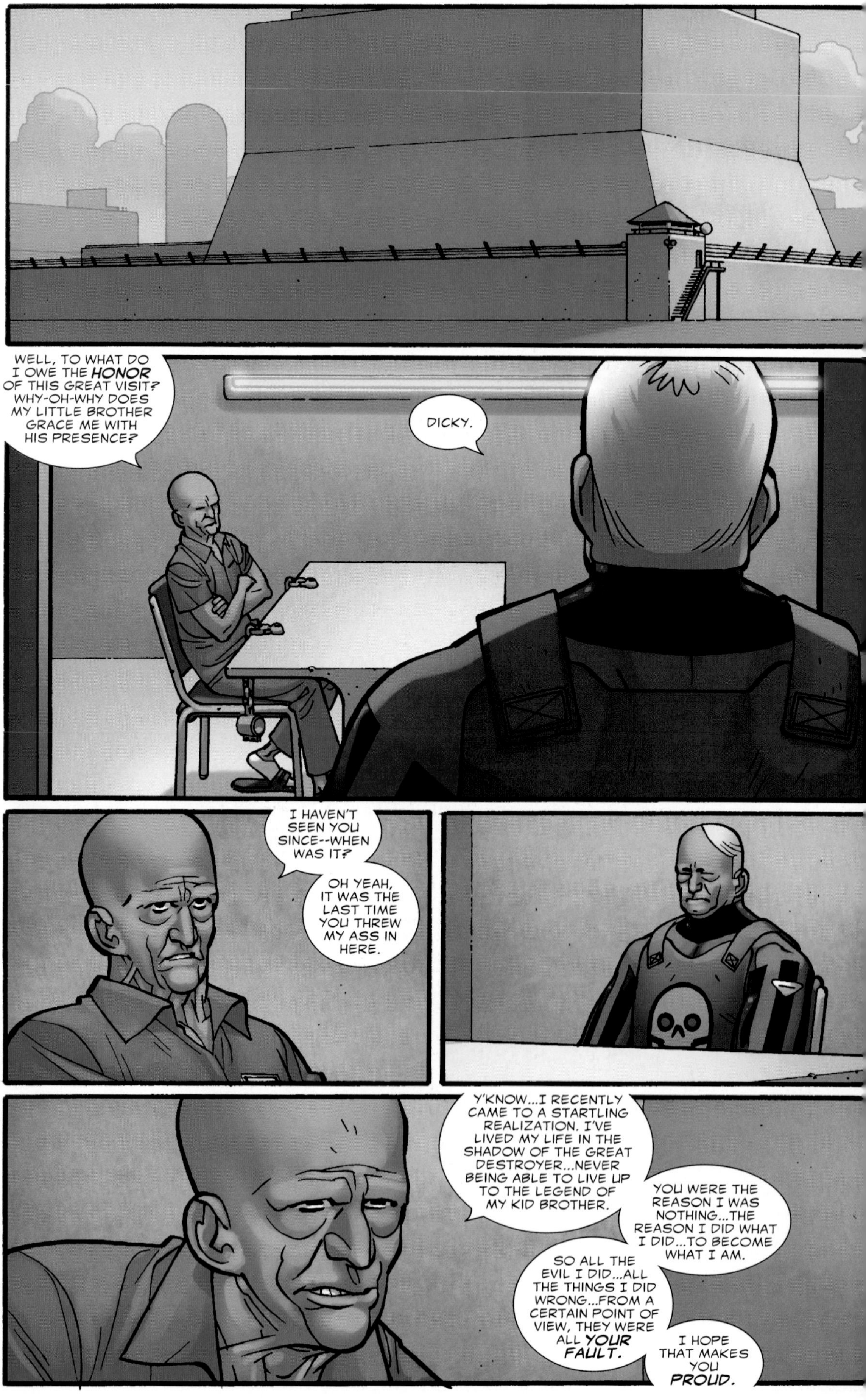

WELL, TO WHAT DO I OWE THE HONOR OF THIS GREAT VISIT? WHY-OH-WHY DOES MY LITTLE BROTHER GRACE ME WITH HIS PRESENCE?
DICKY.
I HAVEN'T SEEN YOU SINCE--WHEN WAS IT?
OH YEAH, IT WAS THE LAST TIME YOU THREW MY ASS IN HERE.
Y'KNOW...I RECENTLY CAME TO A STARTLING REALIZATION. I'VE LIVED MY LIFE IN THE SHADOW OF THE GREAT DESTROYER...NEVER BEING ABLE TO LIVE UP TO THE LEGEND OF MY KID BROTHER.
YOU WERE THE REASON I WAS NOTHING...THE REASON I DID WHAT I DID...TO BECOME WHAT I AM.
SO ALL THE EVIL I DID...ALL THE THINGS I DID WRONG...FROM A CERTAIN POINT OF VIEW, THEY WERE ALL YOUR FAULT.
I HOPE THAT MAKES YOU PROUD.

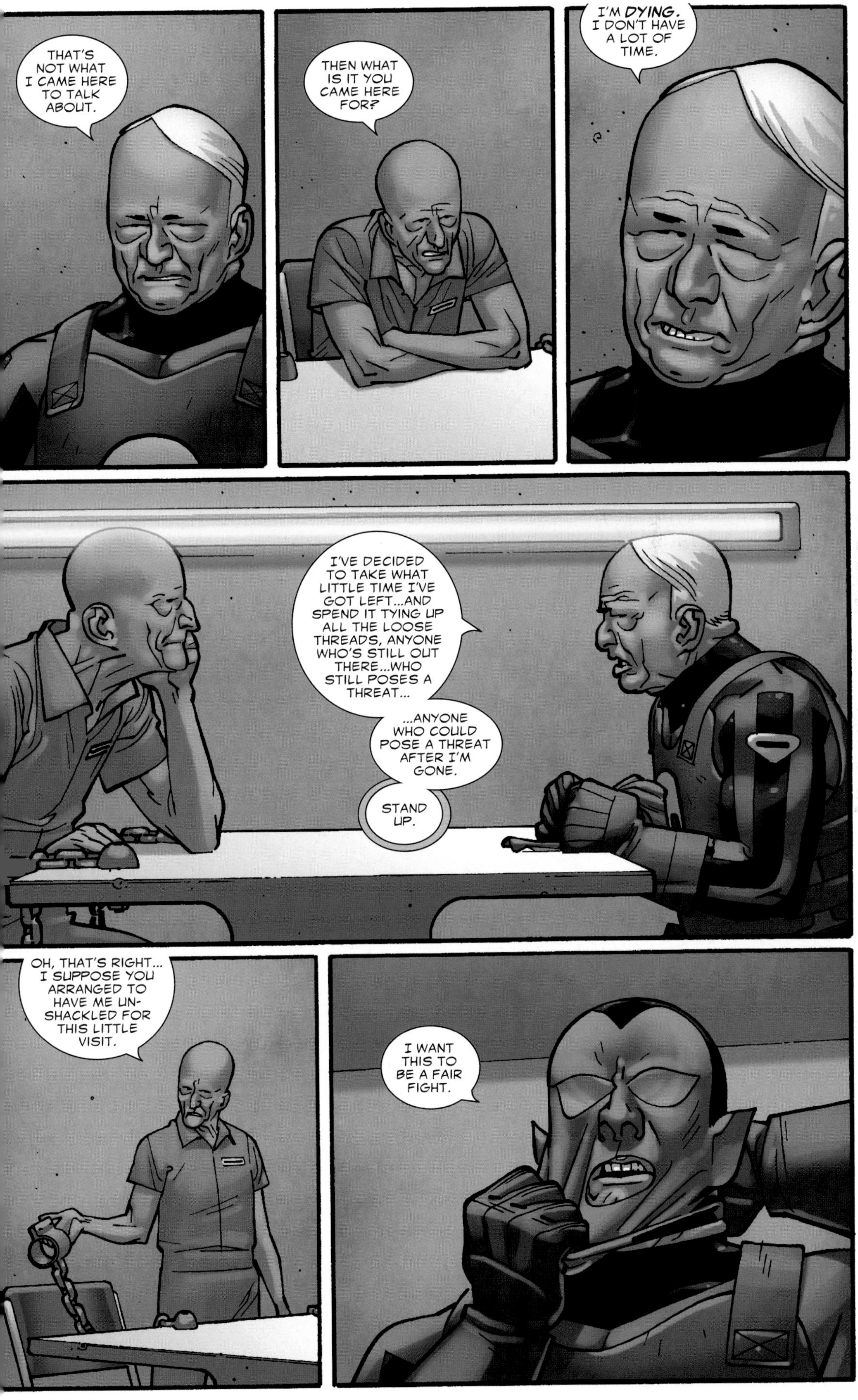
THAT'S NOT WHAT I CAME HERE TO TALK ABOUT.
THEN WHAT IS IT YOU CAME HERE FOR?
I'M *DYING.* I DON'T HAVE A LOT OF TIME.
I'VE DECIDED TO TAKE WHAT LITTLE TIME I'VE GOT LEFT...AND SPEND IT TYING UP ALL THE LOOSE THREADS, ANYONE WHO'S STILL OUT THERE...WHO STILL POSES A THREAT...
...ANYONE WHO COULD POSE A THREAT AFTER I'M GONE.
STAND UP.
OH, THAT'S RIGHT... I SUPPOSE YOU ARRANGED TO HAVE ME UN-SHACKLED FOR THIS LITTLE VISIT.
I WANT THIS TO BE A FAIR FIGHT.

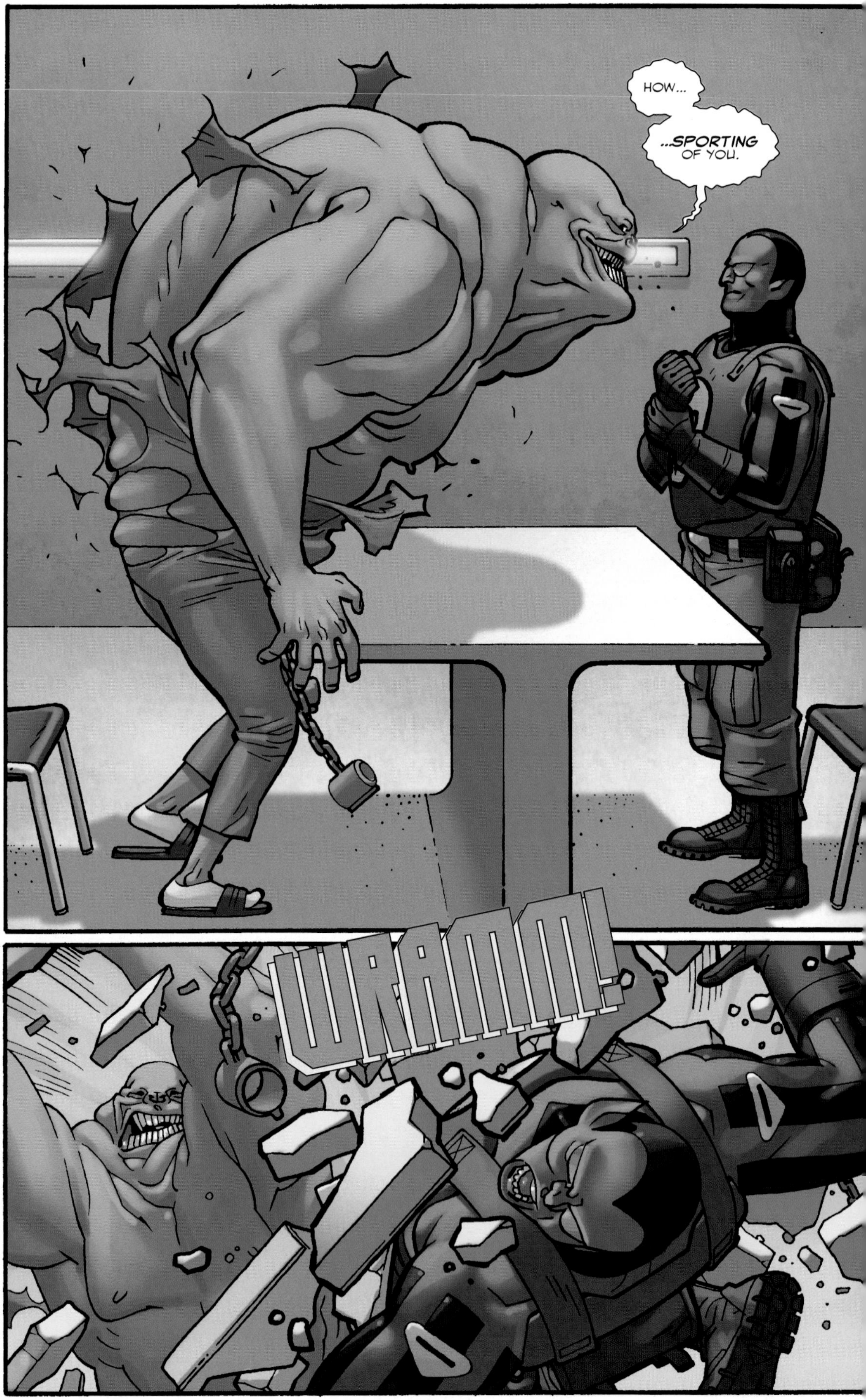
HOW...
...SPORTING OF YOU.
WRAMM!

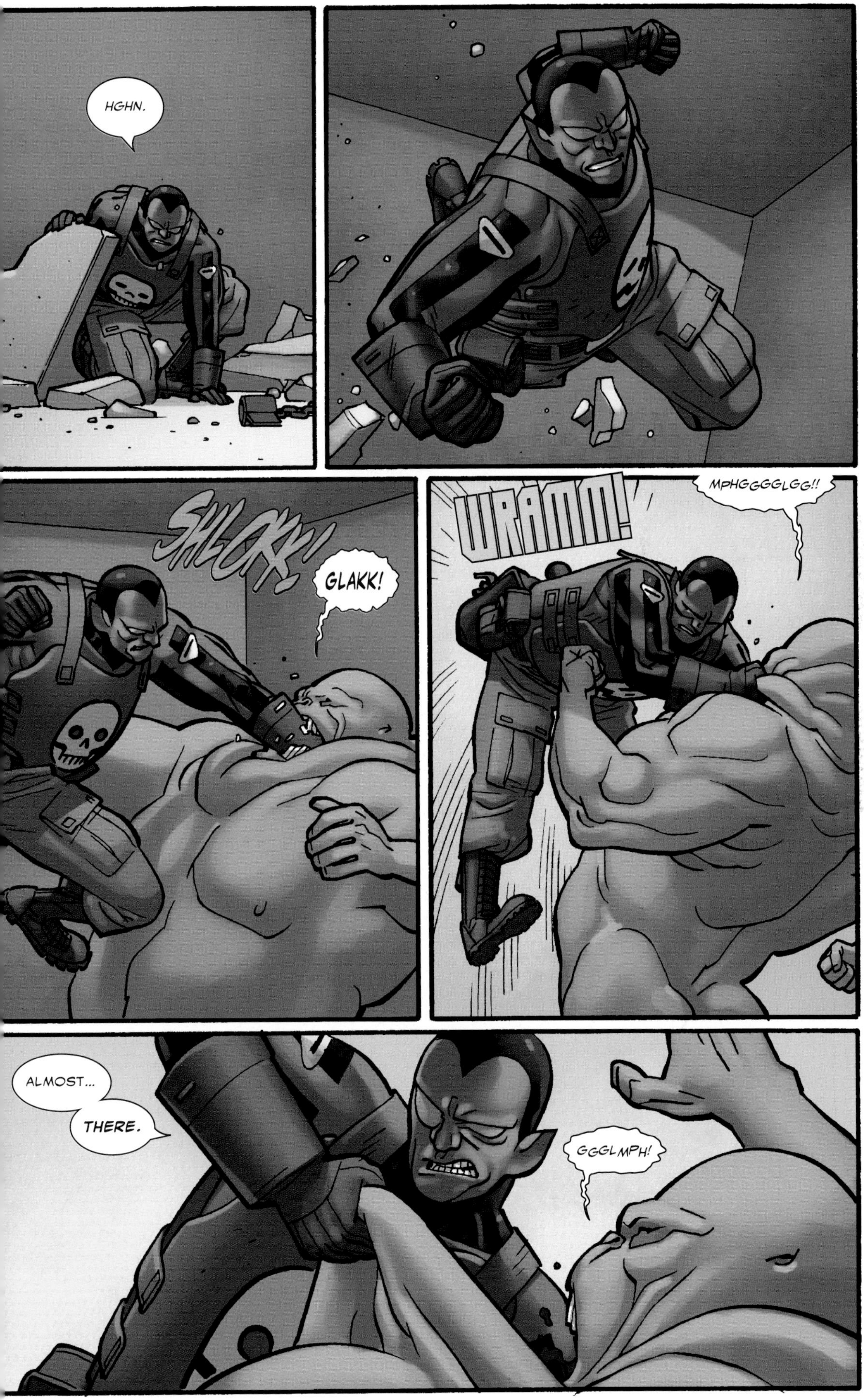
HGHN.
SHLOKK!
GLAKK!
WRAMM!
MPHGGGGLGG!!
ALMOST...
THERE.
GGGLMPH!

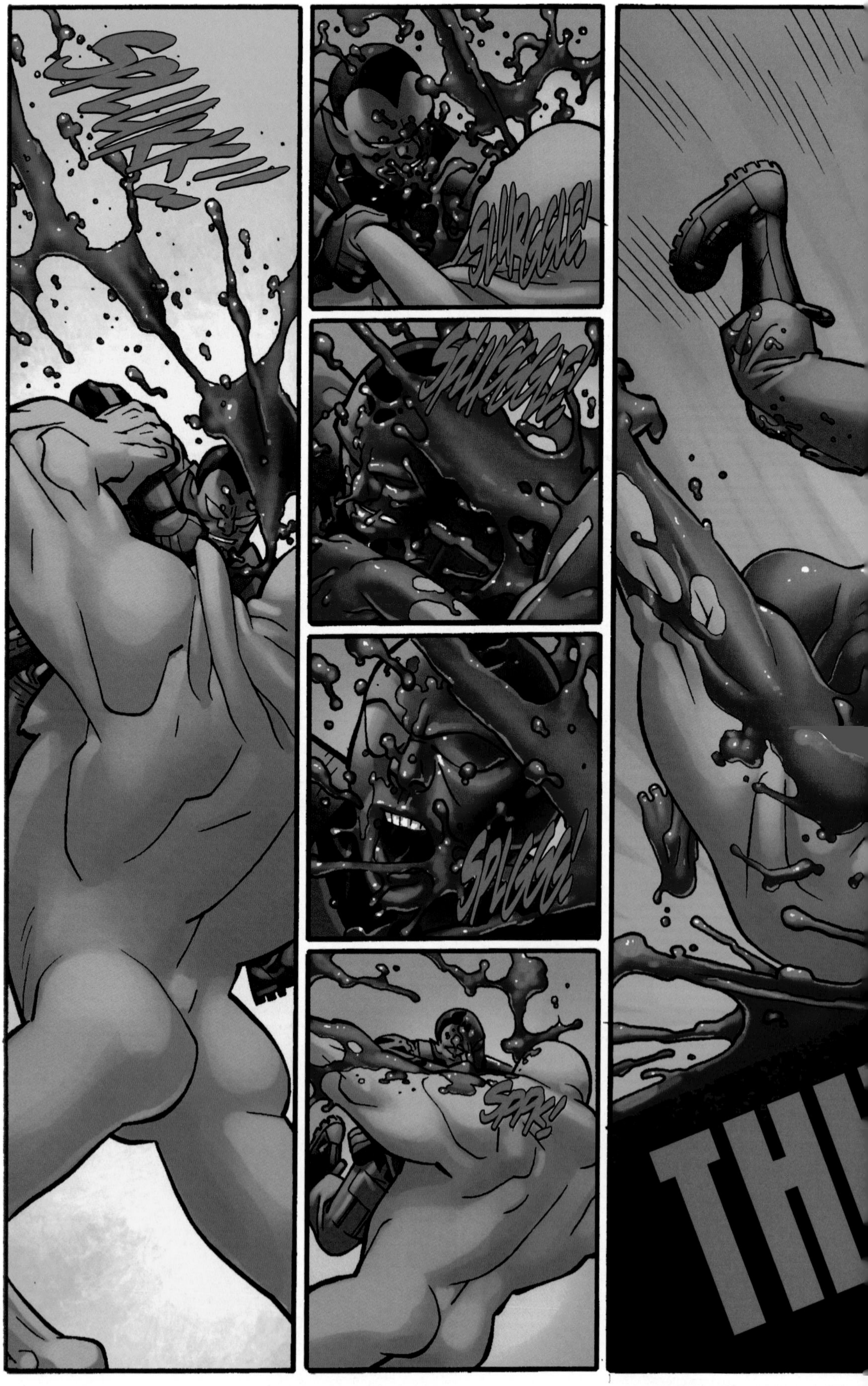
SLURGGLE!
SPLURGGLE!
SPLGGG!
SPPK!

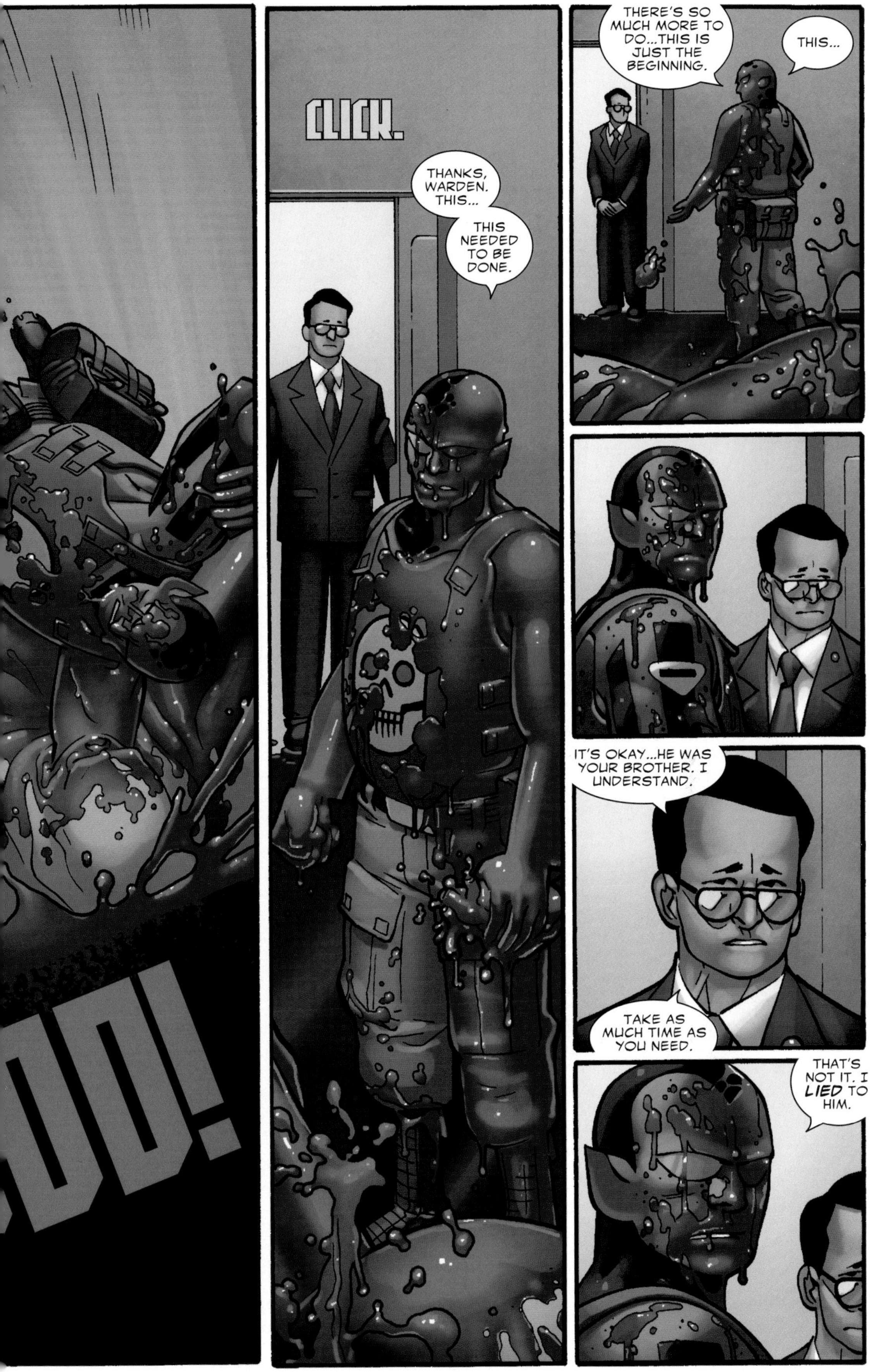

DOD!
CLICK.
THANKS, WARDEN. THIS...
THIS NEEDED TO BE DONE.
THERE'S SO MUCH MORE TO DO...THIS IS JUST THE BEGINNING.
THIS...
IT'S OKAY...HE WAS YOUR BROTHER. I UNDERSTAND.
TAKE AS MUCH TIME AS YOU NEED.
THAT'S NOT IT. I LIED TO HIM.

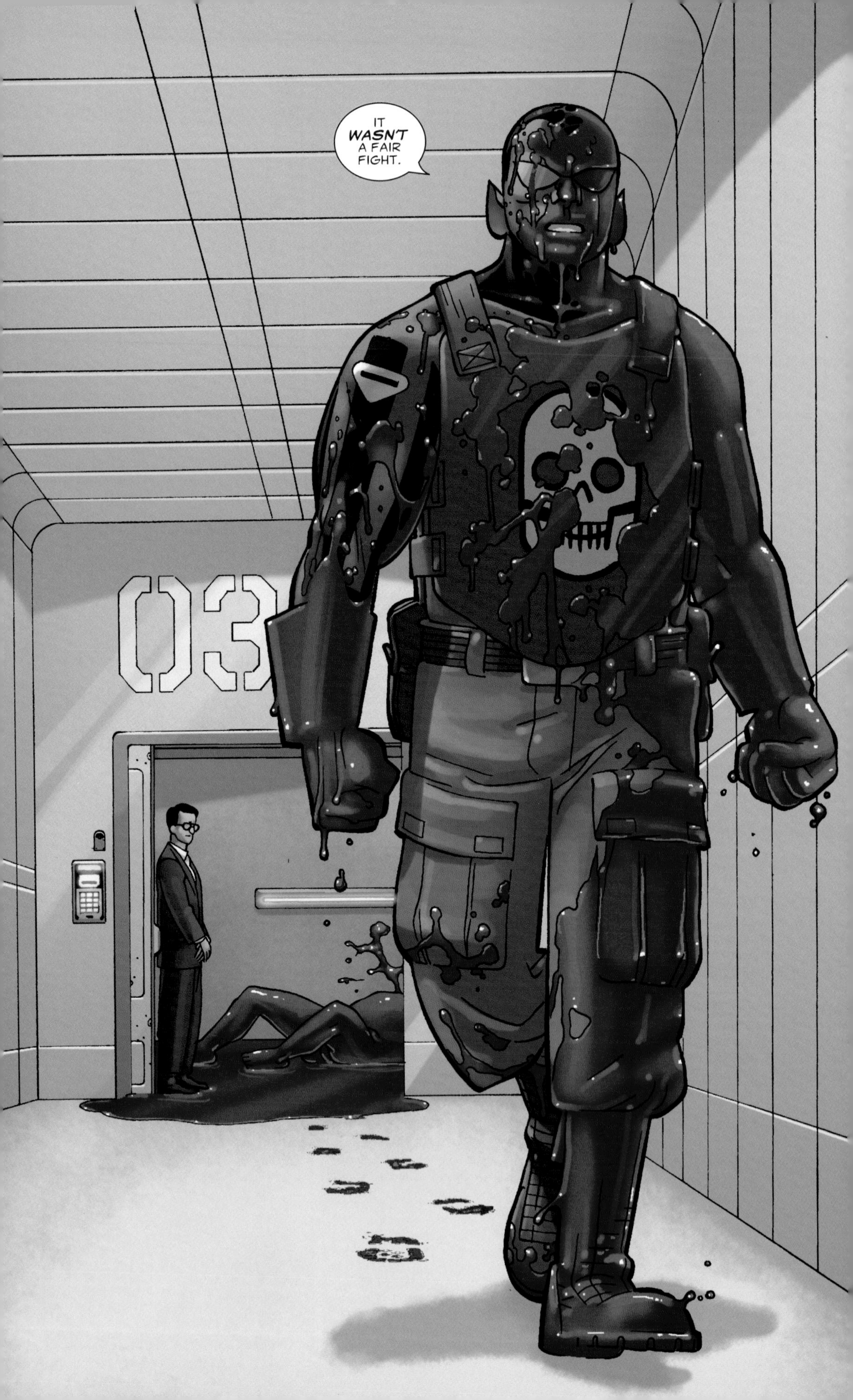
IT WASN'T A FAIR FIGHT.
03

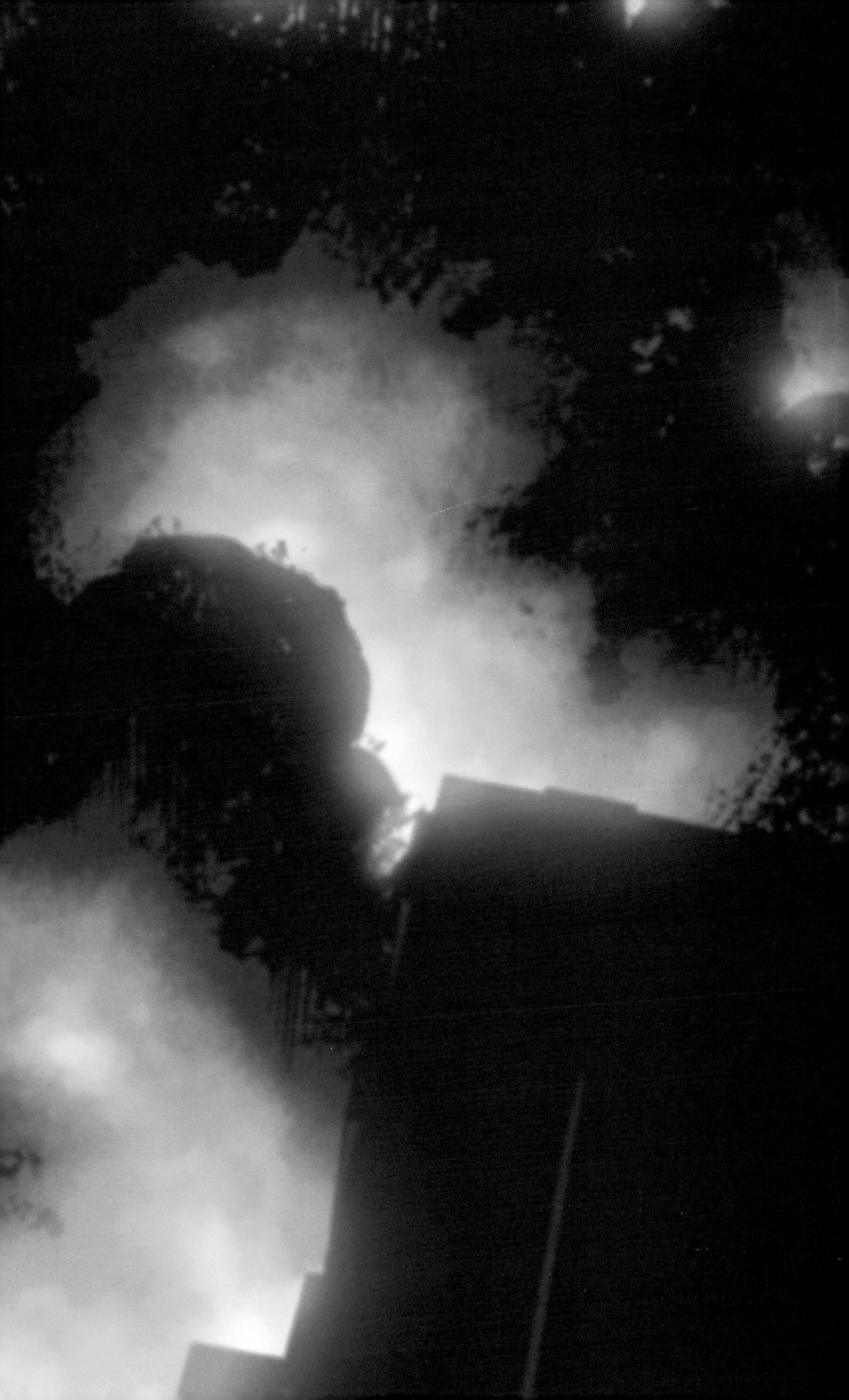

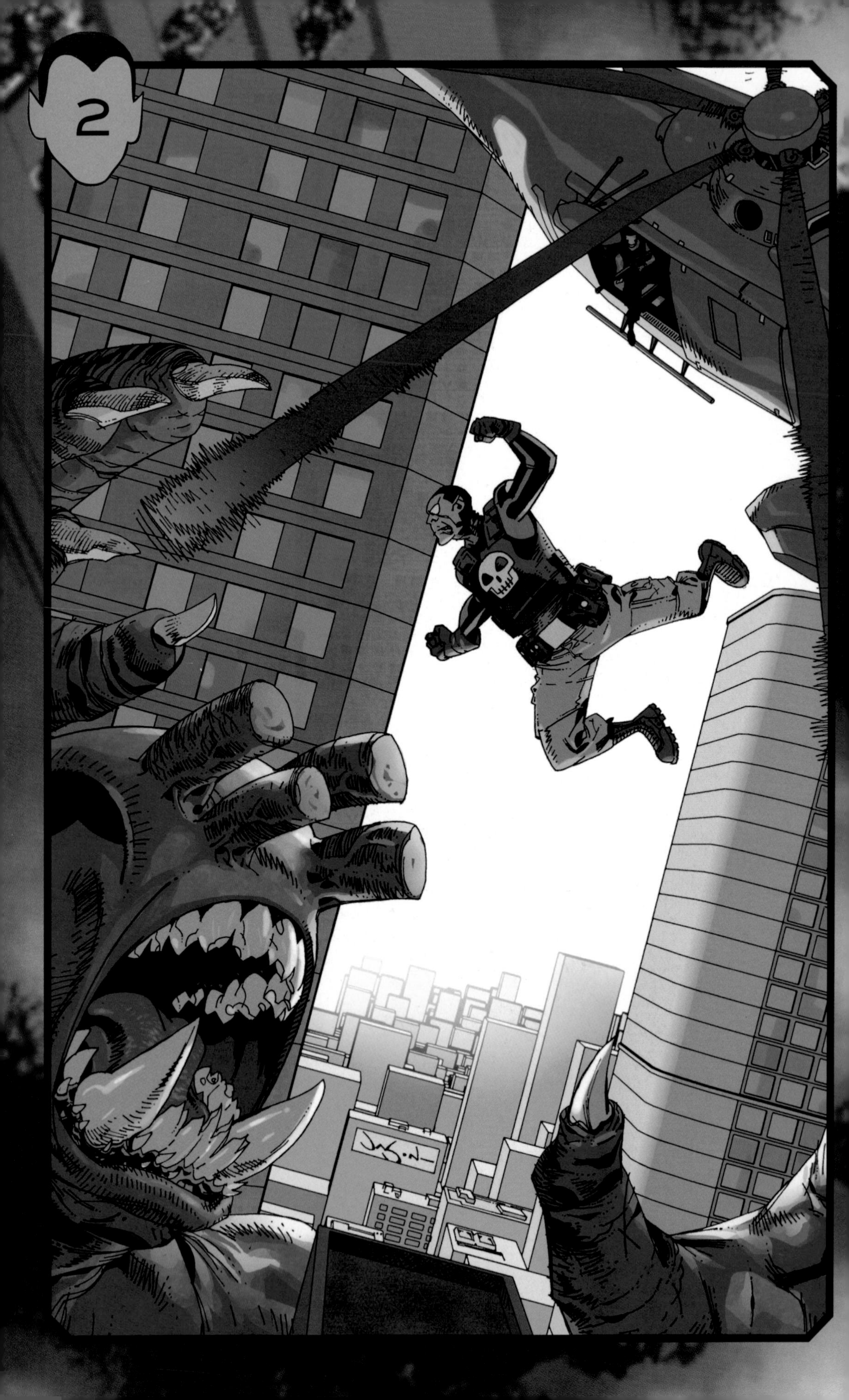
2

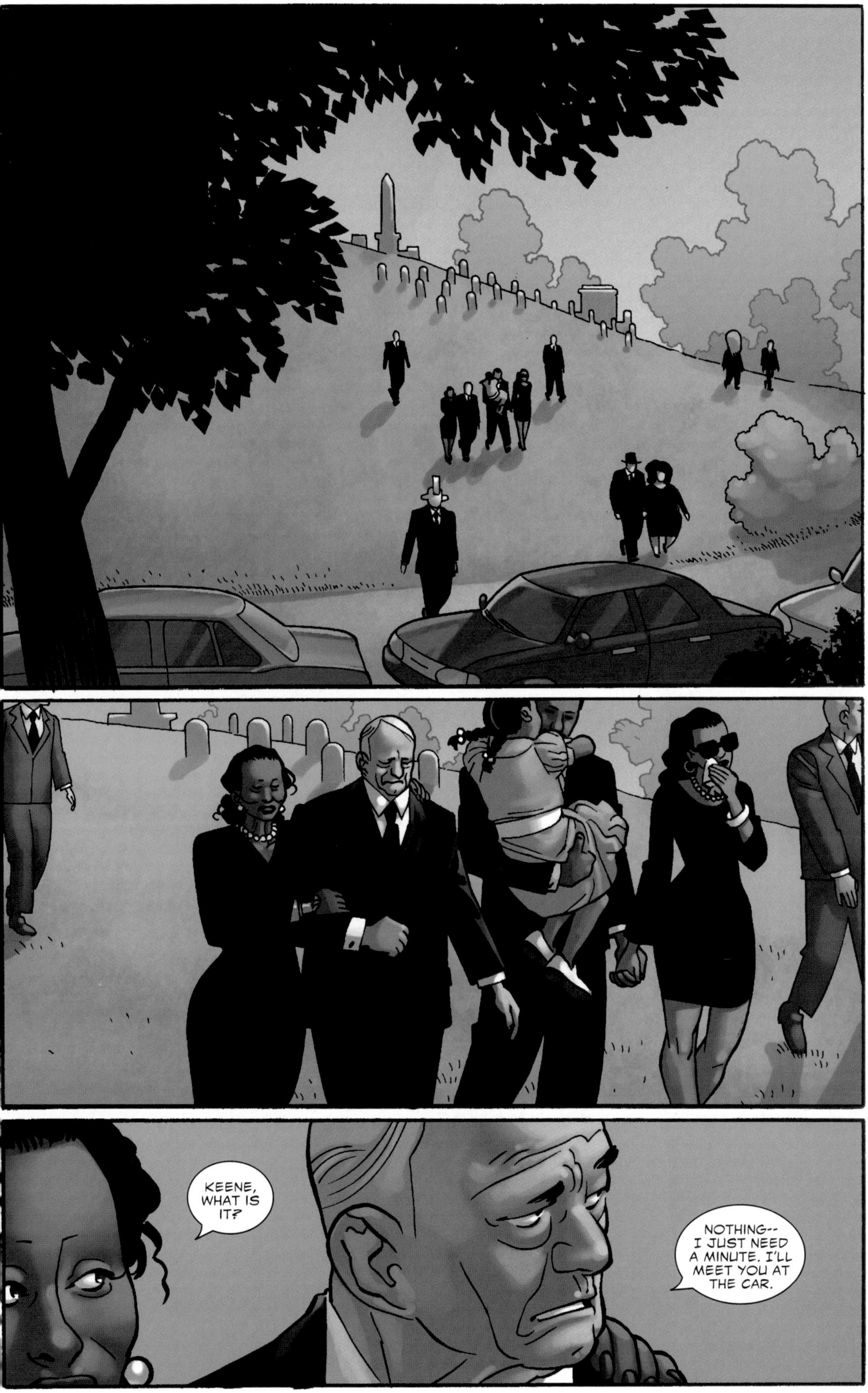
KEENE, WHAT IS IT?
NOTHING-- I JUST NEED A MINUTE. I'LL MEET YOU AT THE CAR.

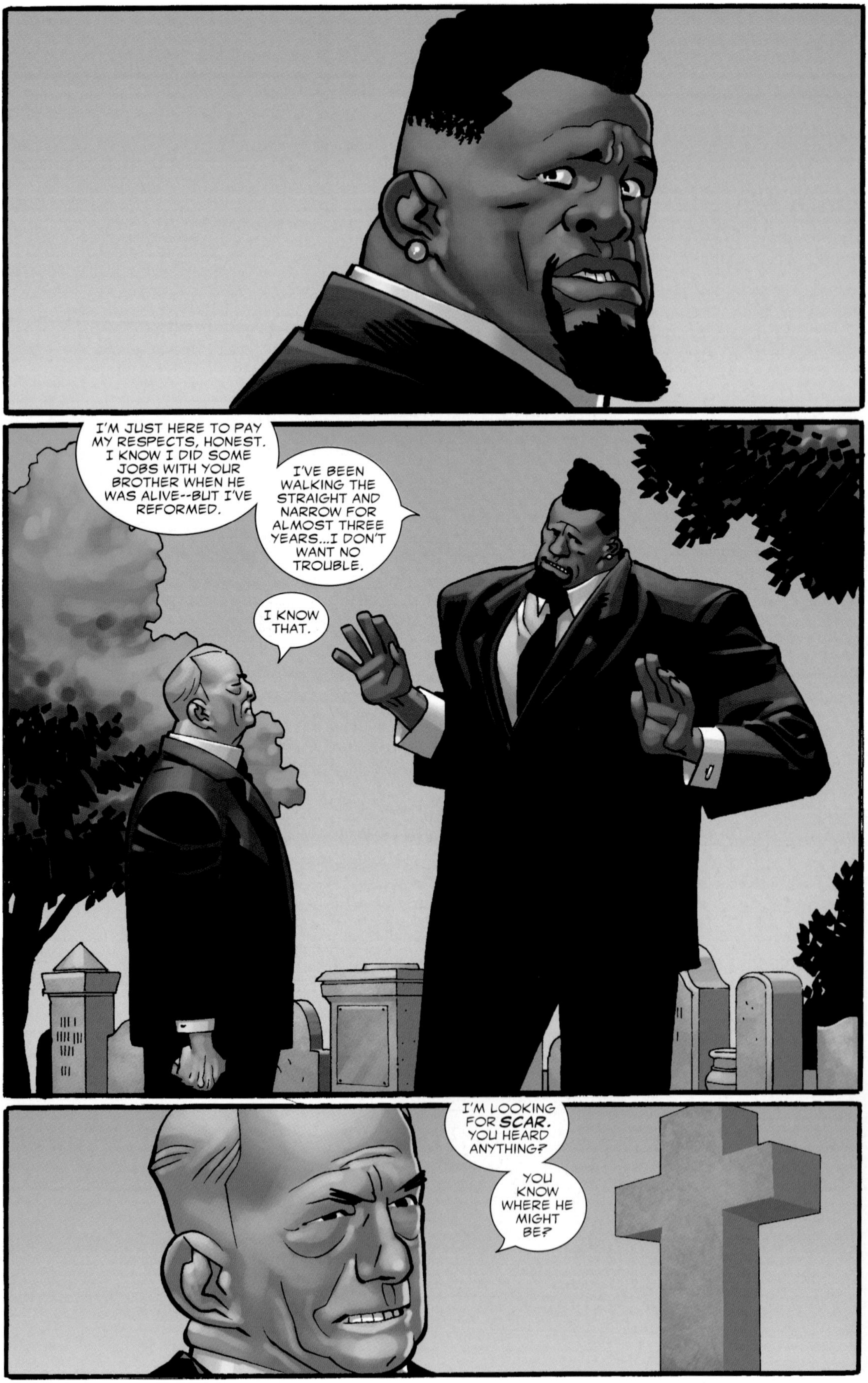
I'M JUST HERE TO PAY MY RESPECTS, HONEST. I KNOW I DID SOME JOBS WITH YOUR BROTHER WHEN HE WAS ALIVE--BUT I'VE REFORMED.
I'VE BEEN WALKING THE STRAIGHT AND NARROW FOR ALMOST THREE YEARS...I DON'T WANT NO TROUBLE.
I KNOW THAT.
I'M LOOKING FOR SCAR. YOU HEARD ANYTHING?
YOU KNOW WHERE HE MIGHT BE?

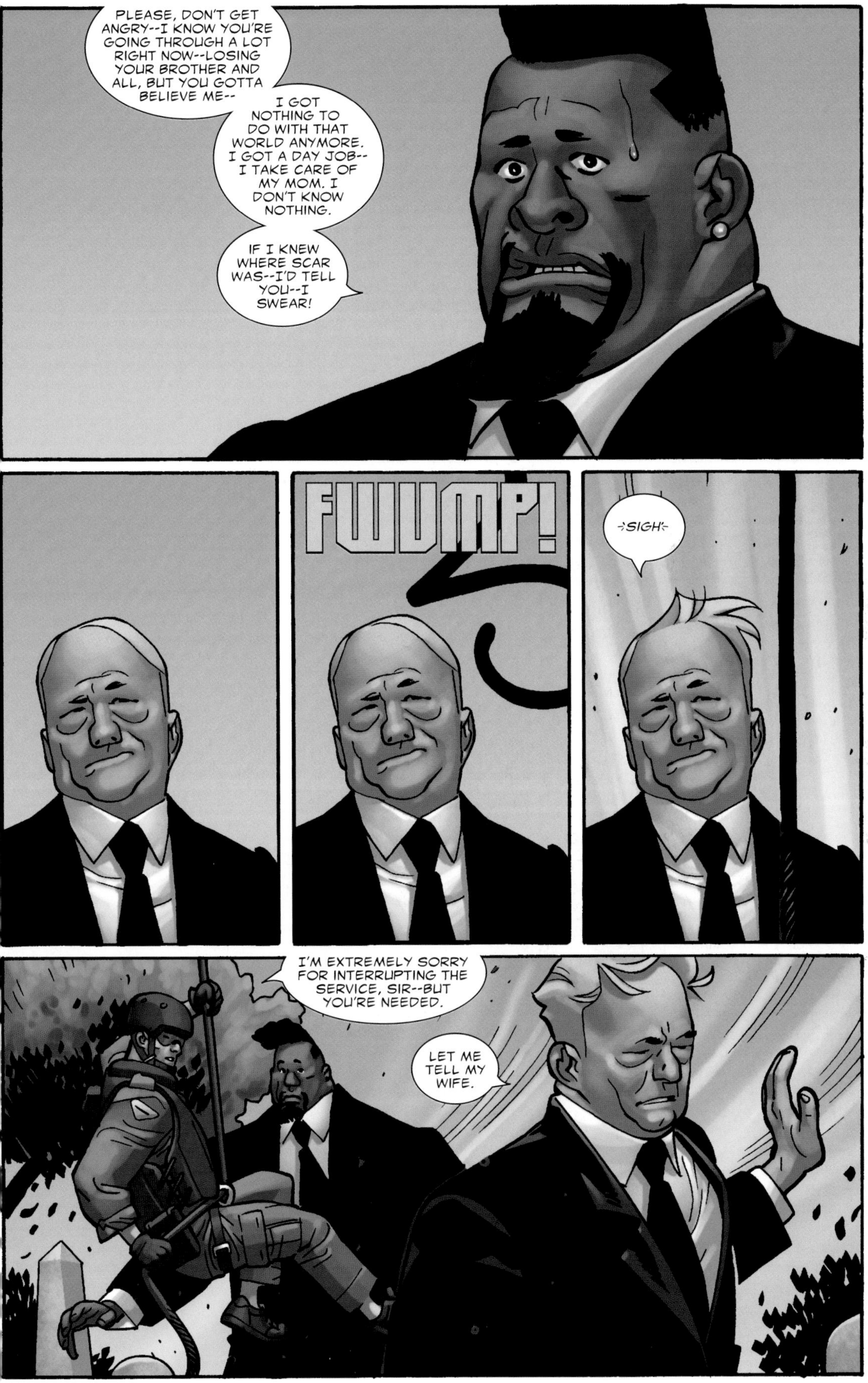
PLEASE, DON'T GET ANGRY--I KNOW YOU'RE GOING THROUGH A LOT RIGHT NOW--LOSING YOUR BROTHER AND ALL, BUT YOU GOTTA BELIEVE ME--
I GOT NOTHING TO DO WITH THAT WORLD ANYMORE. I GOT A DAY JOB-- I TAKE CARE OF MY MOM. I DON'T KNOW NOTHING.
IF I KNEW WHERE SCAR WAS--I'D TELL YOU--I SWEAR!
FWUMP!
SIGH
I'M EXTREMELY SORRY FOR INTERRUPTING THE SERVICE, SIR--BUT YOU'RE NEEDED.
LET ME TELL MY WIFE.

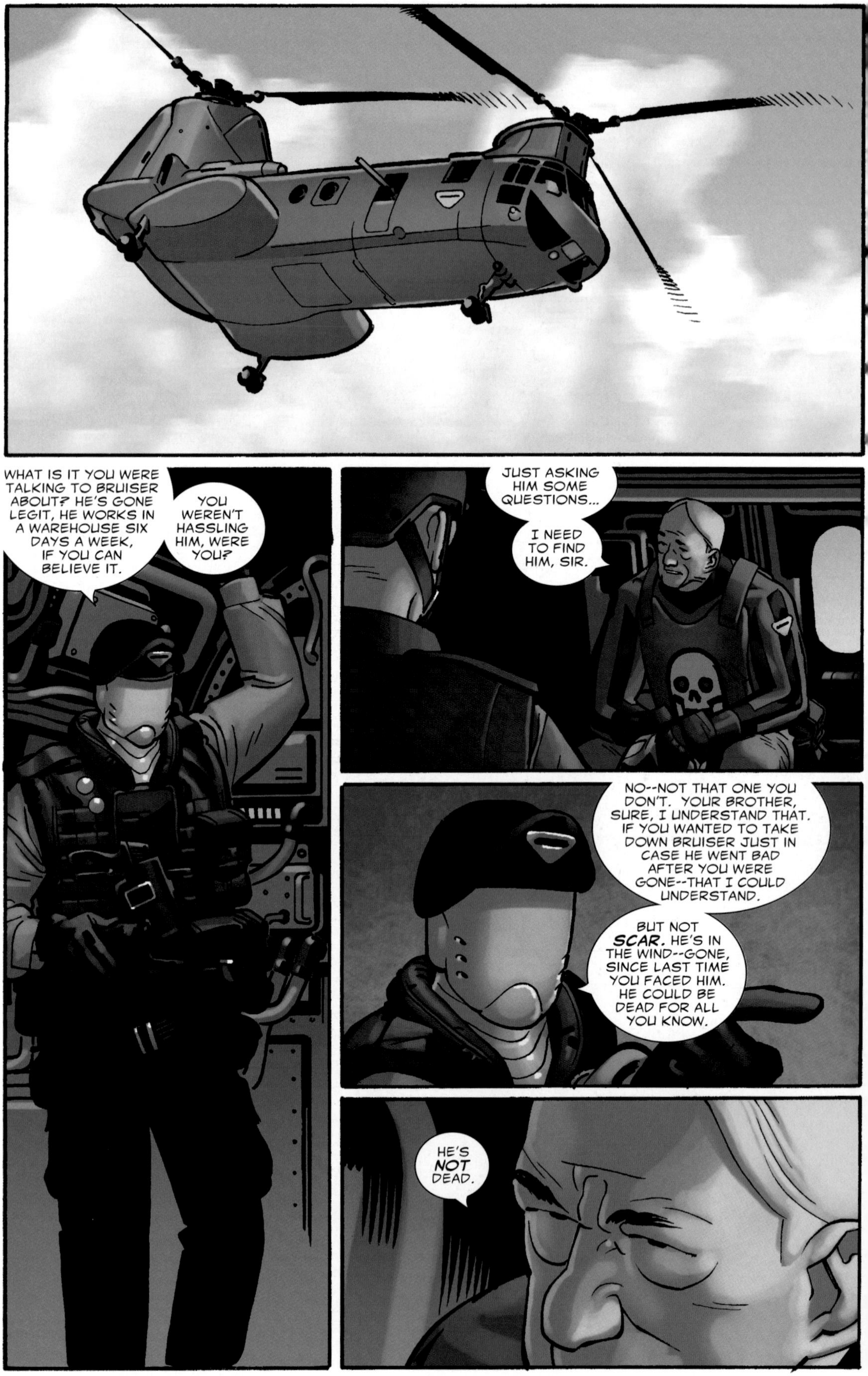
WHAT IS IT YOU WERE TALKING TO BRUISER ABOUT? HE'S GONE LEGIT, HE WORKS IN A WAREHOUSE SIX DAYS A WEEK, IF YOU CAN BELIEVE IT.
YOU WEREN'T HASSLING HIM, WERE YOU?
JUST ASKING HIM SOME QUESTIONS...
I NEED TO FIND HIM, SIR.
NO--NOT THAT ONE YOU DON'T. YOUR BROTHER, SURE, I UNDERSTAND THAT. IF YOU WANTED TO TAKE DOWN BRUISER JUST IN CASE HE WENT BAD AFTER YOU WERE GONE--THAT I COULD UNDERSTAND.
BUT NOT SCAR. HE'S IN THE WIND--GONE, SINCE LAST TIME YOU FACED HIM. HE COULD BE DEAD FOR ALL YOU KNOW.
HE'S NOT DEAD.

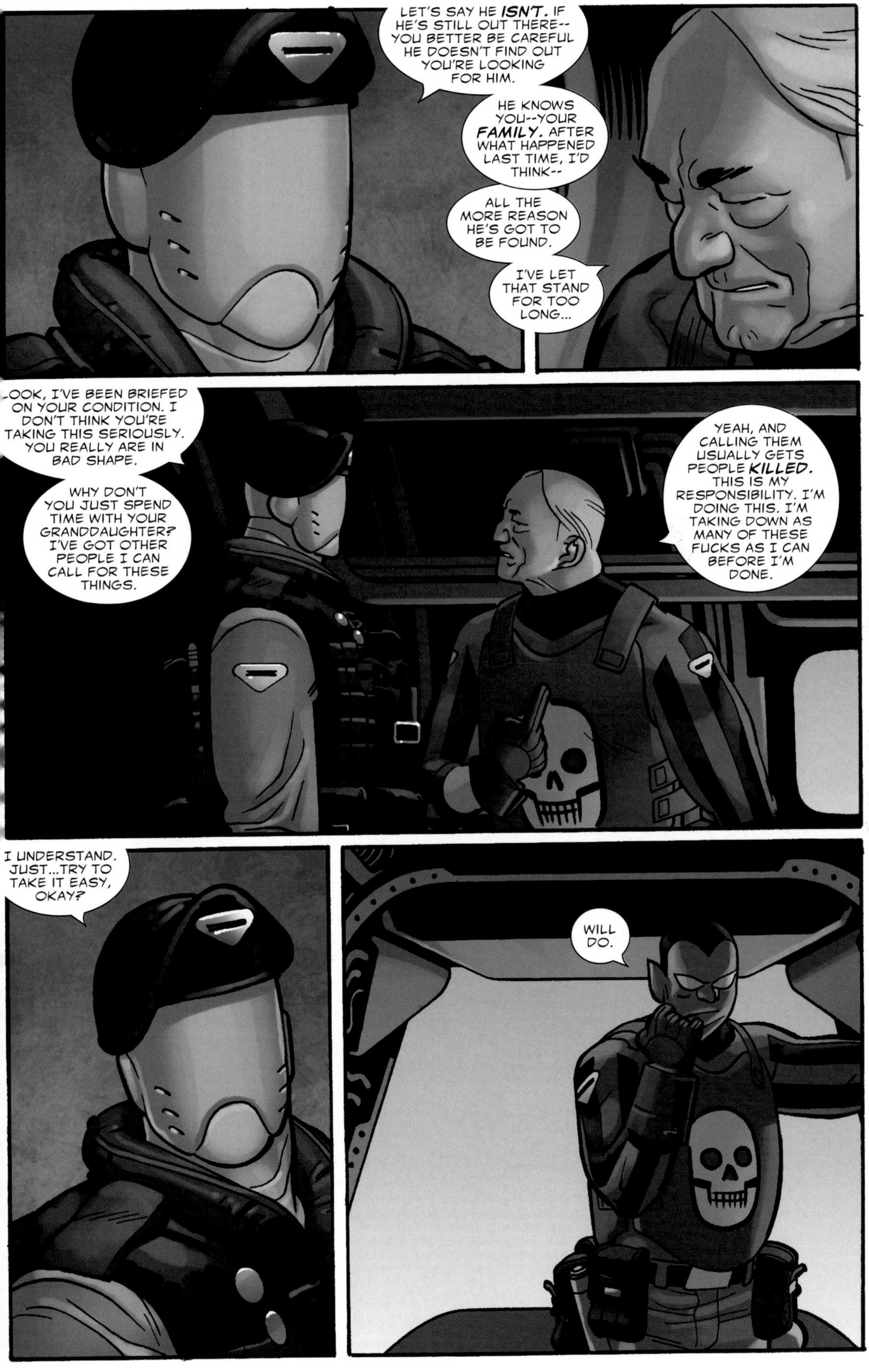
LET'S SAY HE ISN'T. IF HE'S STILL OUT THERE--YOU BETTER BE CAREFUL HE DOESN'T FIND OUT YOU'RE LOOKING FOR HIM.
HE KNOWS YOU--YOUR FAMILY. AFTER WHAT HAPPENED LAST TIME, I'D THINK--
ALL THE MORE REASON HE'S GOT TO BE FOUND.
I'VE LET THAT STAND FOR TOO LONG...
LOOK, I'VE BEEN BRIEFED ON YOUR CONDITION. I DON'T THINK YOU'RE TAKING THIS SERIOUSLY. YOU REALLY ARE IN BAD SHAPE.
WHY DON'T YOU JUST SPEND TIME WITH YOUR GRANDDAUGHTER? I'VE GOT OTHER PEOPLE I CAN CALL FOR THESE THINGS.
YEAH, AND CALLING THEM USUALLY GETS PEOPLE KILLED. THIS IS MY RESPONSIBILITY. I'M DOING THIS. I'M TAKING DOWN AS MANY OF THESE FUCKS AS I CAN BEFORE I'M DONE.
I UNDERSTAND. JUST...TRY TO TAKE IT EASY, OKAY?
WILL DO.

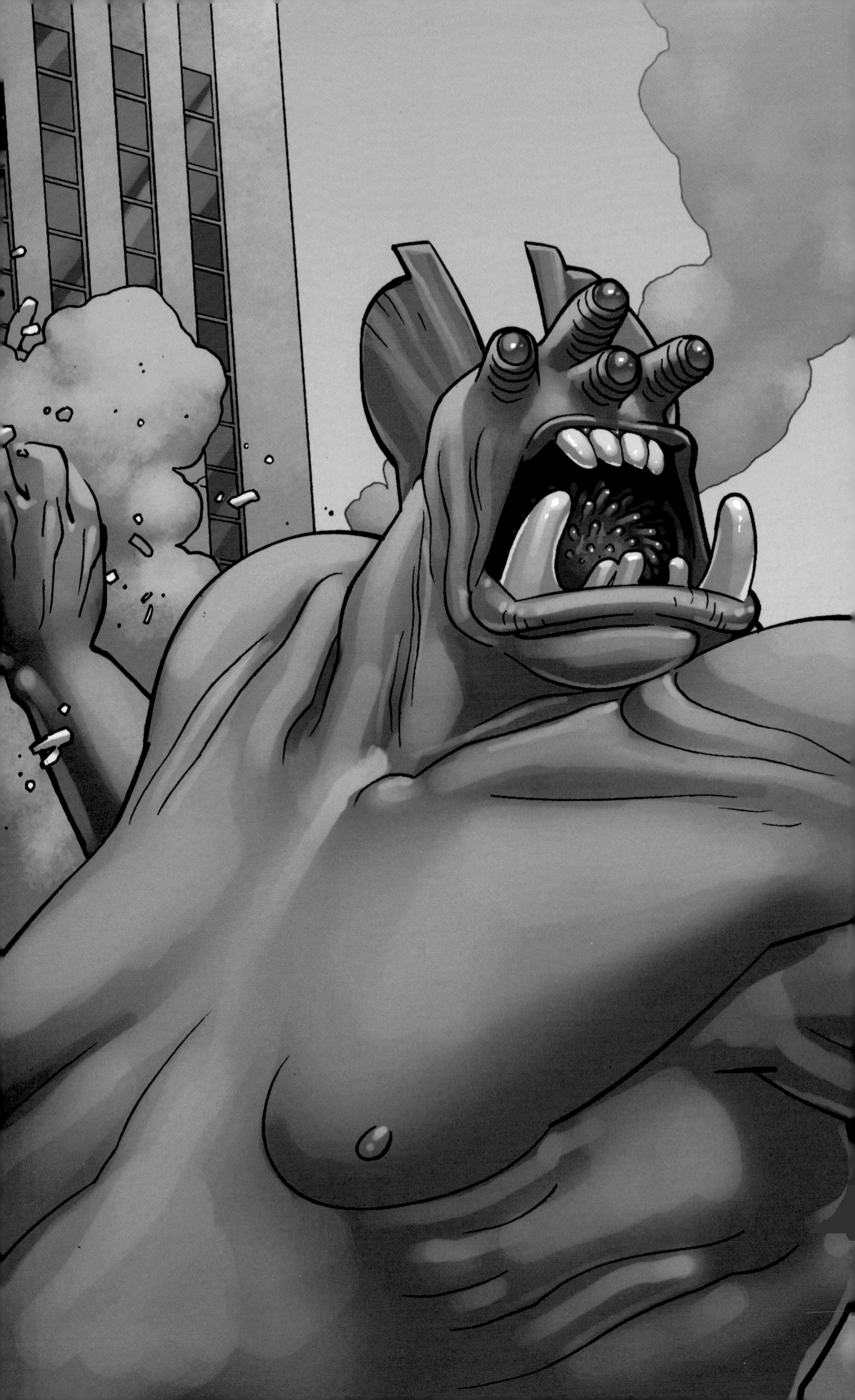

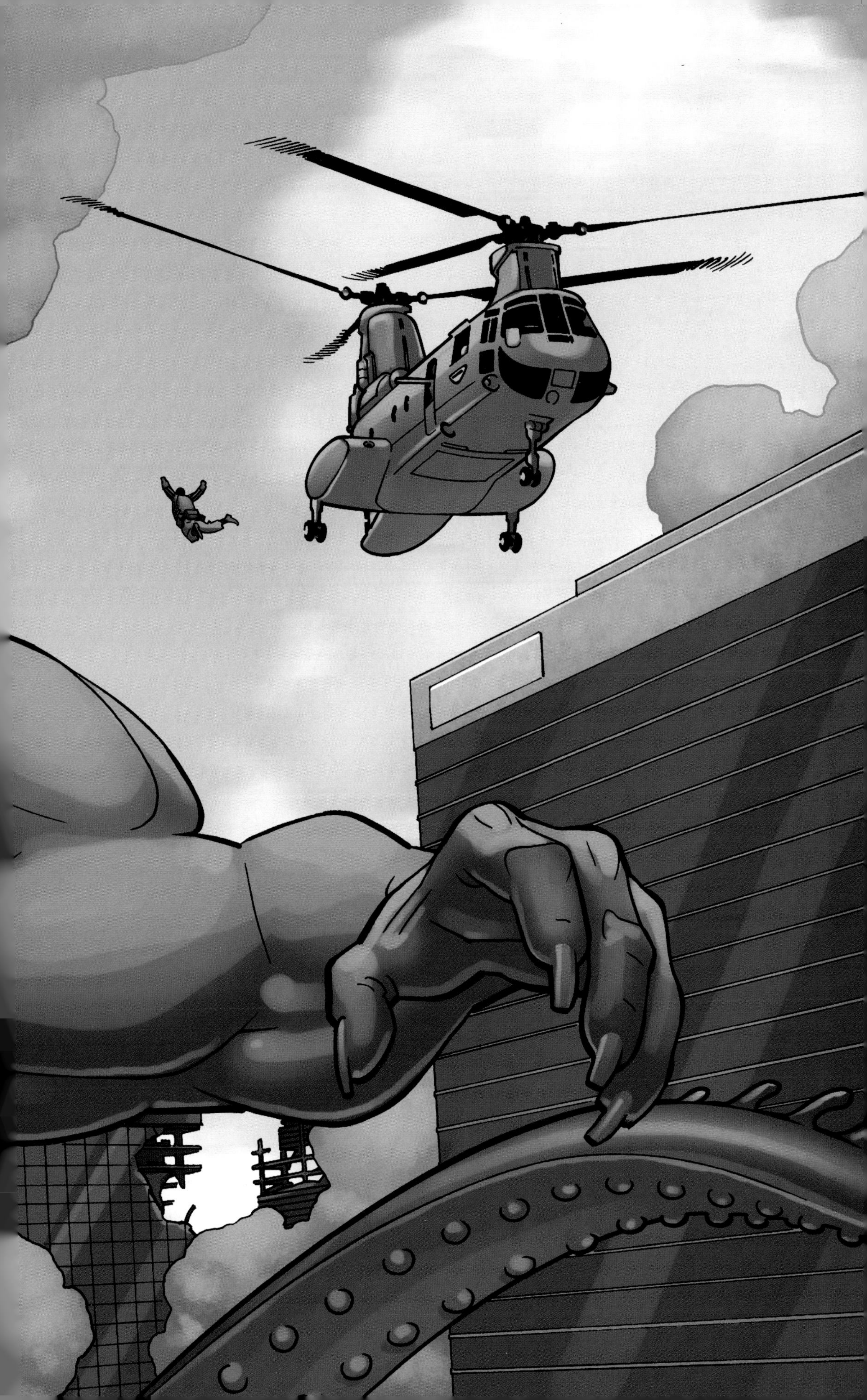

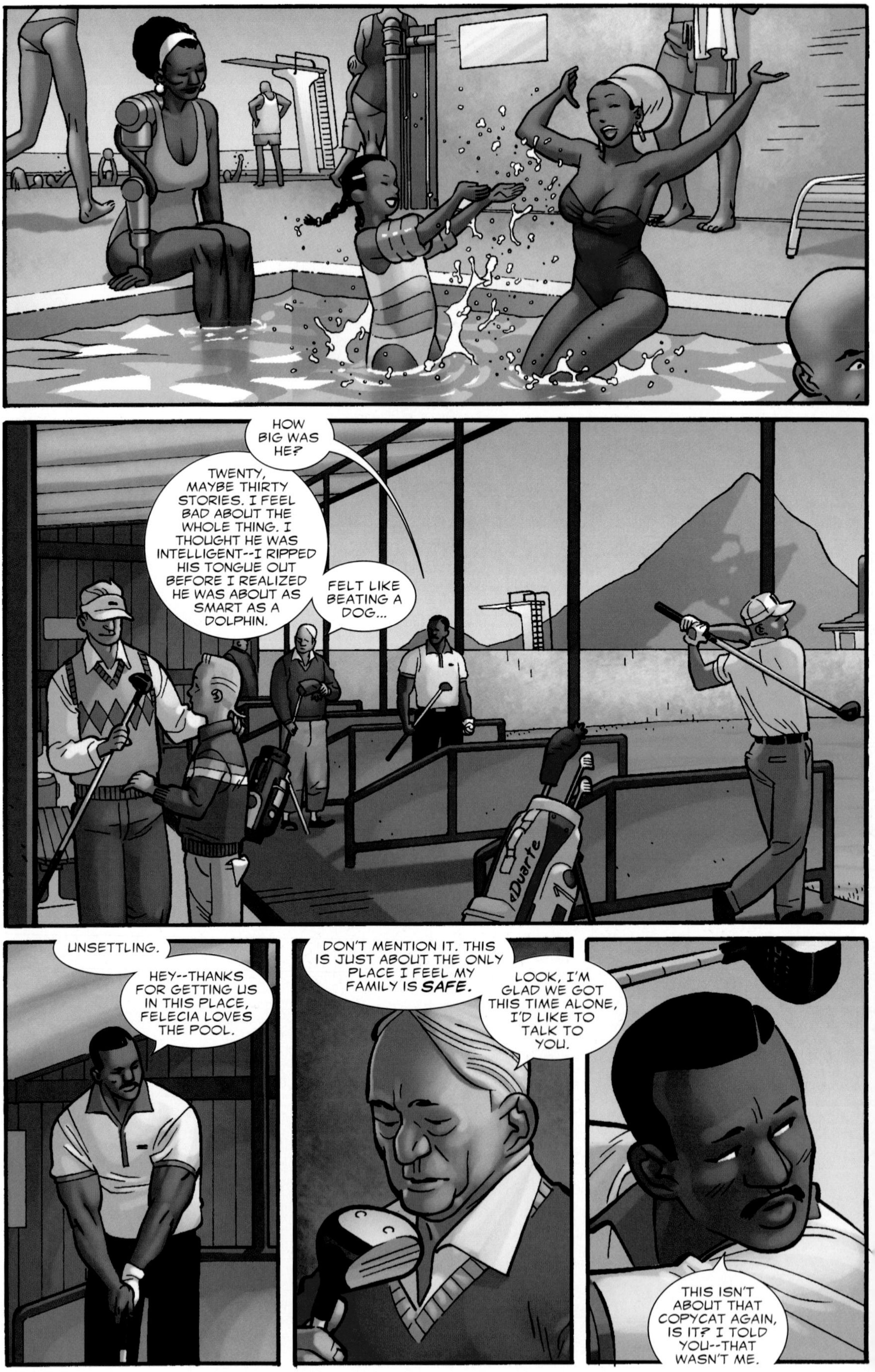
HOW BIG WAS HE?
TWENTY, MAYBE THIRTY STORIES. I FEEL BAD ABOUT THE WHOLE THING. I THOUGHT HE WAS INTELLIGENT--I RIPPED HIS TONGUE OUT BEFORE I REALIZED HE WAS ABOUT AS SMART AS A DOLPHIN.
FELT LIKE BEATING A DOG...
Duarte
UNSETTLING.
HEY--THANKS FOR GETTING US IN THIS PLACE, FELECIA LOVES THE POOL.
DON'T MENTION IT. THIS IS JUST ABOUT THE ONLY PLACE I FEEL MY FAMILY IS SAFE.
LOOK, I'M GLAD WE GOT THIS TIME ALONE, I'D LIKE TO TALK TO YOU.
THIS ISN'T ABOUT THAT COPYCAT AGAIN, IS IT? I TOLD YOU--THAT WASN'T ME.

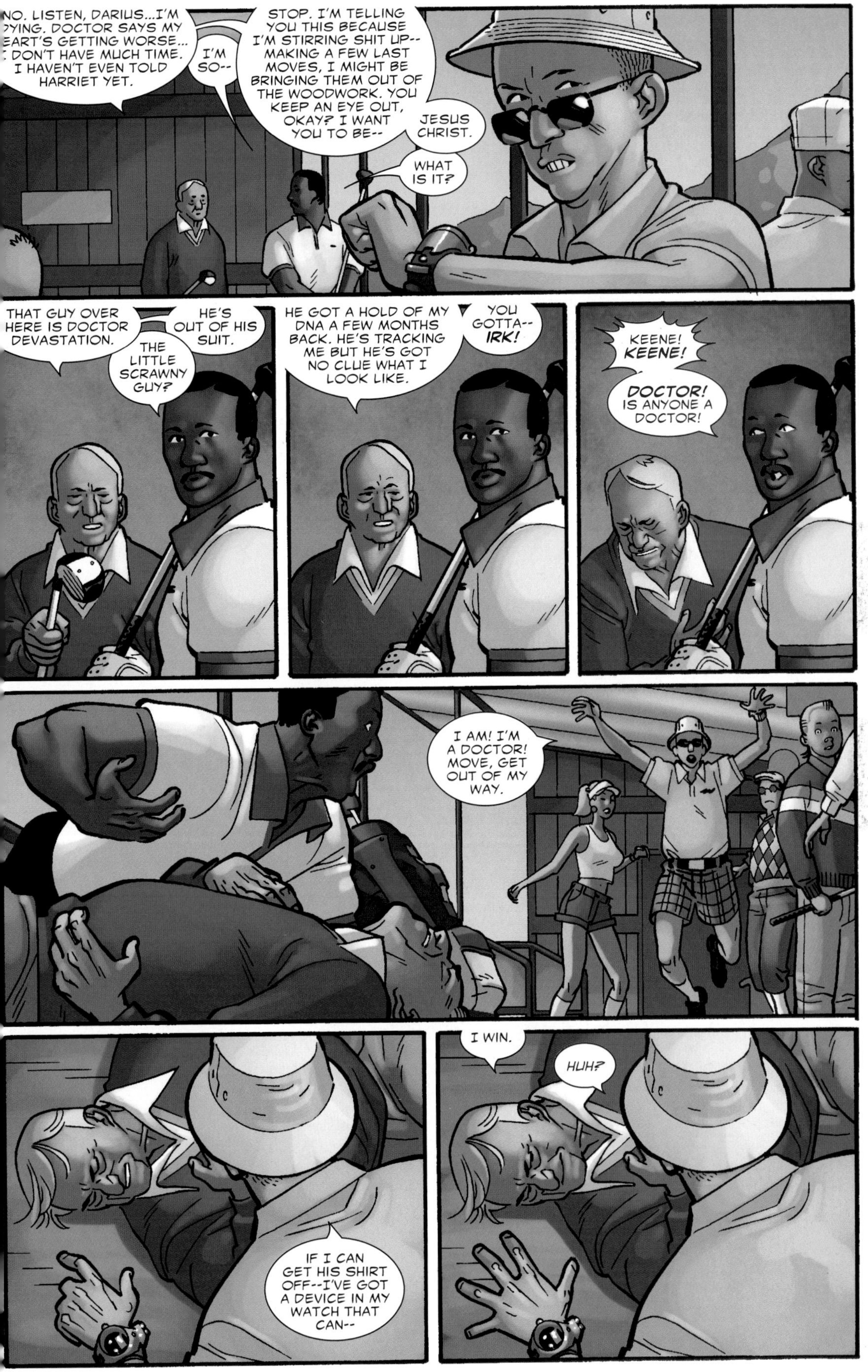
NO. LISTEN, DARIUS...I'M DYING. DOCTOR SAYS MY EART'S GETTING WORSE... DON'T HAVE MUCH TIME. I HAVEN'T EVEN TOLD HARRIET YET.
I'M SO--
STOP. I'M TELLING YOU THIS BECAUSE I'M STIRRING SHIT UP-- MAKING A FEW LAST MOVES, I MIGHT BE BRINGING THEM OUT OF THE WOODWORK. YOU KEEP AN EYE OUT, OKAY? I WANT YOU TO BE--
JESUS CHRIST.
WHAT IS IT?
THAT GUY OVER HERE IS DOCTOR DEVASTATION.
THE LITTLE SCRAWNY GUY?
HE'S OUT OF HIS SUIT.
HE GOT A HOLD OF MY DNA A FEW MONTHS BACK. HE'S TRACKING ME BUT HE'S GOT NO CLUE WHAT I LOOK LIKE.
YOU GOTTA-- IRK!
KEENE! KEENE!
DOCTOR! IS ANYONE A DOCTOR!
I AM! I'M A DOCTOR! MOVE, GET OUT OF MY WAY.
IF I CAN GET HIS SHIRT OFF--I'VE GOT A DEVICE IN MY WATCH THAT CAN--
I WIN.
HUH?

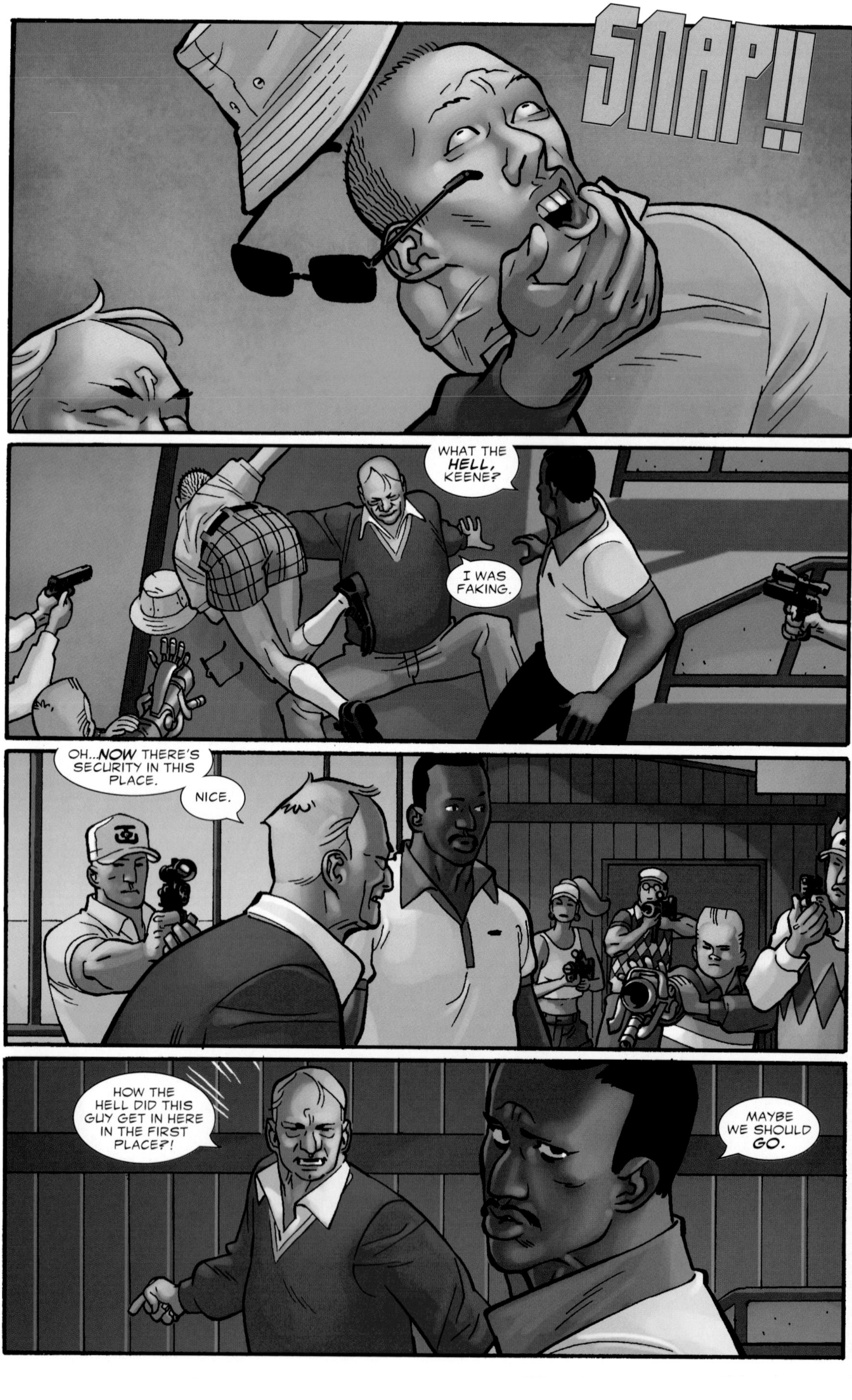
SNAP!!
WHAT THE HELL, KEENE?
I WAS FAKING.
OH...NOW THERE'S SECURITY IN THIS PLACE.
NICE.
HOW THE HELL DID THIS GUY GET IN HERE IN THE FIRST PLACE?!
MAYBE WE SHOULD GO.

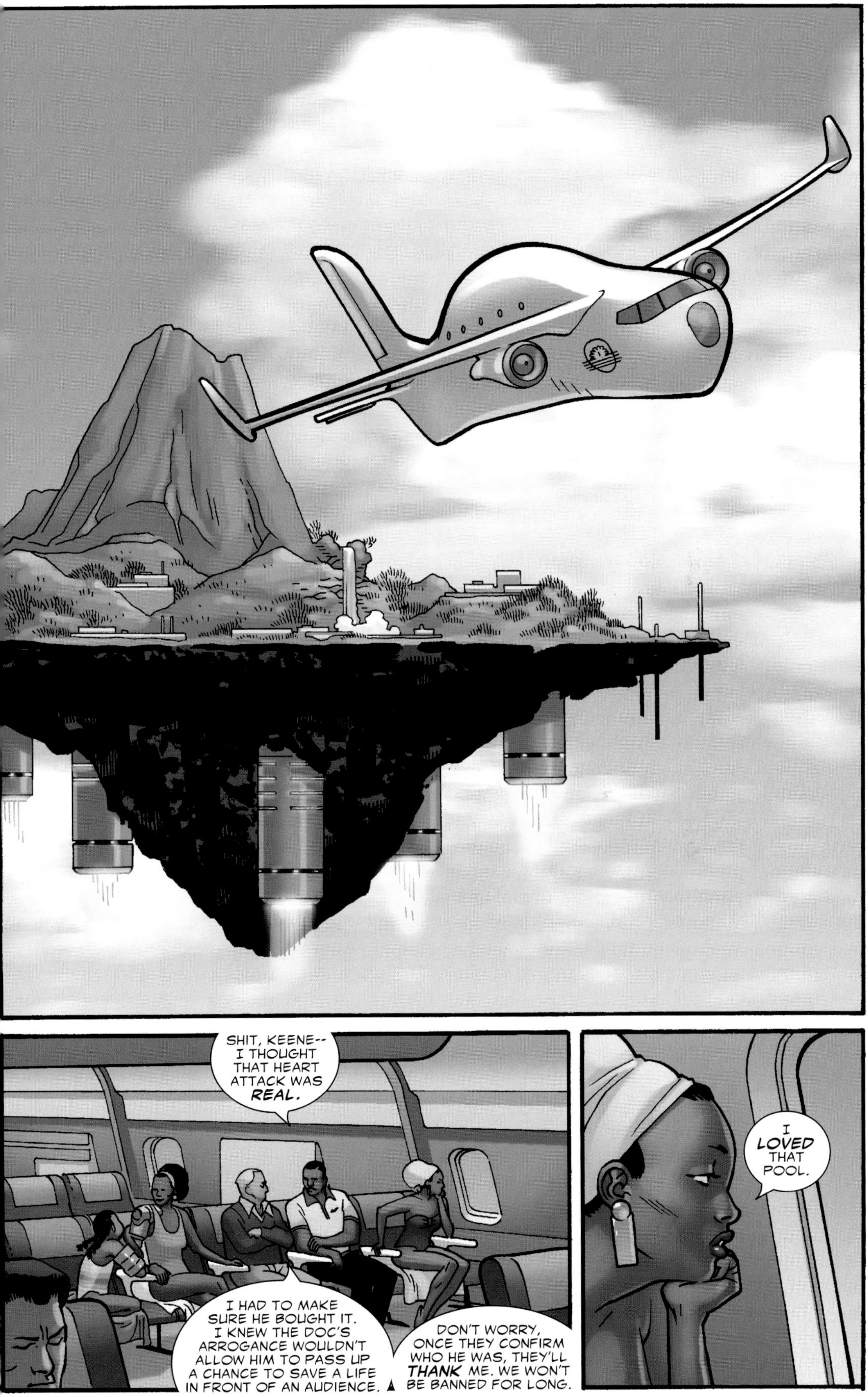
SHIT, KEENE-- I THOUGHT THAT HEART ATTACK WAS REAL.
I HAD TO MAKE SURE HE BOUGHT IT. I KNEW THE DOC'S ARROGANCE WOULDN'T ALLOW HIM TO PASS UP A CHANCE TO SAVE A LIFE IN FRONT OF AN AUDIENCE.
DON'T WORRY, ONCE THEY CONFIRM WHO HE WAS, THEY'LL THANK ME. WE WON'T BE BANNED FOR LONG.
I LOVED THAT POOL.

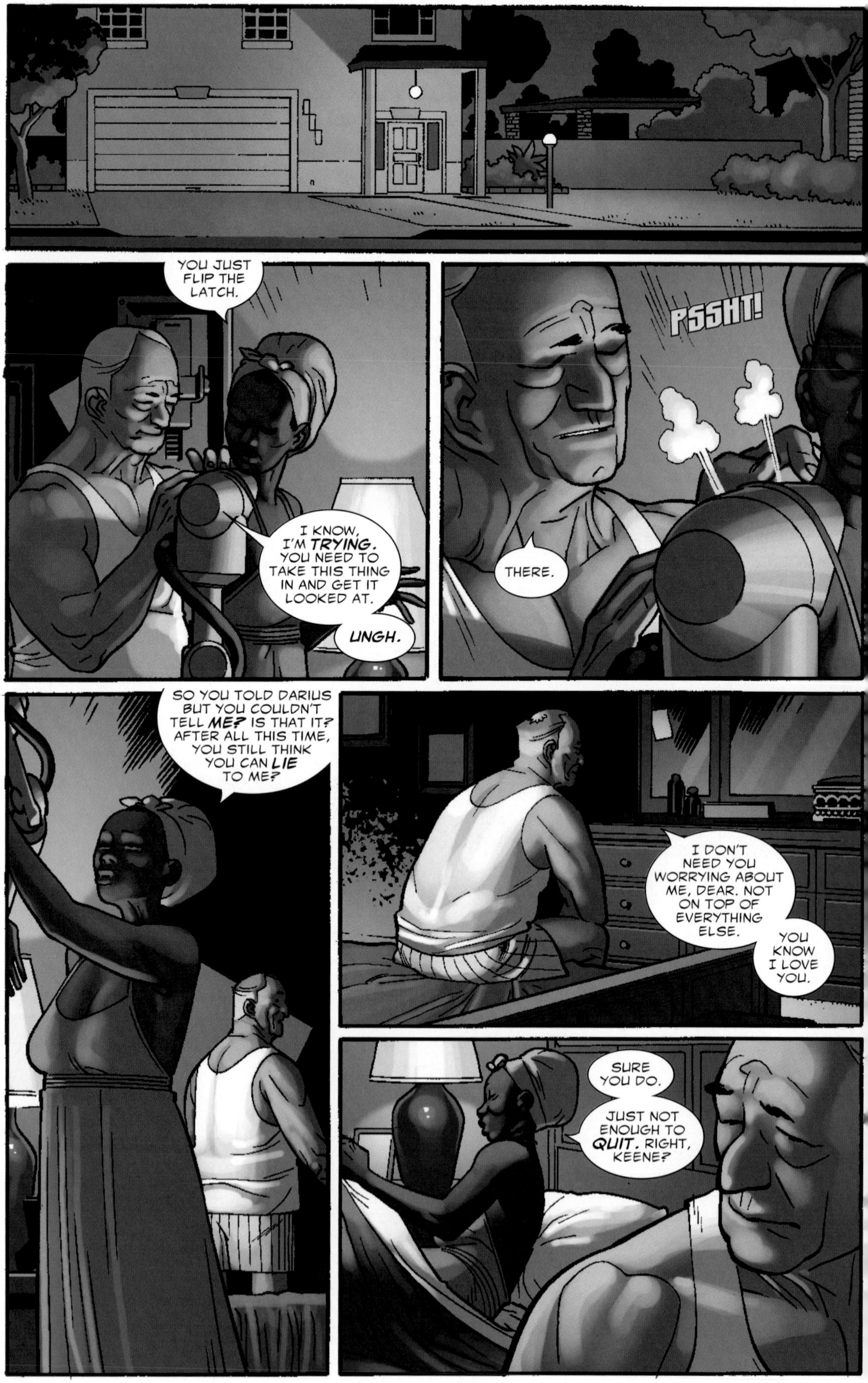
YOU JUST FLIP THE LATCH.
I KNOW, I'M **TRYING.** YOU NEED TO TAKE THIS THING IN AND GET IT LOOKED AT.
UNGH.
PSSHT!
THERE.
SO YOU TOLD DARIUS BUT YOU COULDN'T TELL **ME?** IS THAT IT? AFTER ALL THIS TIME, YOU STILL THINK YOU CAN **LIE** TO ME?
I DON'T NEED YOU WORRYING ABOUT ME, DEAR. NOT ON TOP OF EVERYTHING ELSE.
YOU KNOW I LOVE YOU.
SURE YOU DO.
JUST NOT ENOUGH TO **QUIT.** RIGHT, KEENE?

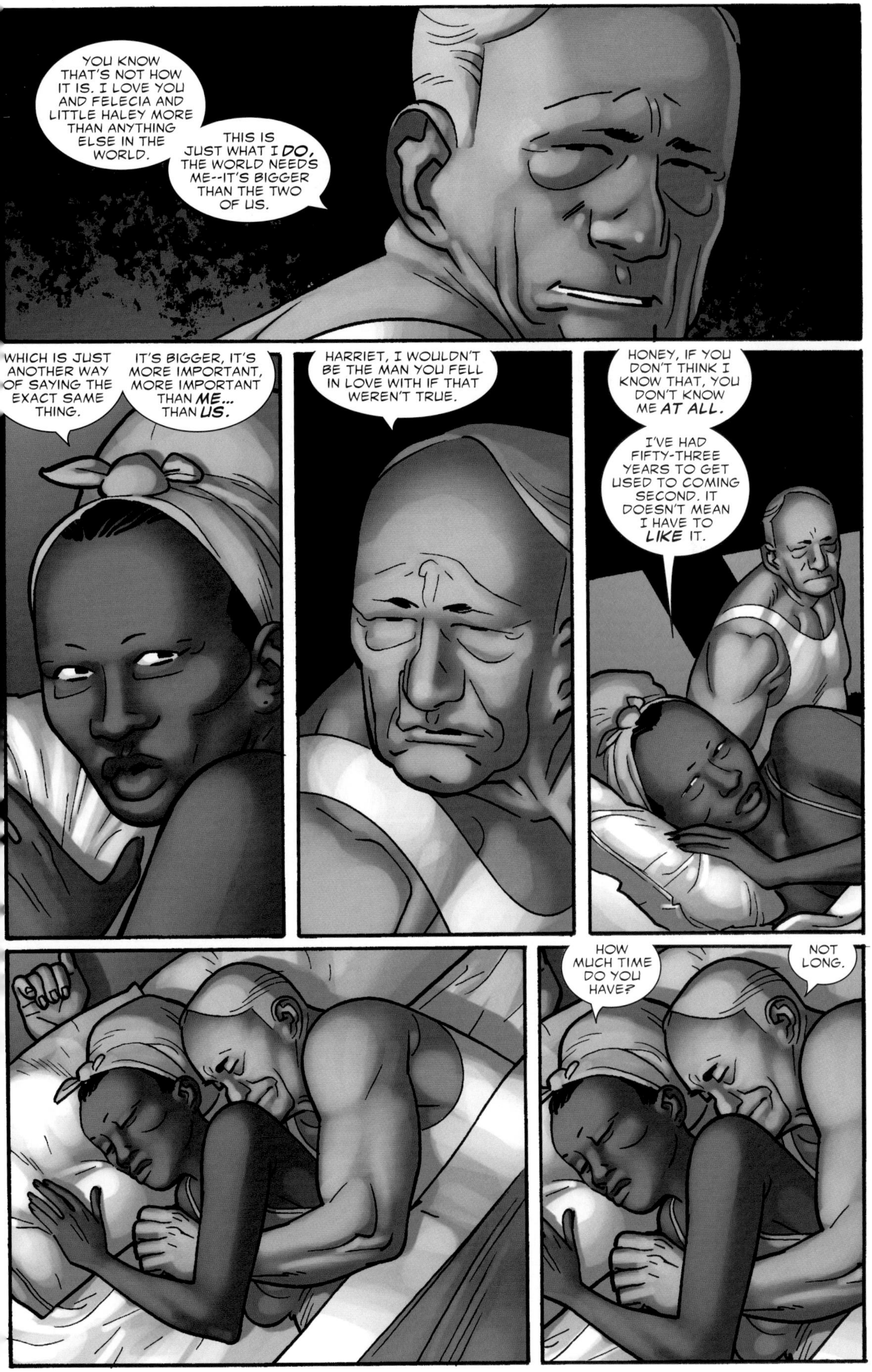
YOU KNOW THAT'S NOT HOW IT IS. I LOVE YOU AND FELECIA AND LITTLE HALEY MORE THAN ANYTHING ELSE IN THE WORLD.
THIS IS JUST WHAT I DO, THE WORLD NEEDS ME--IT'S BIGGER THAN THE TWO OF US.
WHICH IS JUST ANOTHER WAY OF SAYING THE EXACT SAME THING.
IT'S BIGGER, IT'S MORE IMPORTANT, MORE IMPORTANT THAN ME... THAN US.
HARRIET, I WOULDN'T BE THE MAN YOU FELL IN LOVE WITH IF THAT WEREN'T TRUE.
HONEY, IF YOU DON'T THINK I KNOW THAT, YOU DON'T KNOW ME AT ALL.
I'VE HAD FIFTY-THREE YEARS TO GET USED TO COMING SECOND. IT DOESN'T MEAN I HAVE TO LIKE IT.
HOW MUCH TIME DO YOU HAVE?
NOT LONG.

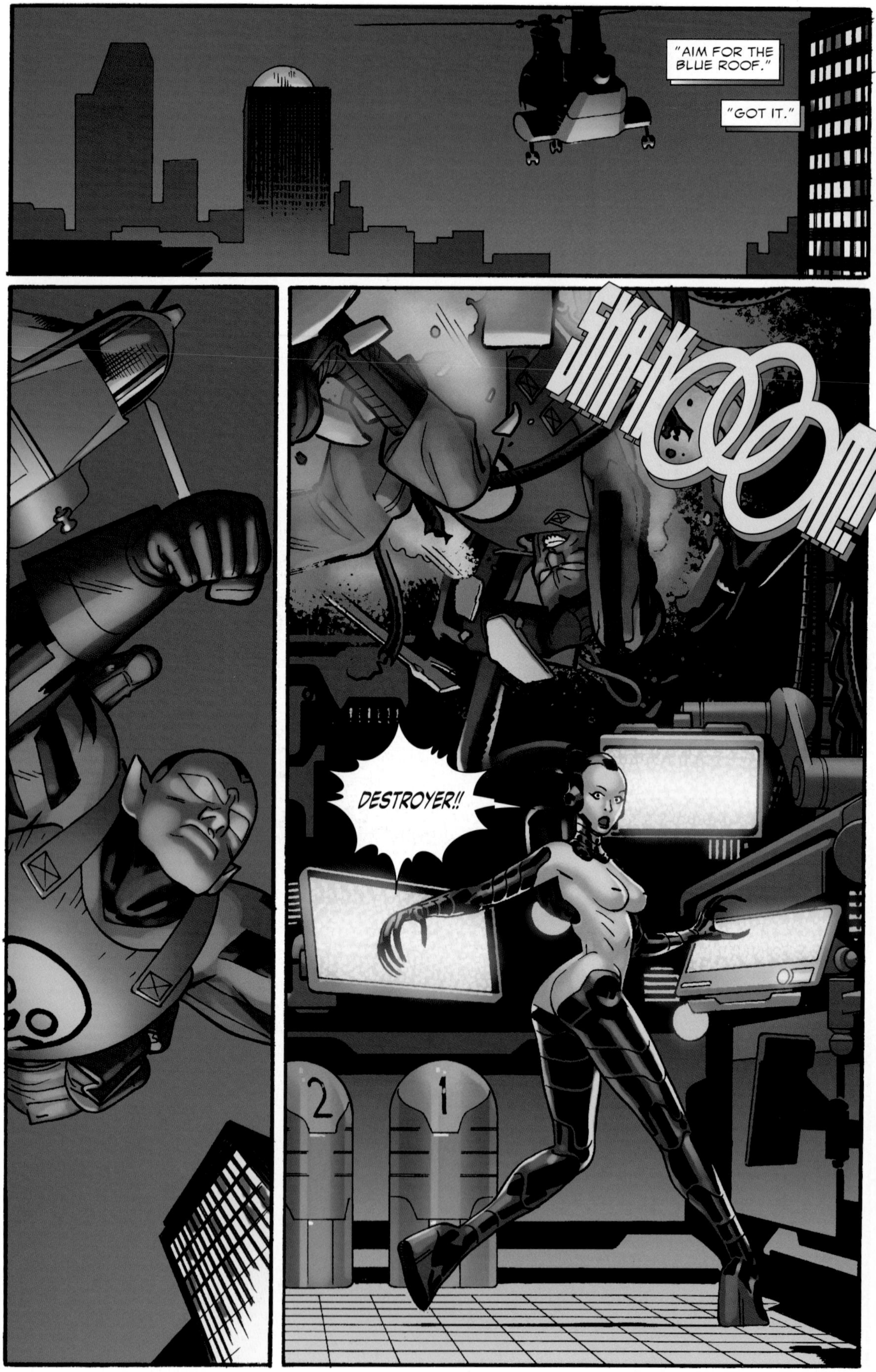
"AIM FOR THE BLUE ROOF."
"GOT IT."
SKA-KOOOM!!
DESTROYER!!

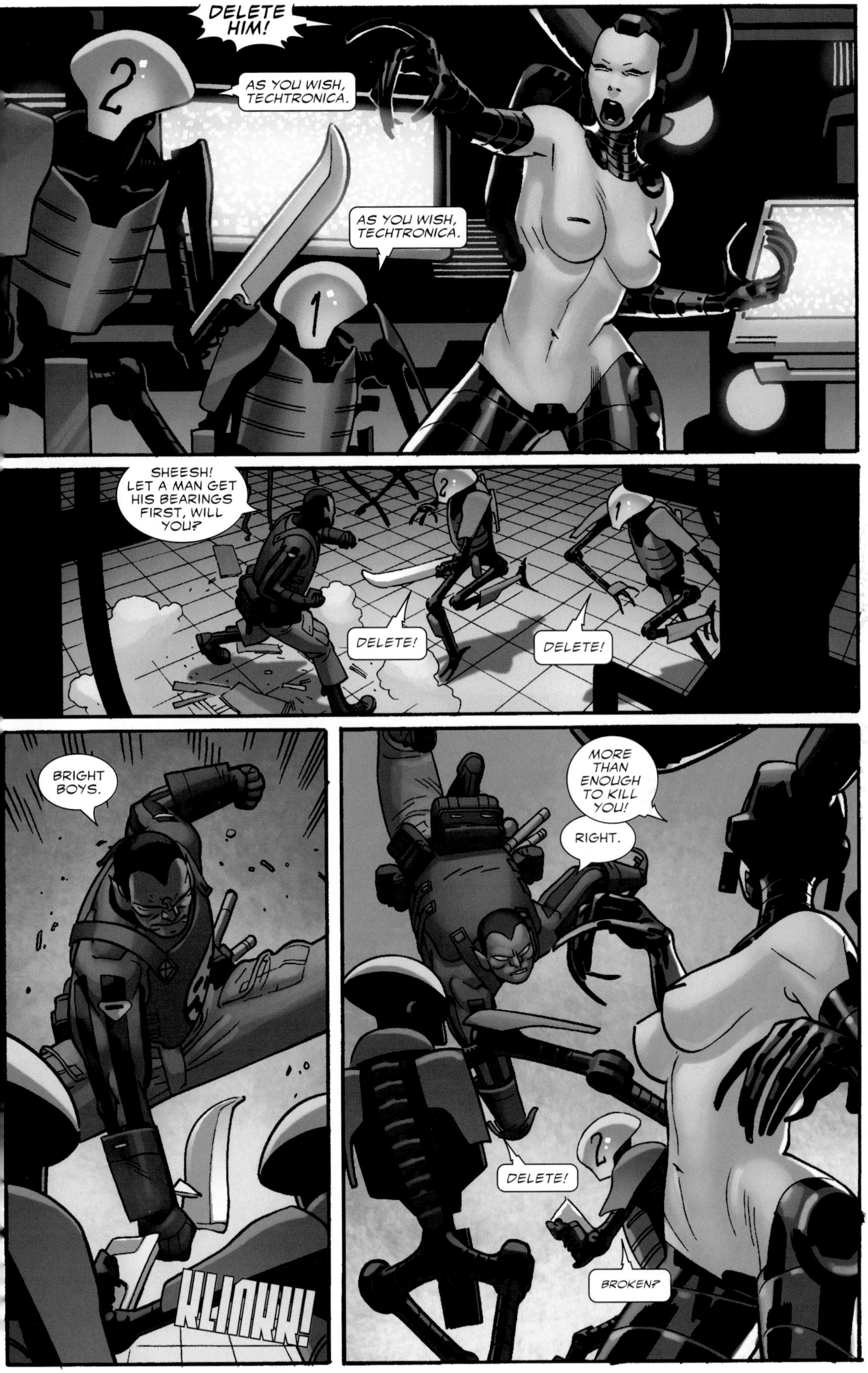
DELETE HIM!
AS YOU WISH, TECHTRONICA.
AS YOU WISH, TECHTRONICA.
SHEESH! LET A MAN GET HIS BEARINGS FIRST, WILL YOU?
DELETE!
DELETE!
BRIGHT BOYS.
KLINKK!
MORE THAN ENOUGH TO KILL YOU!
RIGHT.
DELETE!
BROKEN?

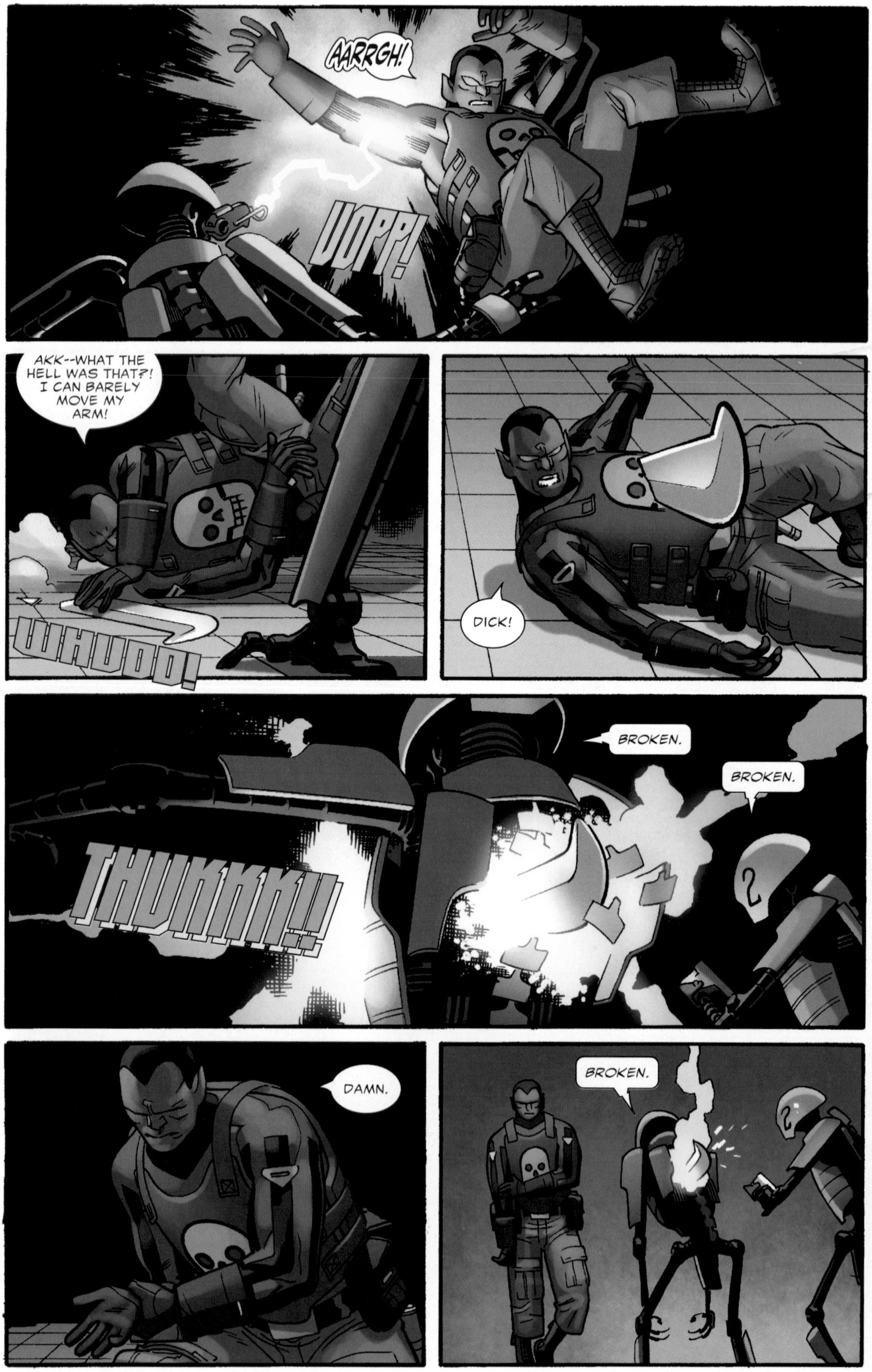
AARRGH!
UOPP!
AKK--WHAT THE HELL WAS THAT?! I CAN BARELY MOVE MY ARM!
WHUDD!
DICK!
BROKEN.
BROKEN.
THUKKK!!
DAMN.
BROKEN.

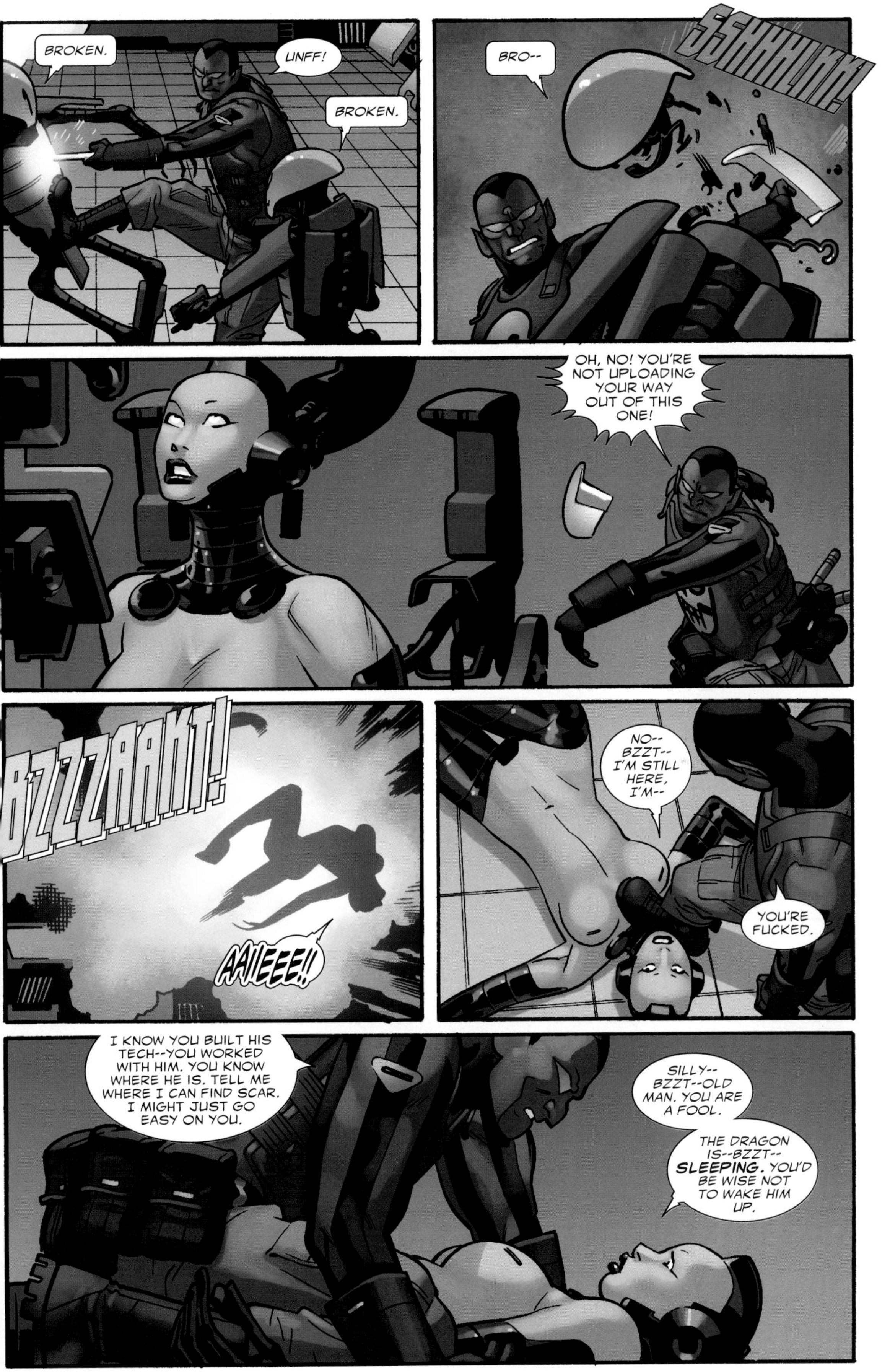
BROKEN.
UNFF!
BROKEN.
BRO--
SSHHHUNK!
OH, NO! YOU'RE NOT UPLOADING YOUR WAY OUT OF THIS ONE!
BZZZAAKT!
AAIIEEE!!
NO-- BZZT-- I'M STILL HERE, I'M--
YOU'RE FUCKED.
I KNOW YOU BUILT HIS TECH--YOU WORKED WITH HIM. YOU KNOW WHERE HE IS. TELL ME WHERE I CAN FIND SCAR. I MIGHT JUST GO EASY ON YOU.
SILLY-- BZZT--OLD MAN. YOU ARE A FOOL.
THE DRAGON IS--BZZT-- **SLEEPING.** YOU'D BE WISE NOT TO WAKE HIM UP.

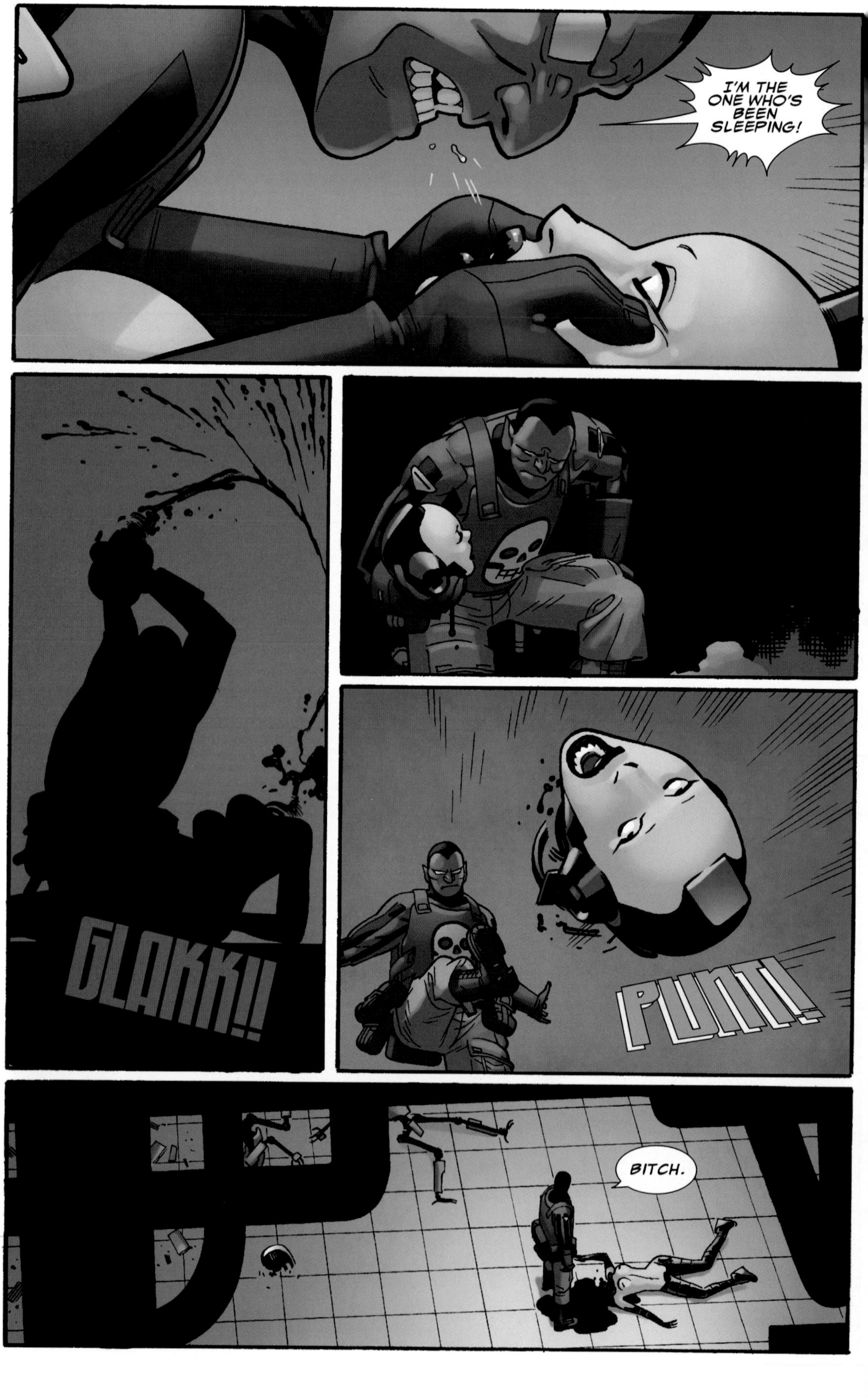
I'M THE ONE WHO'S BEEN SLEEPING!
GLAKK!!
PUNT!
BITCH.

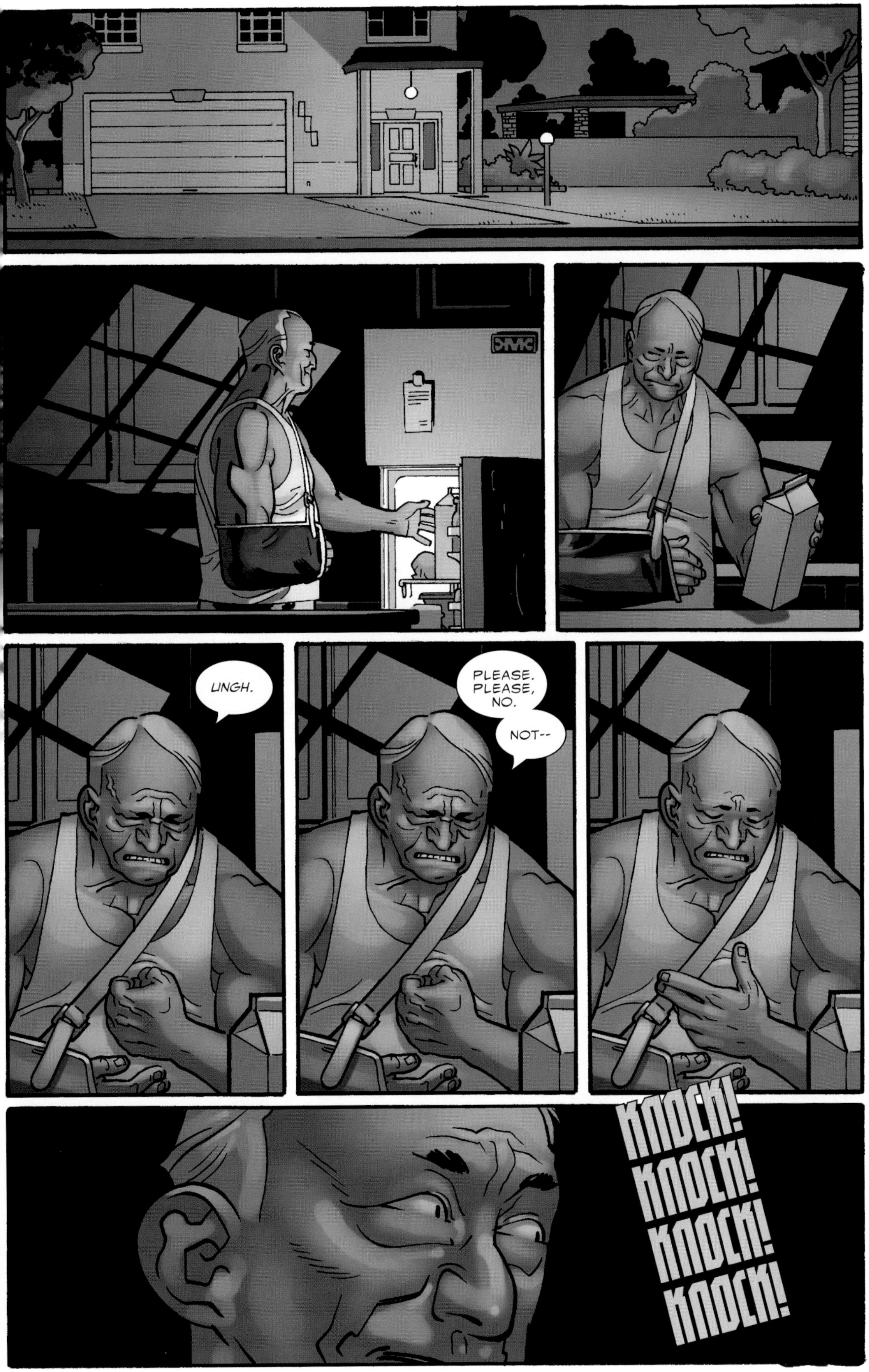
UNGH.
PLEASE. PLEASE, NO.
NOT--
KNOCK! KNOCK! KNOCK! KNOCK!

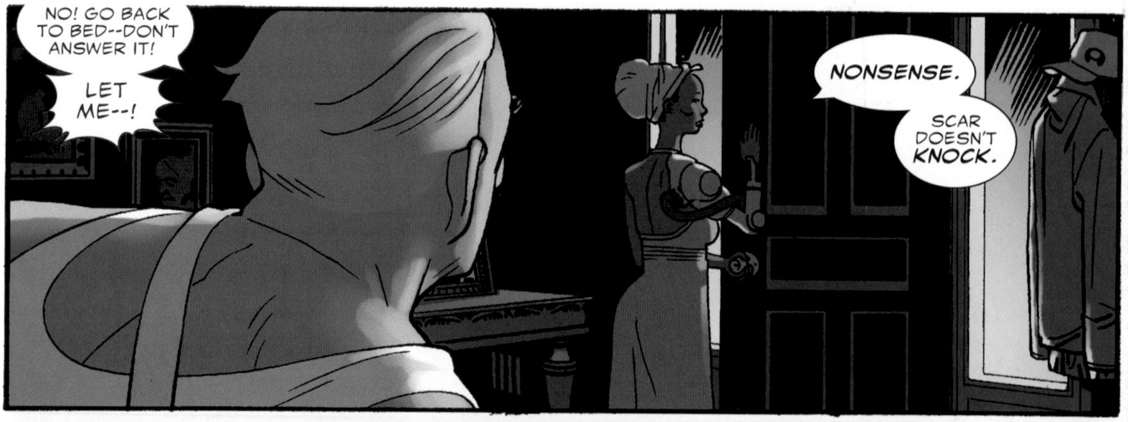
NO! GO BACK TO BED--DON'T ANSWER IT!
LET ME--!
NONSENSE.
SCAR DOESN'T KNOCK.

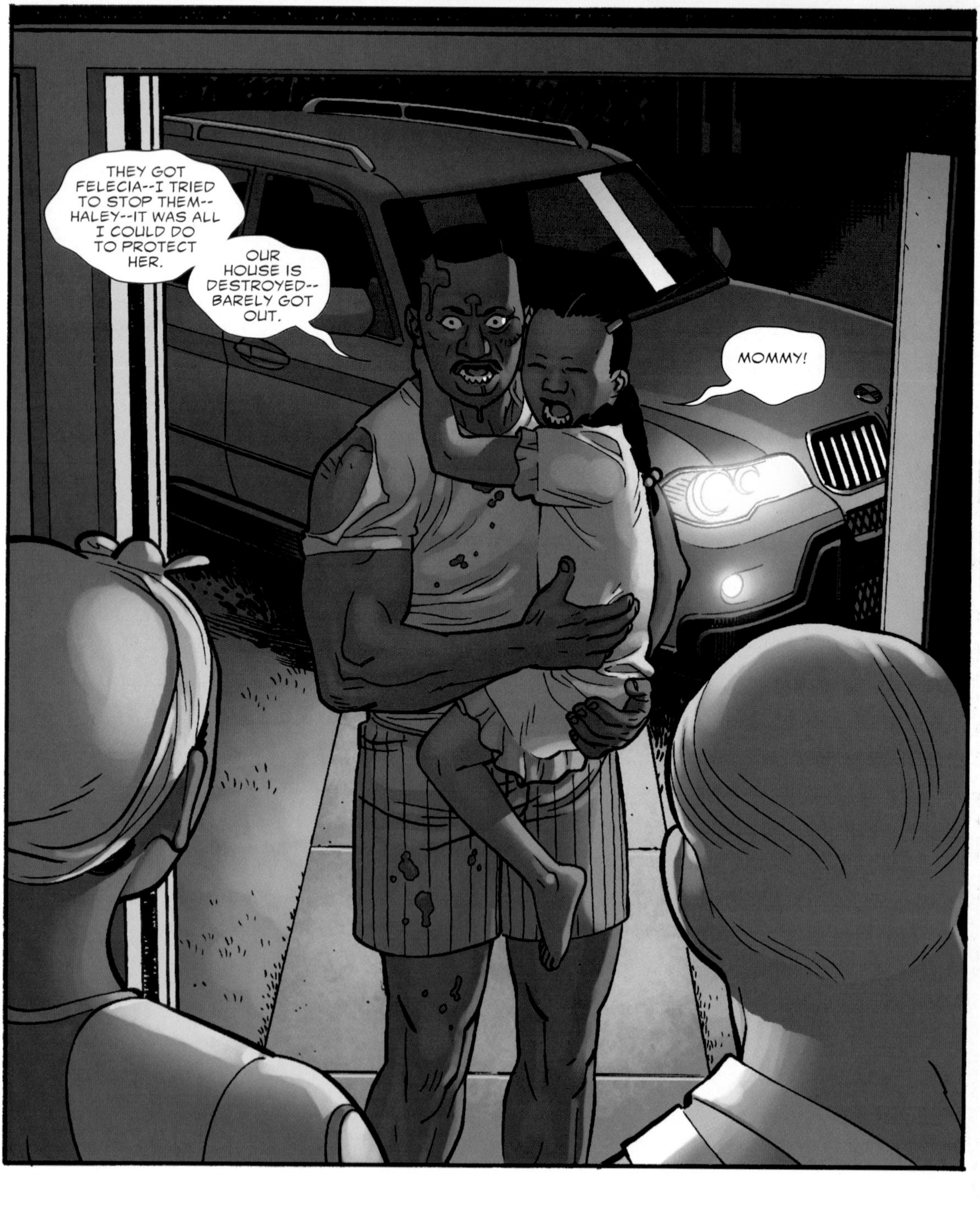
THEY GOT FELECIA--I TRIED TO STOP THEM--HALEY--IT WAS ALL I COULD DO TO PROTECT HER.
OUR HOUSE IS DESTROYED--BARELY GOT OUT.
MOMMY!

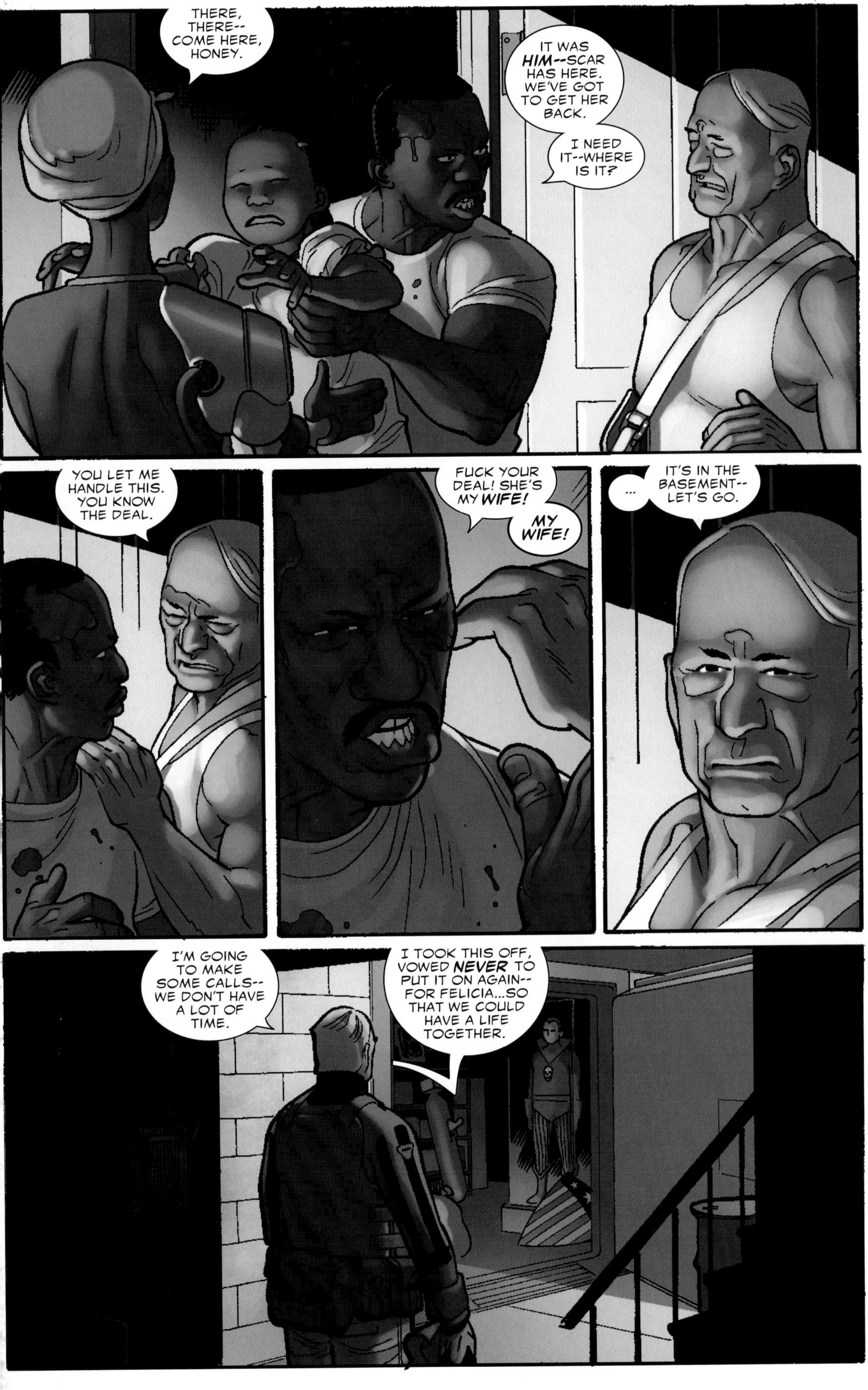
THERE, THERE-- COME HERE, HONEY.
IT WAS HIM--SCAR HAS HERE. WE'VE GOT TO GET HER BACK.
I NEED IT--WHERE IS IT?
YOU LET ME HANDLE THIS. YOU KNOW THE DEAL.
FUCK YOUR DEAL! SHE'S MY WIFE!
MY WIFE!
...
IT'S IN THE BASEMENT-- LET'S GO.
I'M GOING TO MAKE SOME CALLS-- WE DON'T HAVE A LOT OF TIME.
I TOOK THIS OFF, VOWED NEVER TO PUT IT ON AGAIN-- FOR FELICIA...SO THAT WE COULD HAVE A LIFE TOGETHER.

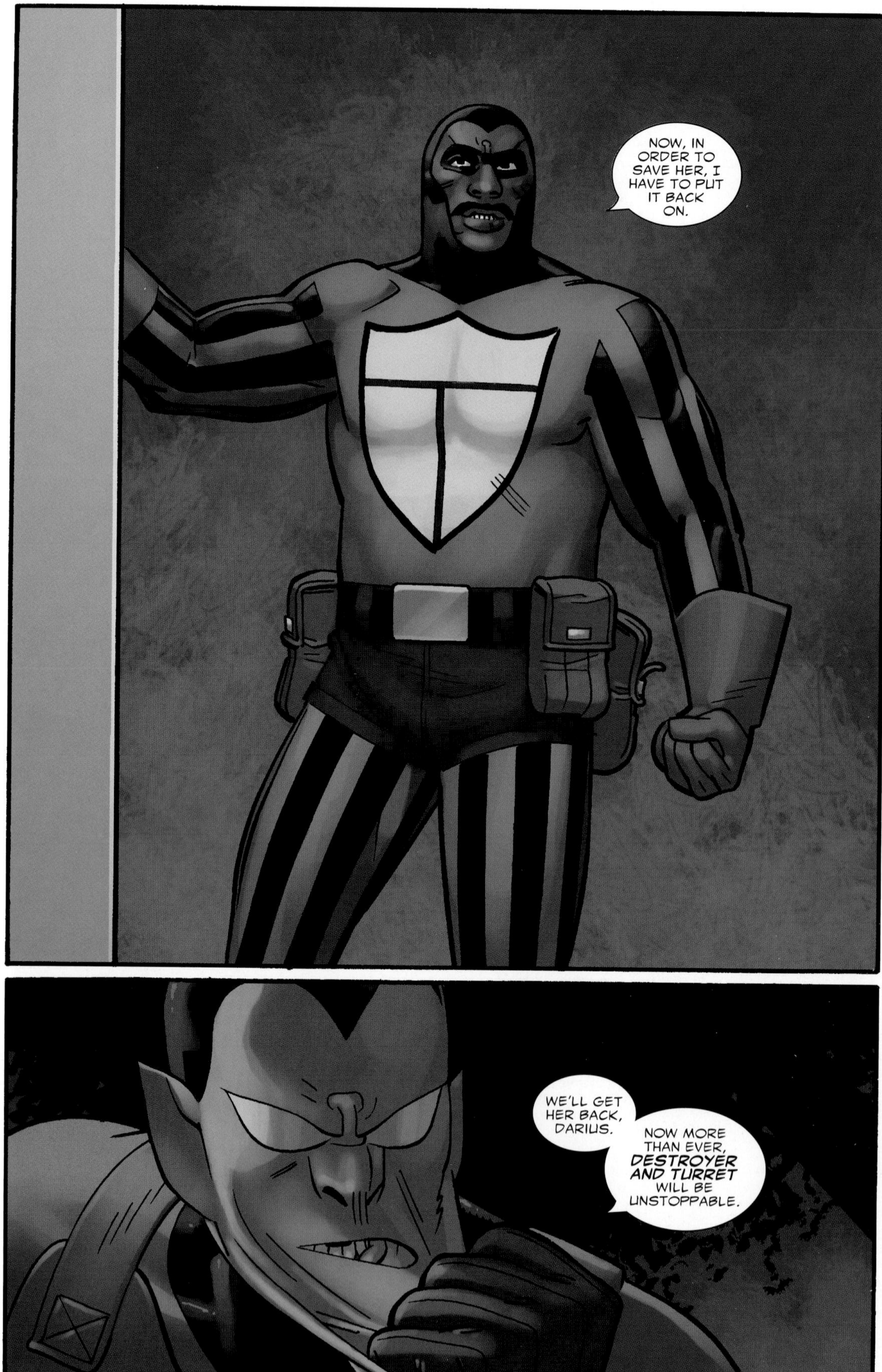
NOW, IN ORDER TO SAVE HER, I HAVE TO PUT IT BACK ON.
WE'LL GET HER BACK, DARIUS.
NOW MORE THAN EVER, ***DESTROYER AND TURRET*** WILL BE UNSTOPPABLE.

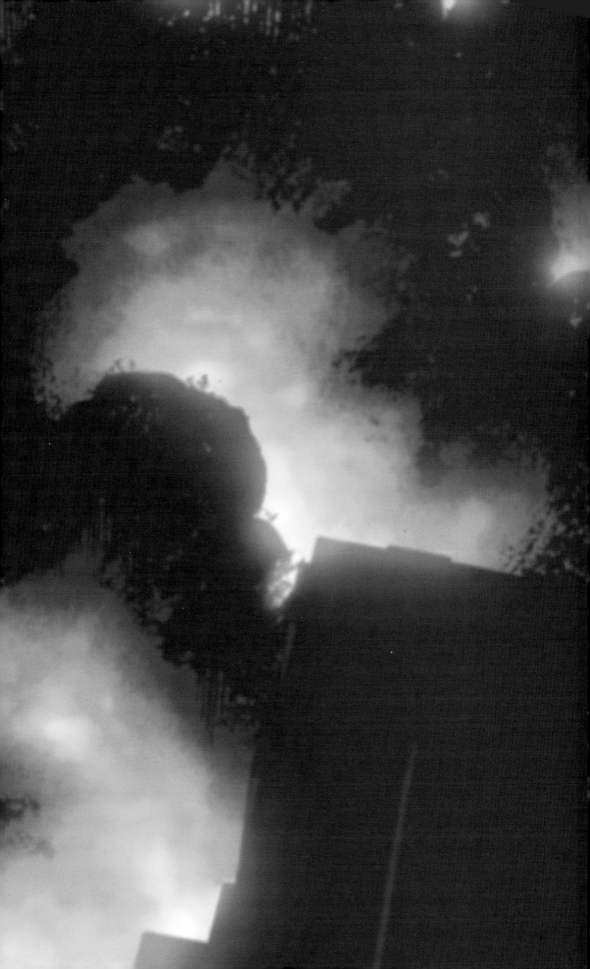

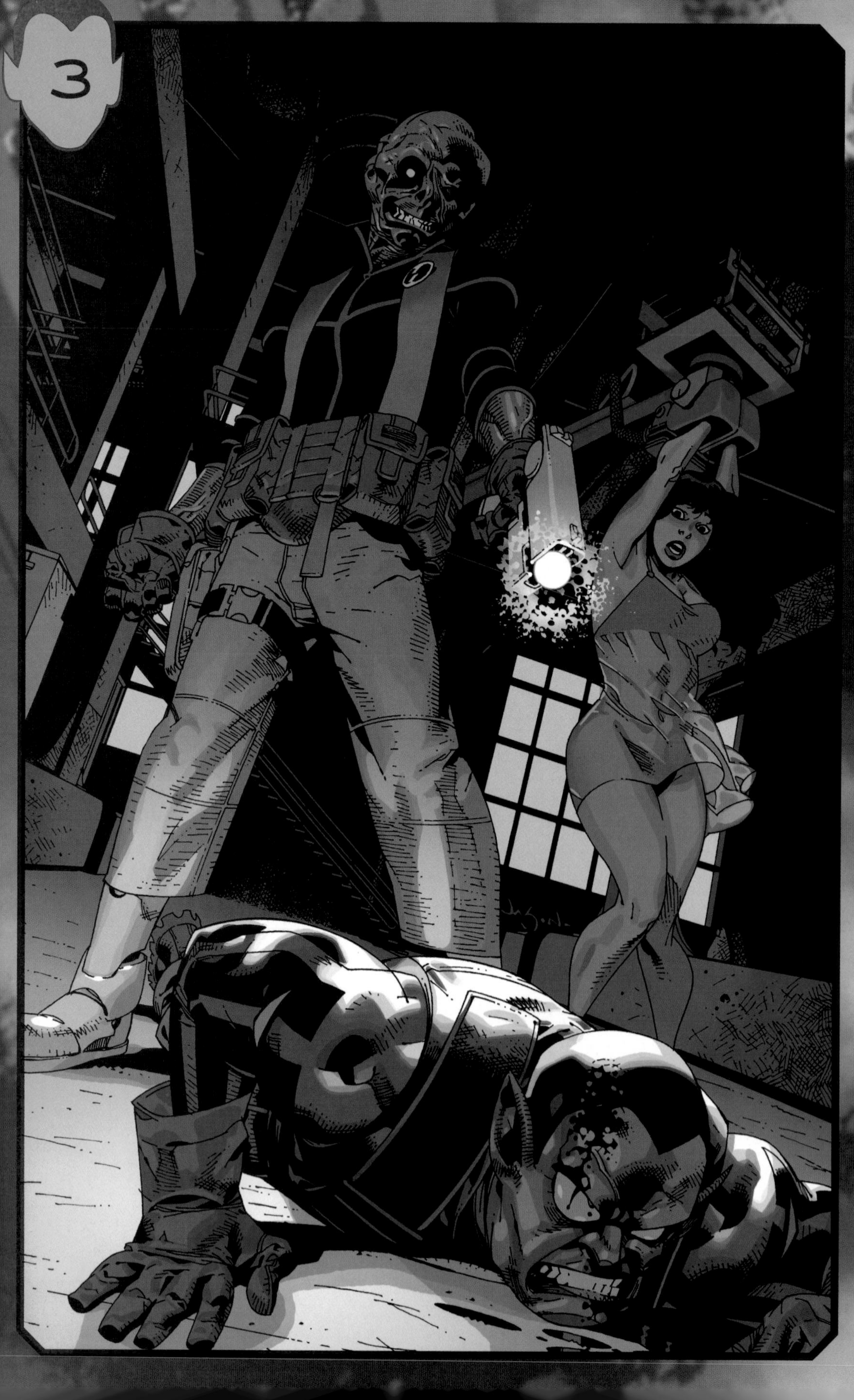
3

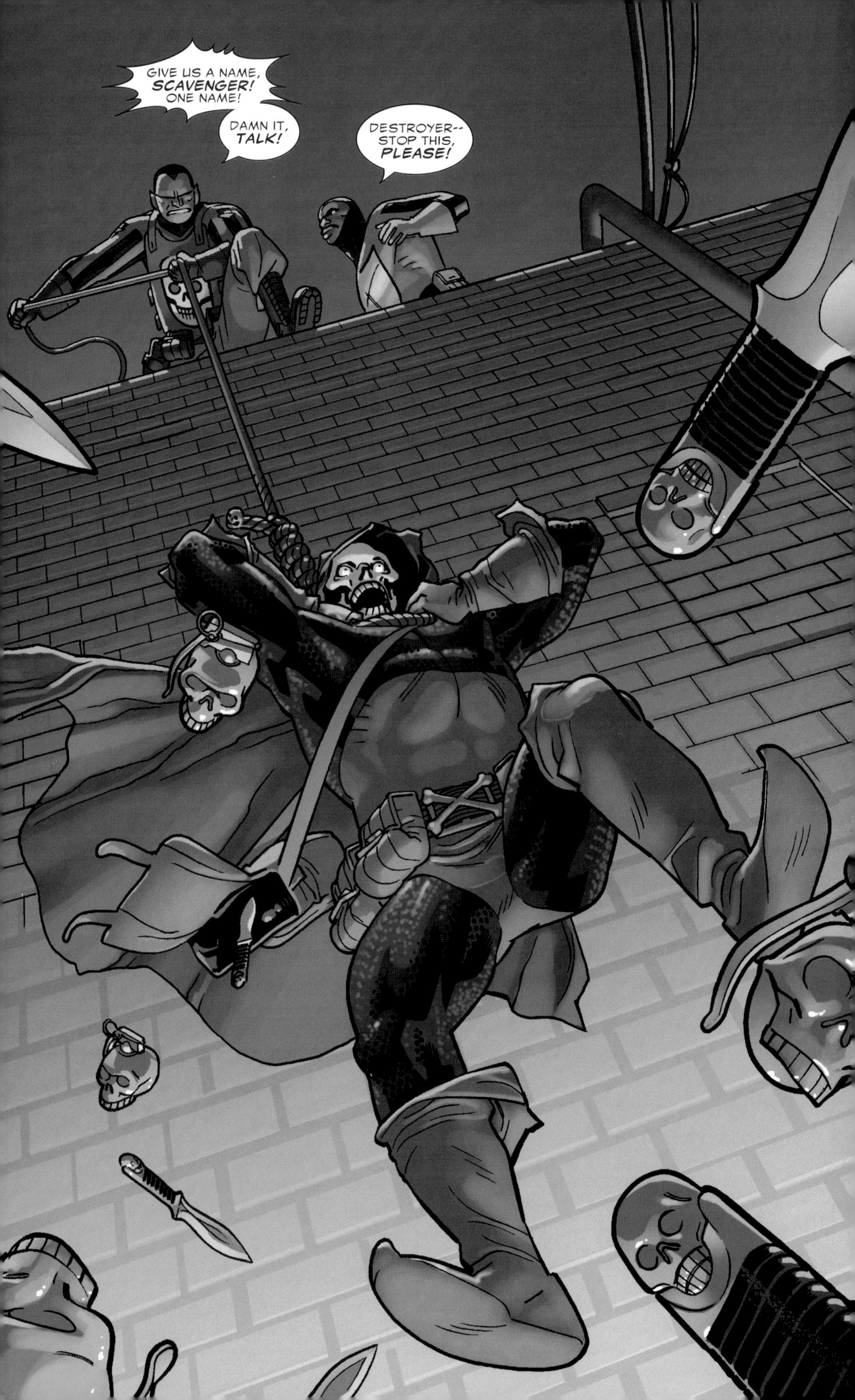
GIVE US A NAME, SCAVENGER! ONE NAME!
DAMN IT, TALK!
DESTROYER-- STOP THIS, PLEASE!

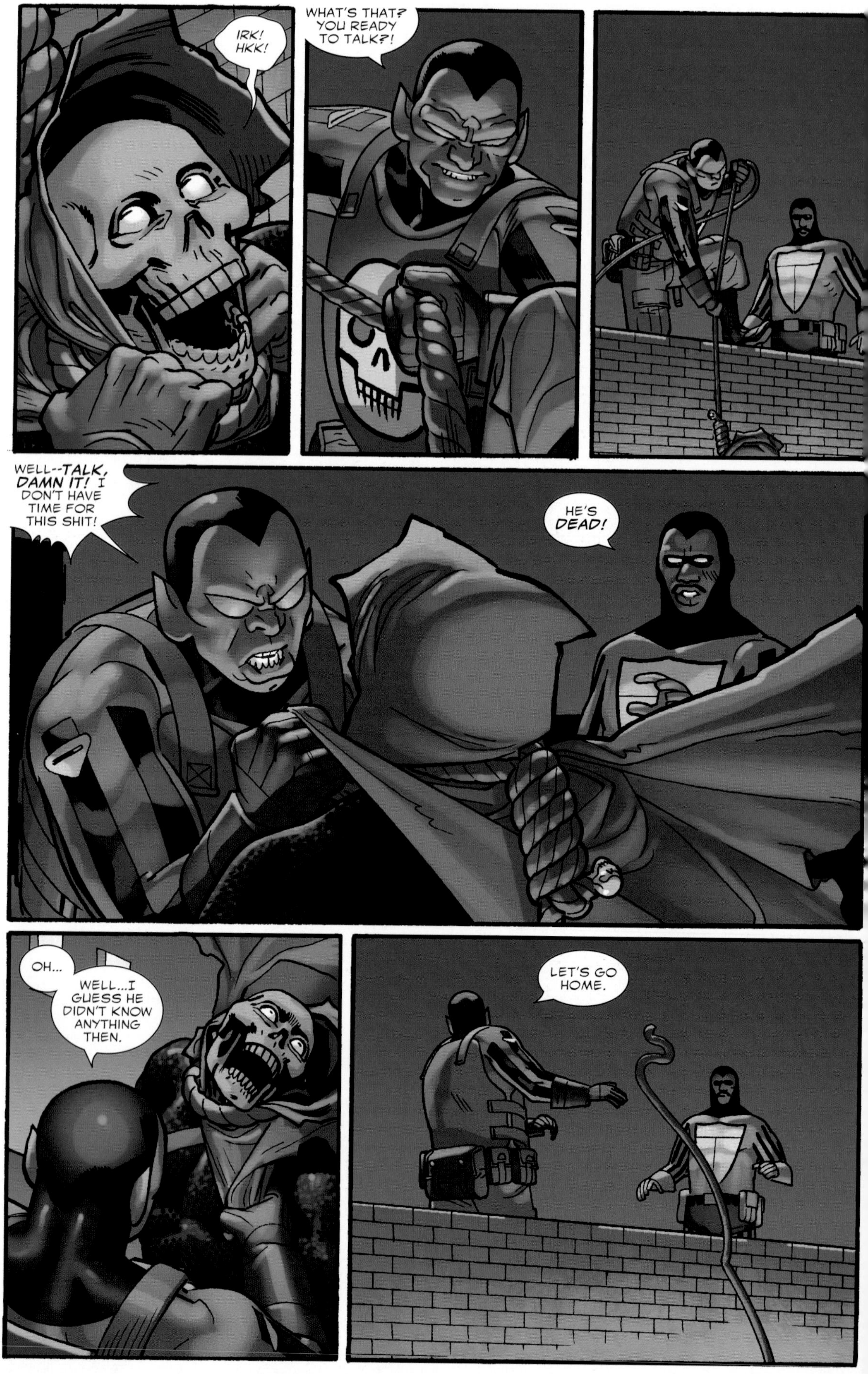
IRK! HKK!
WHAT'S THAT? YOU READY TO TALK?!
WELL--TALK, DAMN IT! I DON'T HAVE TIME FOR THIS SHIT!
HE'S DEAD!
OH...
WELL...I GUESS HE DIDN'T KNOW ANYTHING THEN.
LET'S GO HOME.

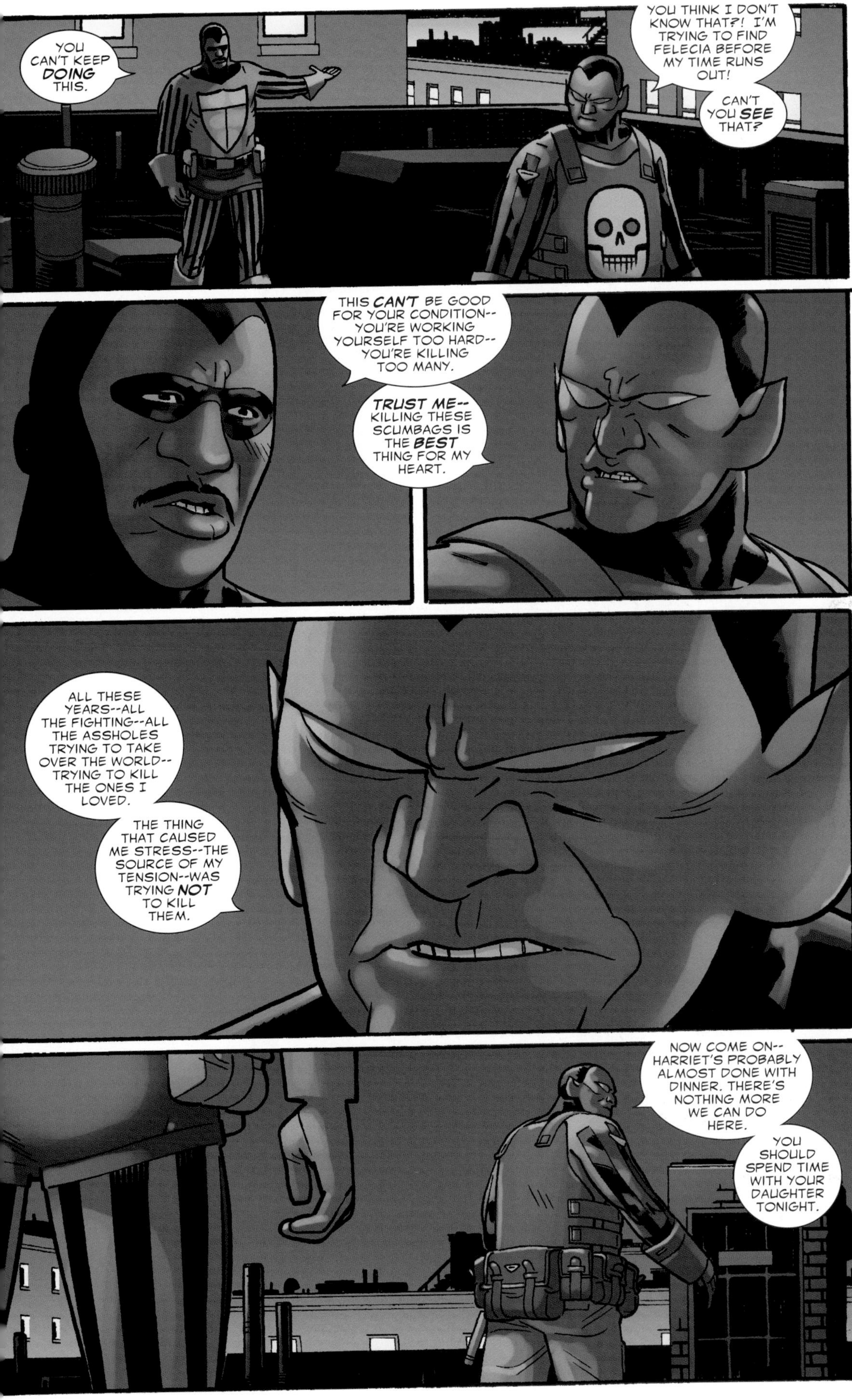
YOU CAN'T KEEP **DOING** THIS.
YOU THINK I DON'T KNOW THAT?! I'M TRYING TO FIND FELECIA BEFORE MY TIME RUNS OUT!
CAN'T YOU **SEE** THAT?
THIS **CAN'T** BE GOOD FOR YOUR CONDITION--YOU'RE WORKING YOURSELF TOO HARD--YOU'RE KILLING TOO MANY.
TRUST ME-- KILLING THESE SCUMBAGS IS THE **BEST** THING FOR MY HEART.
ALL THESE YEARS--ALL THE FIGHTING--ALL THE ASSHOLES TRYING TO TAKE OVER THE WORLD--TRYING TO KILL THE ONES I LOVED.
THE THING THAT CAUSED ME STRESS--THE SOURCE OF MY TENSION--WAS TRYING **NOT** TO KILL THEM.
NOW COME ON--HARRIET'S PROBABLY ALMOST DONE WITH DINNER. THERE'S NOTHING MORE WE CAN DO HERE.
YOU SHOULD SPEND TIME WITH YOUR DAUGHTER TONIGHT.

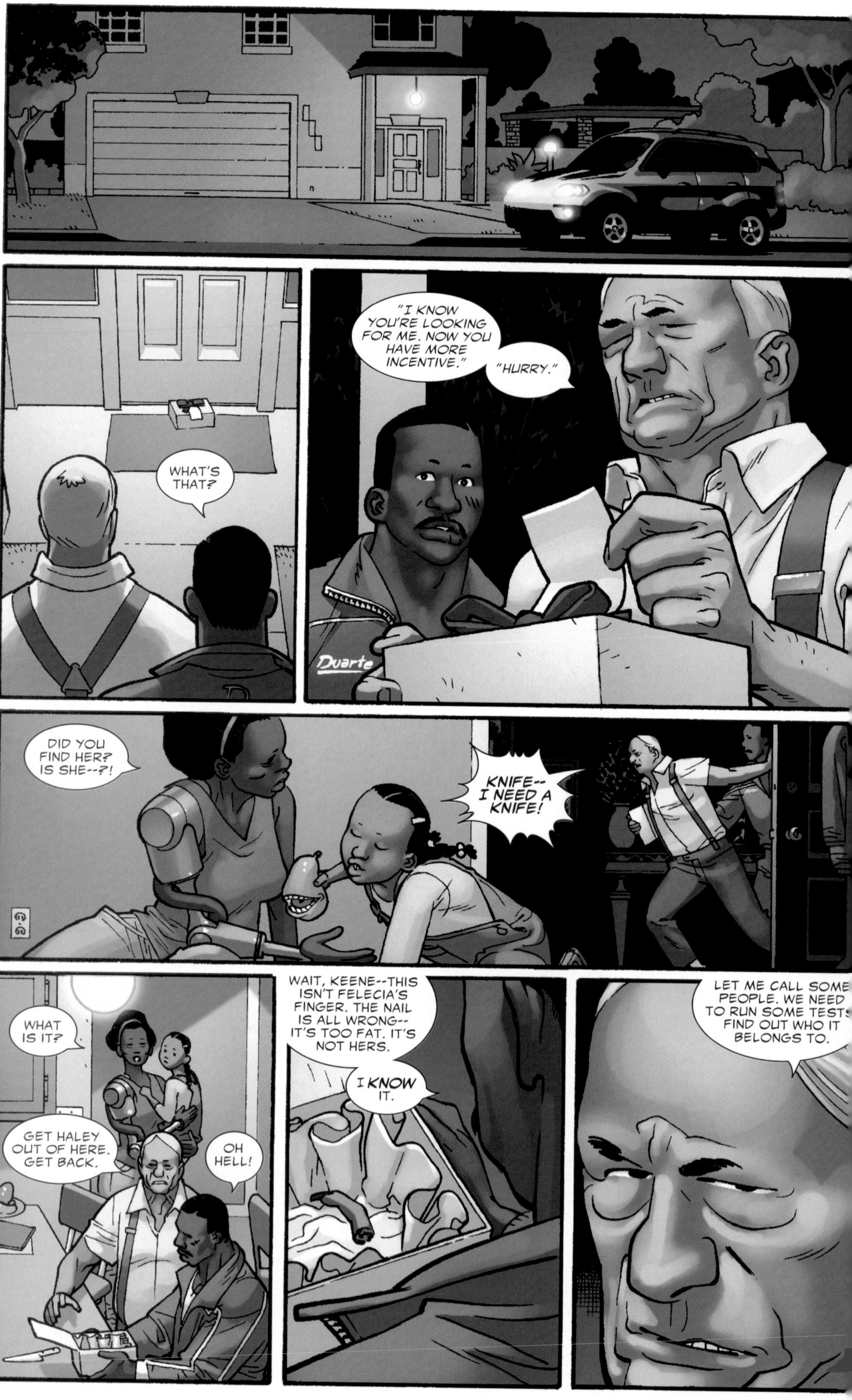
WHAT'S THAT?
"I KNOW YOU'RE LOOKING FOR ME. NOW YOU HAVE MORE INCENTIVE."
"HURRY."
Duarte
DID YOU FIND HER? IS SHE--?!
KNIFE-- I NEED A KNIFE!
WHAT IS IT?
GET HALEY OUT OF HERE. GET BACK.
OH HELL!
WAIT, KEENE--THIS ISN'T FELECIA'S FINGER. THE NAIL IS ALL WRONG-- IT'S TOO FAT. IT'S NOT HERS.
I KNOW IT.
LET ME CALL SOME PEOPLE. WE NEED TO RUN SOME TESTS FIND OUT WHO IT BELONGS TO.

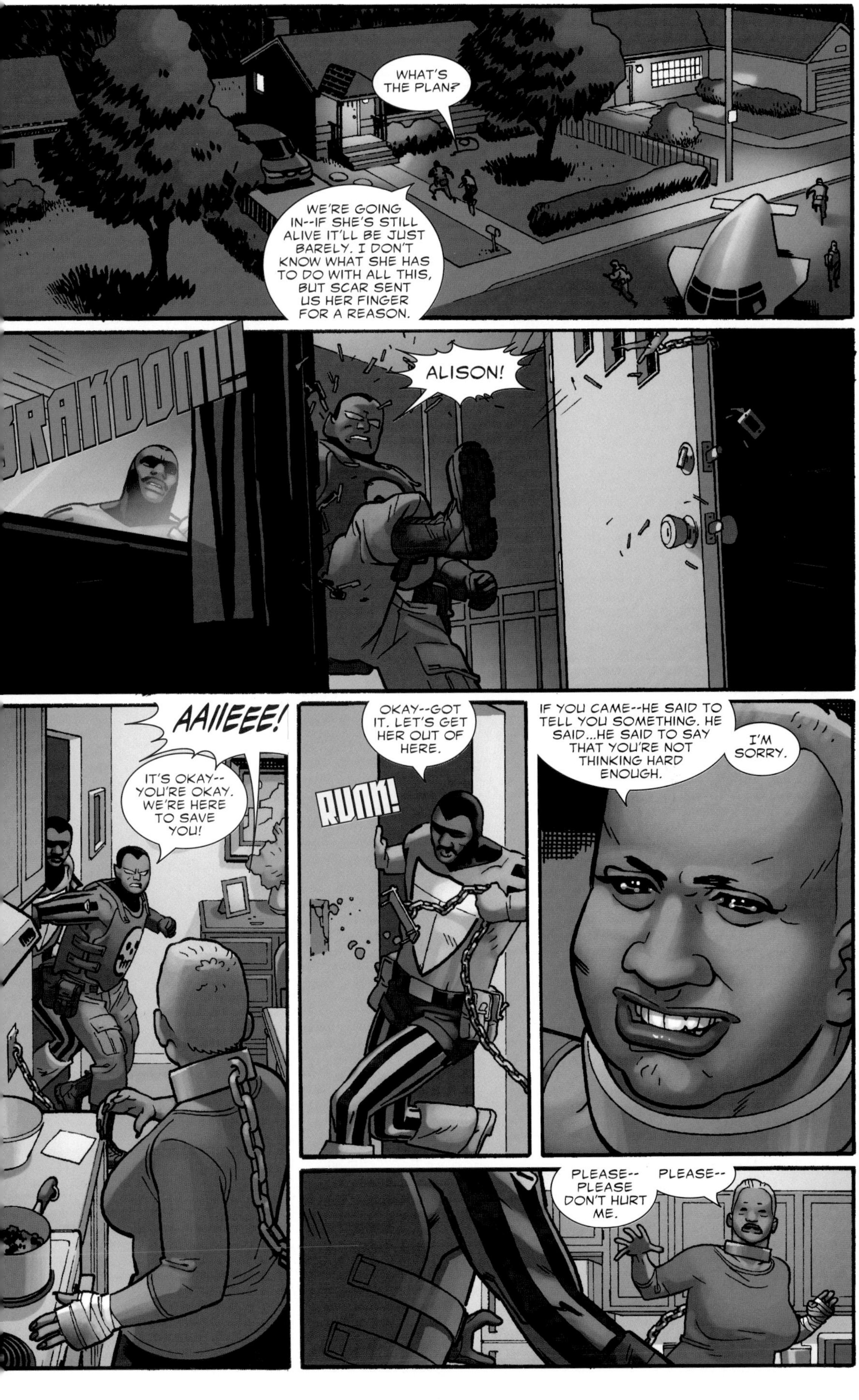

WHAT'S THE PLAN?
WE'RE GOING IN--IF SHE'S STILL ALIVE IT'LL BE JUST BARELY. I DON'T KNOW WHAT SHE HAS TO DO WITH ALL THIS, BUT SCAR SENT US HER FINGER FOR A REASON.
BRAKOOM!!
ALISON!
AAIIEEE!
IT'S OKAY--YOU'RE OKAY. WE'RE HERE TO SAVE YOU!
OKAY--GOT IT. LET'S GET HER OUT OF HERE.
RUNK!
IF YOU CAME--HE SAID TO TELL YOU SOMETHING. HE SAID...HE SAID TO SAY THAT YOU'RE NOT THINKING HARD ENOUGH.
I'M SORRY.
PLEASE--
PLEASE--PLEASE DON'T HURT ME.

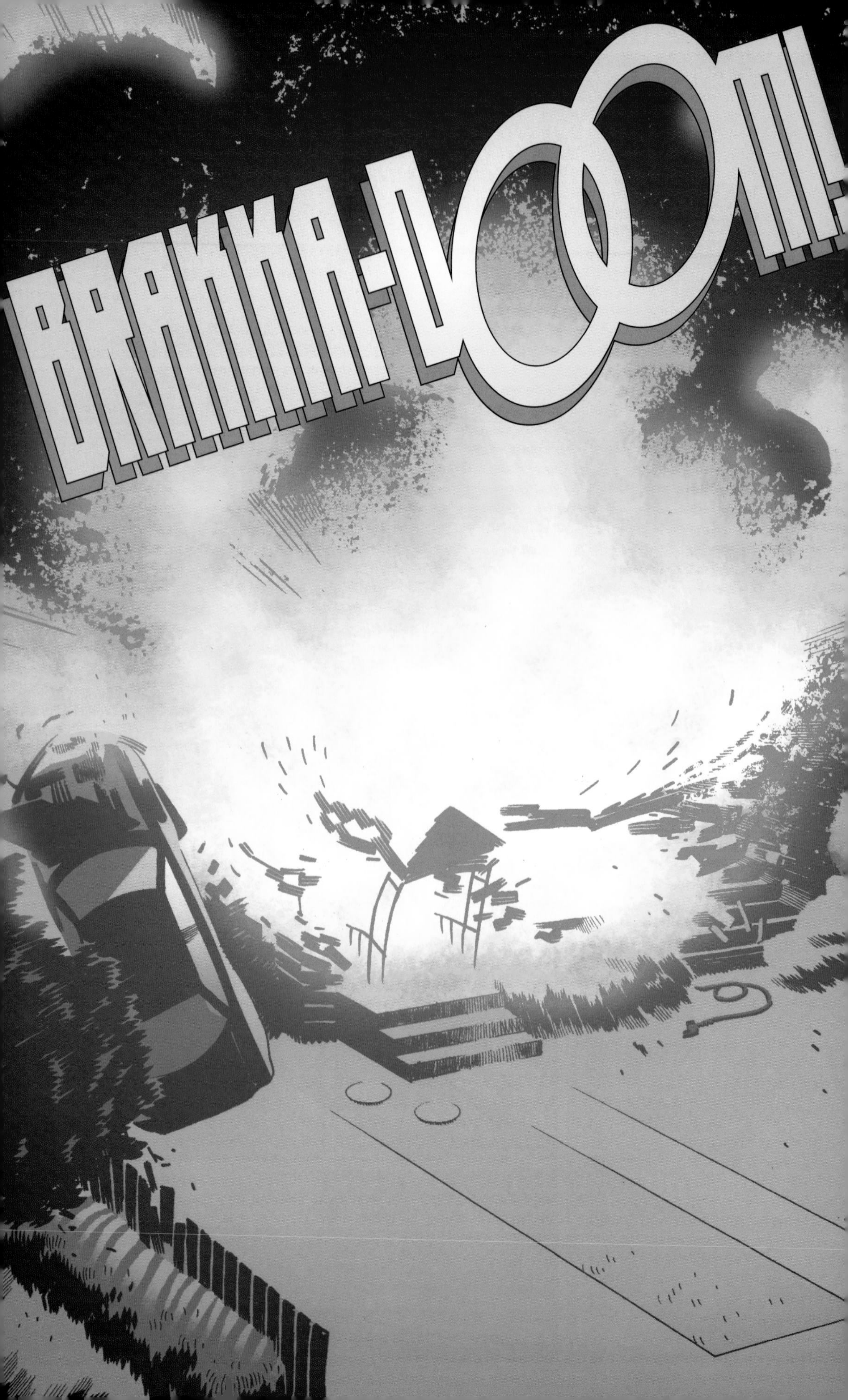
BRAKKA-DOOM!

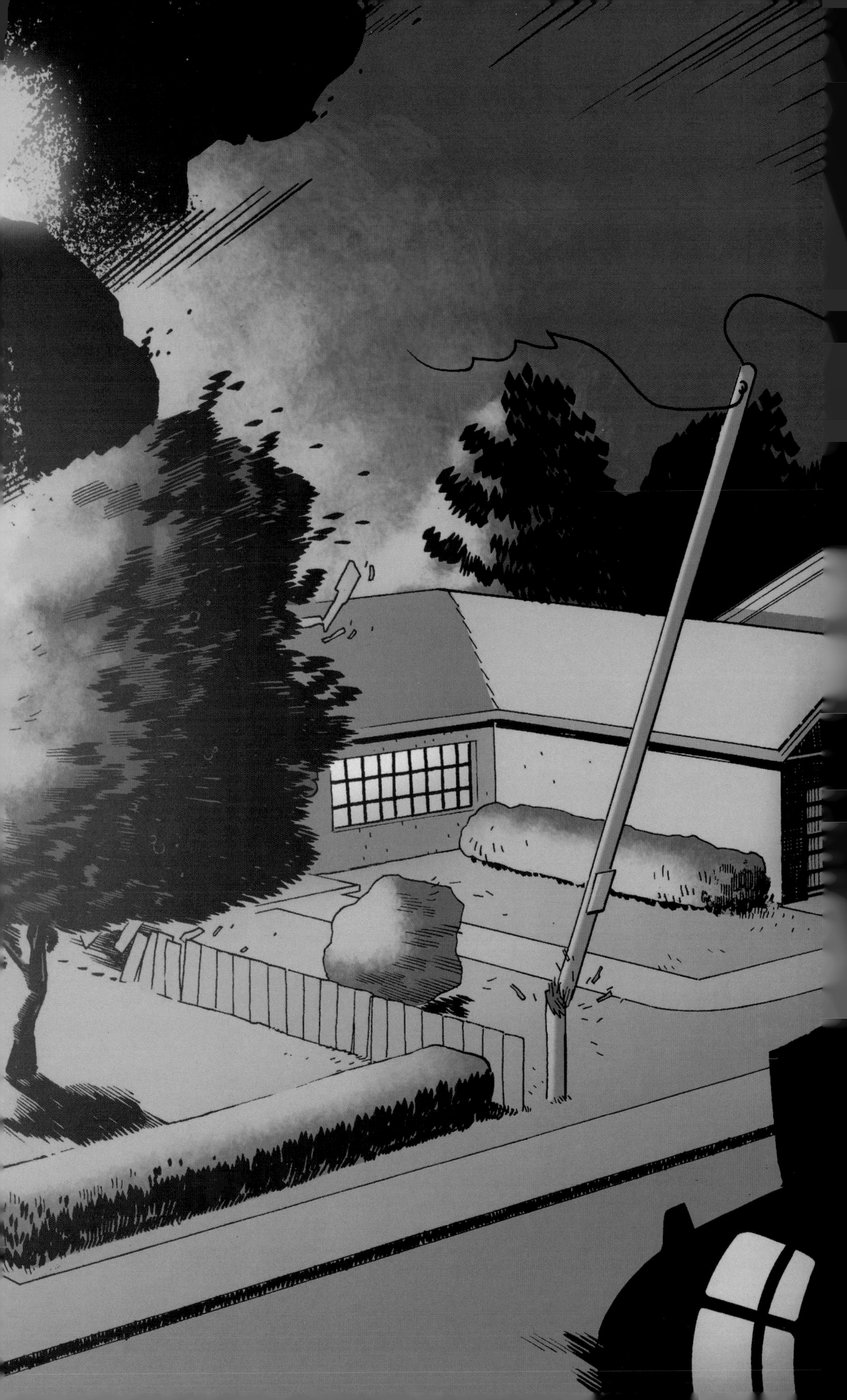

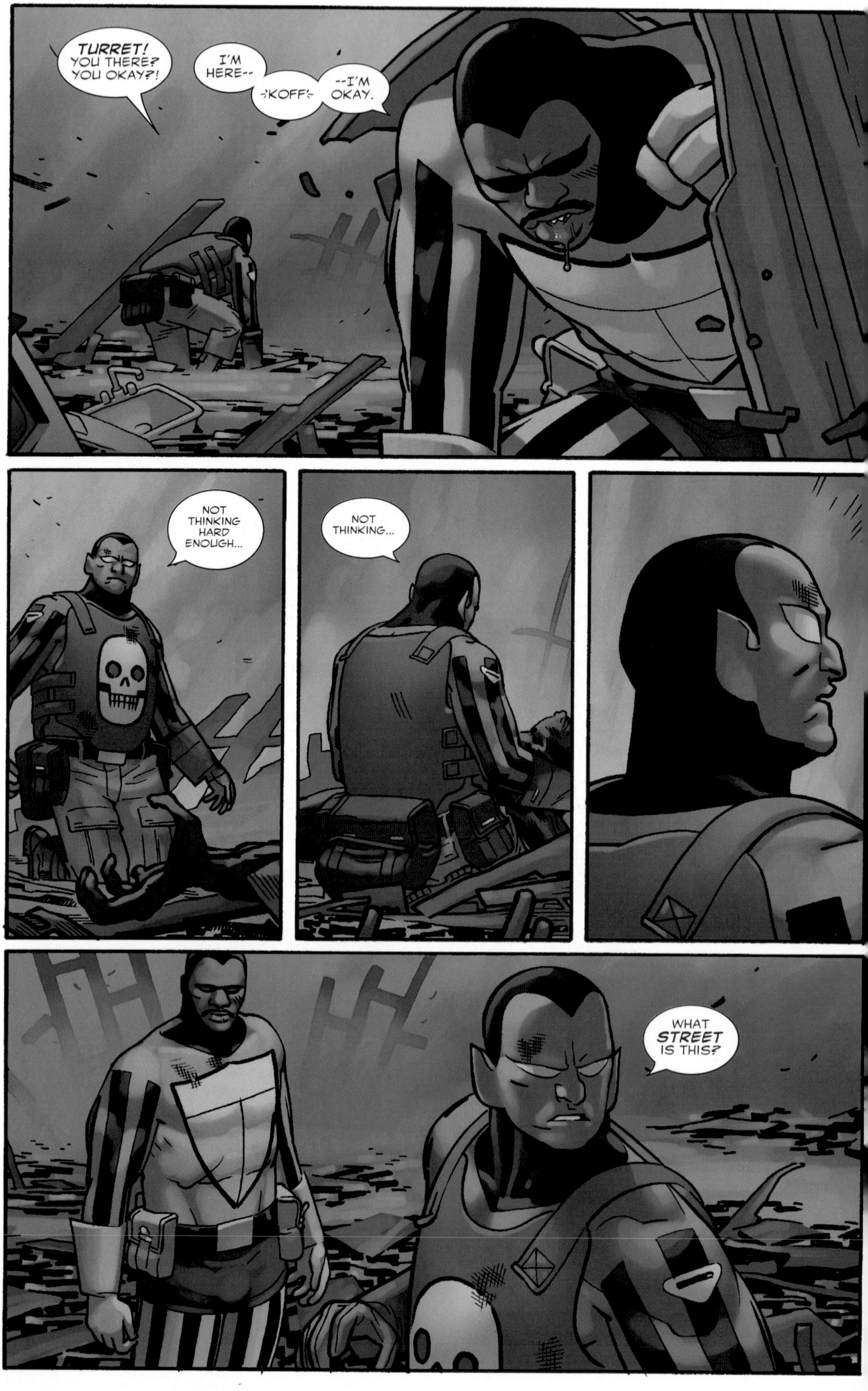
TURRET! YOU THERE? YOU OKAY?!
I'M HERE--
-KOFF-
--I'M OKAY.
NOT THINKING HARD ENOUGH...
NOT THINKING...
WHAT STREET IS THIS?

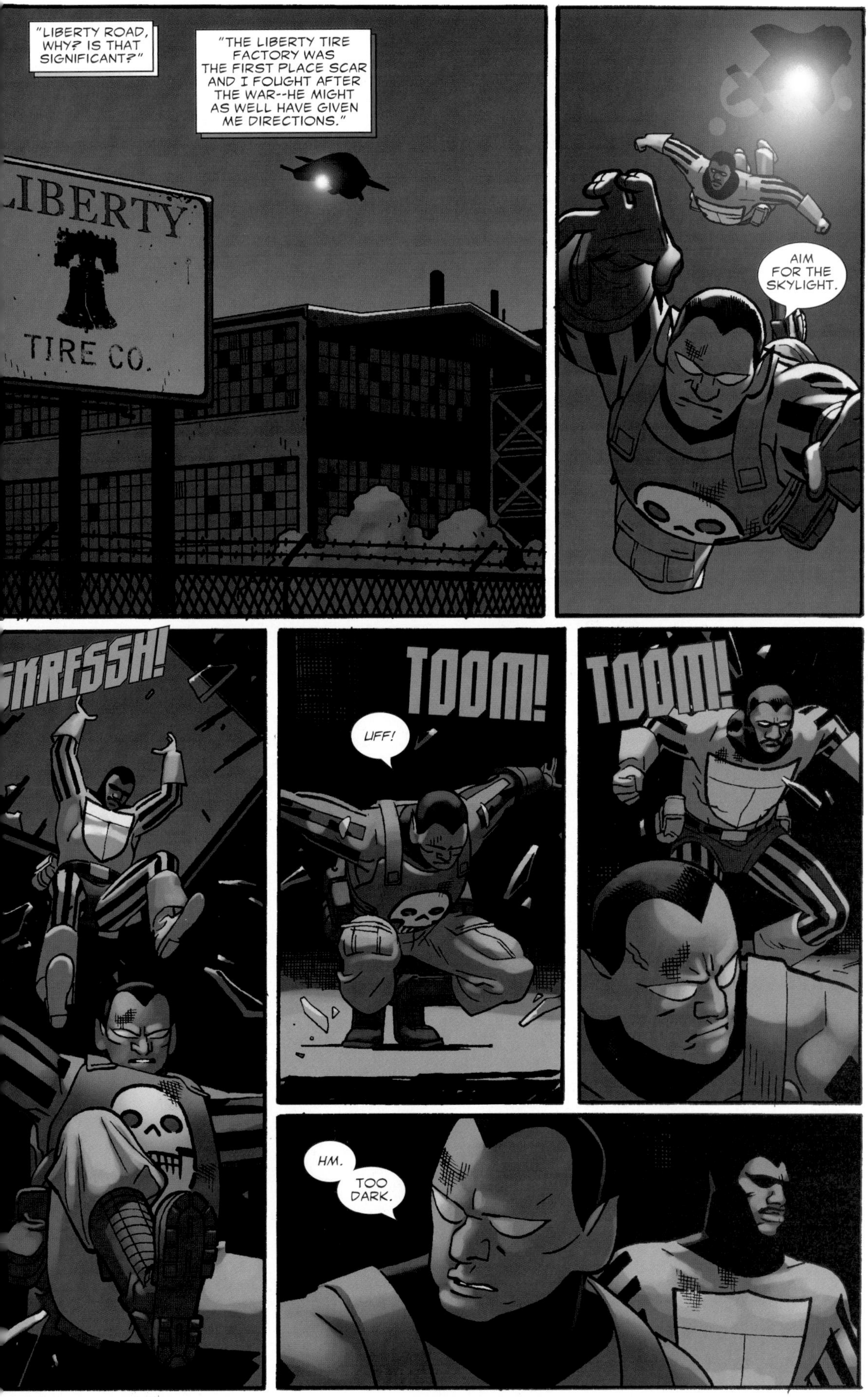
"LIBERTY ROAD, WHY? IS THAT SIGNIFICANT?"
"THE LIBERTY TIRE FACTORY WAS THE FIRST PLACE SCAR AND I FOUGHT AFTER THE WAR--HE MIGHT AS WELL HAVE GIVEN ME DIRECTIONS."
LIBERTY
TIRE CO.
AIM FOR THE SKYLIGHT.
SKRESSH!
TOOM!
UFF!
TOOM!
HM.
TOO DARK.

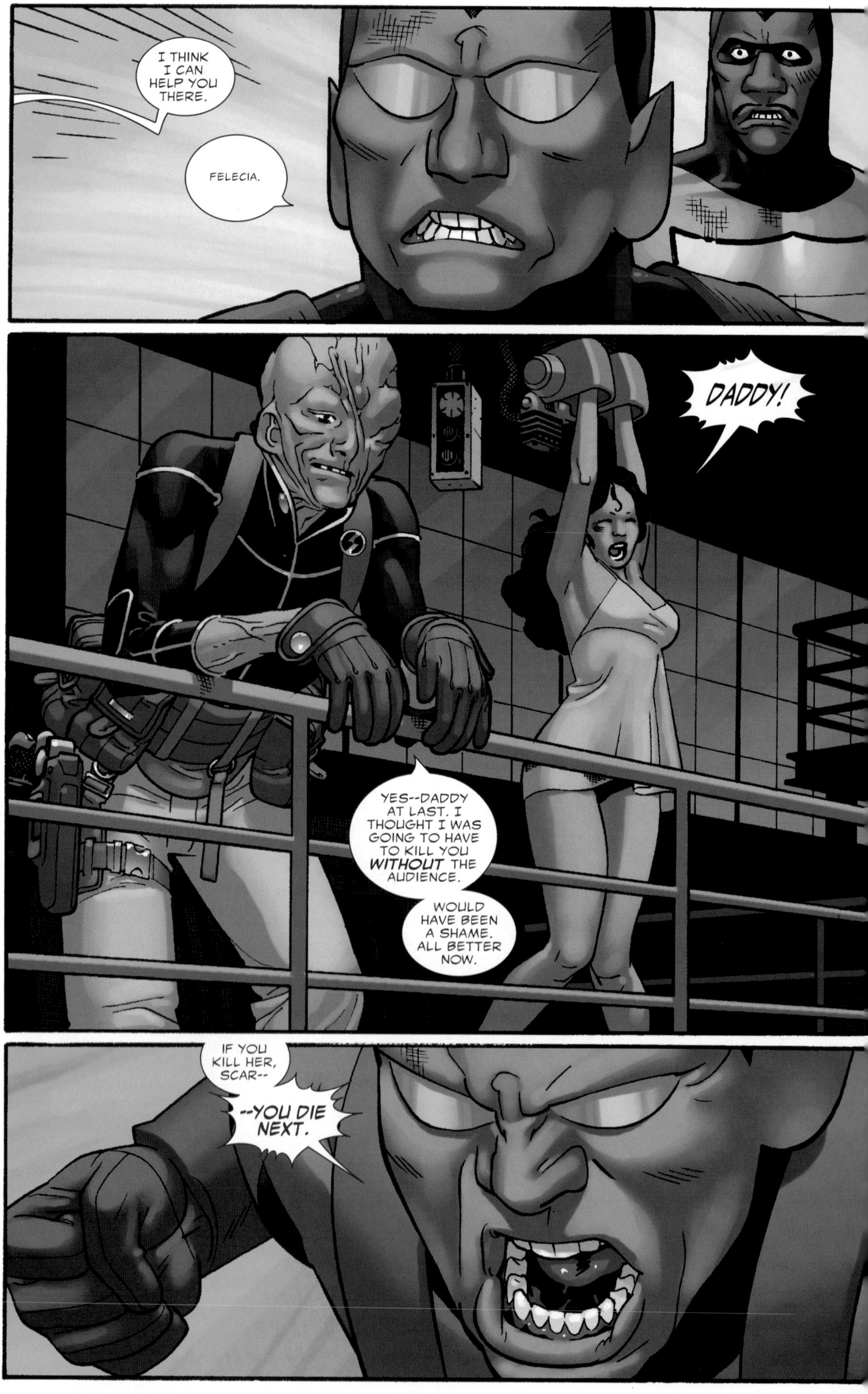
I THINK I CAN HELP YOU THERE.
FELECIA.
DADDY!
YES--DADDY AT LAST. I THOUGHT I WAS GOING TO HAVE TO KILL YOU **WITHOUT** THE AUDIENCE.
WOULD HAVE BEEN A SHAME. ALL BETTER NOW.
IF YOU KILL HER, SCAR--
--YOU DIE NEXT.

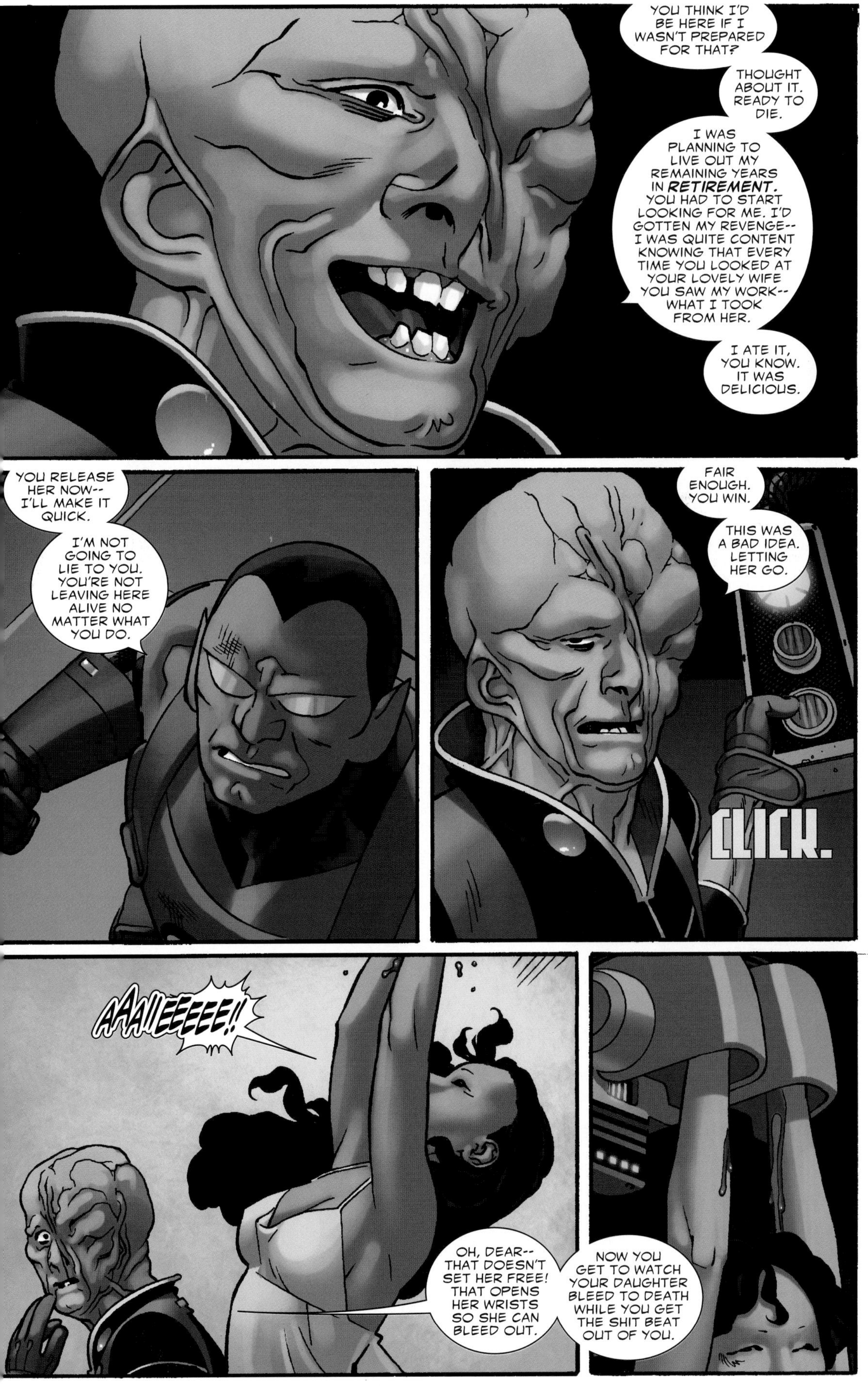

YOU THINK I'D BE HERE IF I WASN'T PREPARED FOR THAT?
THOUGHT ABOUT IT. READY TO DIE.
I WAS PLANNING TO LIVE OUT MY REMAINING YEARS IN RETIREMENT. YOU HAD TO START LOOKING FOR ME. I'D GOTTEN MY REVENGE-- I WAS QUITE CONTENT KNOWING THAT EVERY TIME YOU LOOKED AT YOUR LOVELY WIFE YOU SAW MY WORK-- WHAT I TOOK FROM HER.
I ATE IT, YOU KNOW. IT WAS DELICIOUS.
YOU RELEASE HER NOW-- I'LL MAKE IT QUICK.
I'M NOT GOING TO LIE TO YOU. YOU'RE NOT LEAVING HERE ALIVE NO MATTER WHAT YOU DO.
FAIR ENOUGH. YOU WIN.
THIS WAS A BAD IDEA. LETTING HER GO.
CLICK.
AAAIIEEEEEE!!
OH, DEAR-- THAT DOESN'T SET HER FREE! THAT OPENS HER WRISTS SO SHE CAN BLEED OUT.
NOW YOU GET TO WATCH YOUR DAUGHTER BLEED TO DEATH WHILE YOU GET THE SHIT BEAT OUT OF YOU.

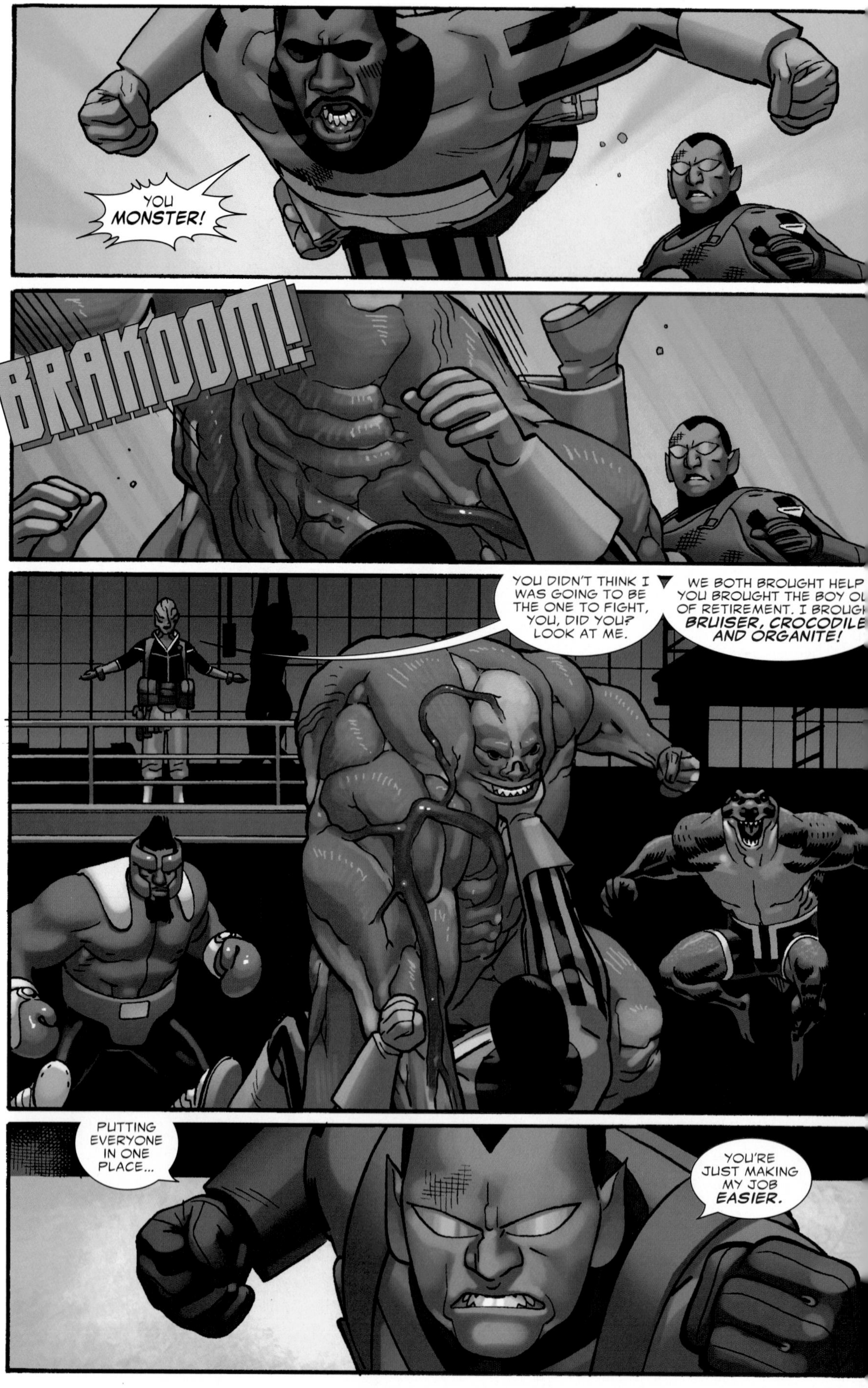
YOU MONSTER!
BRAKOOM!
YOU DIDN'T THINK I WAS GOING TO BE THE ONE TO FIGHT, YOU, DID YOU? LOOK AT ME.
WE BOTH BROUGHT HELP YOU BROUGHT THE BOY OU OF RETIREMENT. I BROUGH BRUISER, CROCODILE AND ORGANITE!
PUTTING EVERYONE IN ONE PLACE...
YOU'RE JUST MAKING MY JOB EASIER.

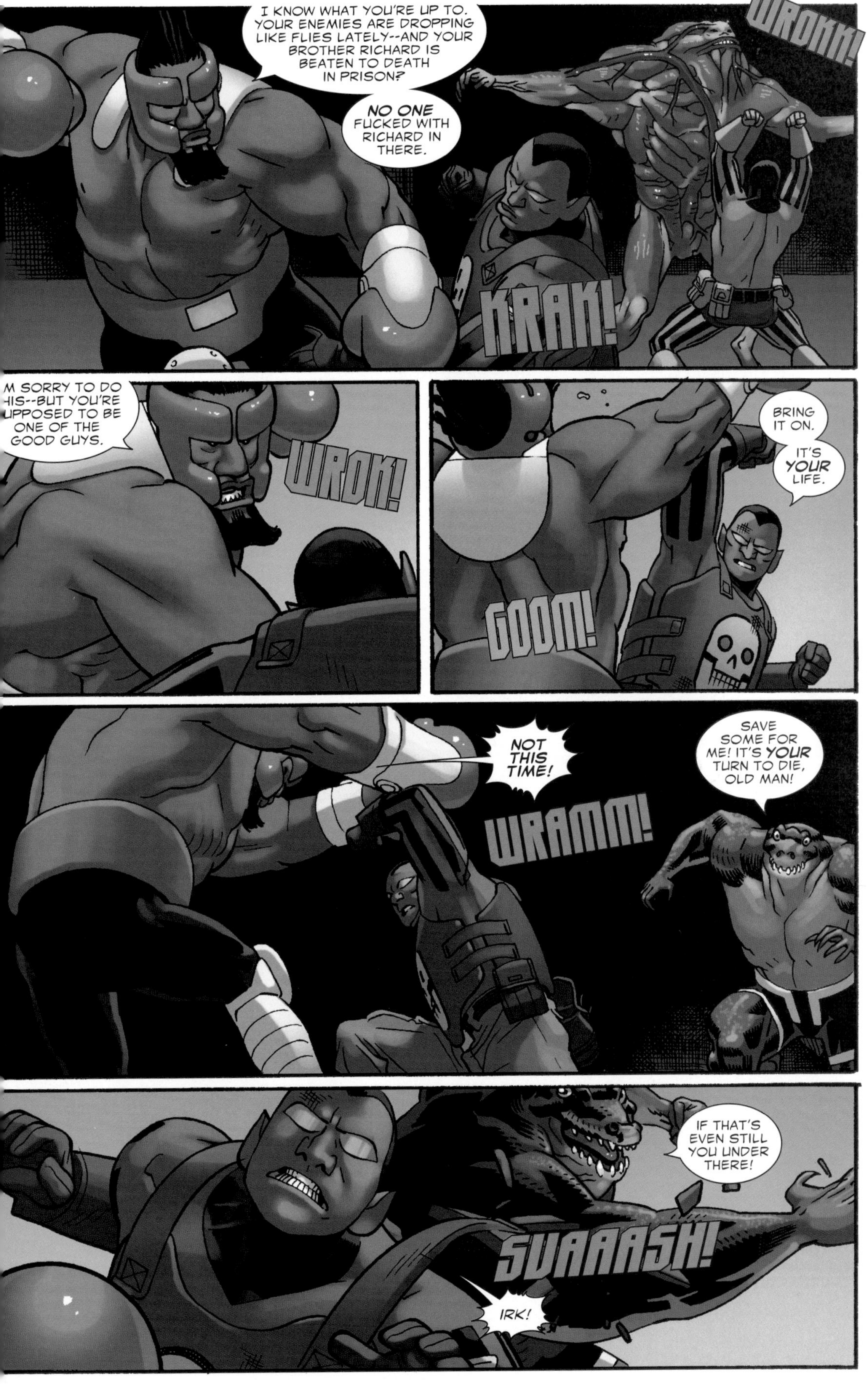
I KNOW WHAT YOU'RE UP TO. YOUR ENEMIES ARE DROPPING LIKE FLIES LATELY--AND YOUR BROTHER RICHARD IS BEATEN TO DEATH IN PRISON?
NO ONE FUCKED WITH RICHARD IN THERE.
WROKK!
KRAK!
M SORRY TO DO HIS--BUT YOU'RE UPPOSED TO BE ONE OF THE GOOD GUYS.
WROK!
BRING IT ON.
IT'S YOUR LIFE.
GOOM!
NOT THIS TIME!
SAVE SOME FOR ME! IT'S YOUR TURN TO DIE, OLD MAN!
WRAMM!
IF THAT'S EVEN STILL YOU UNDER THERE!
SUAAASH!
IRK!

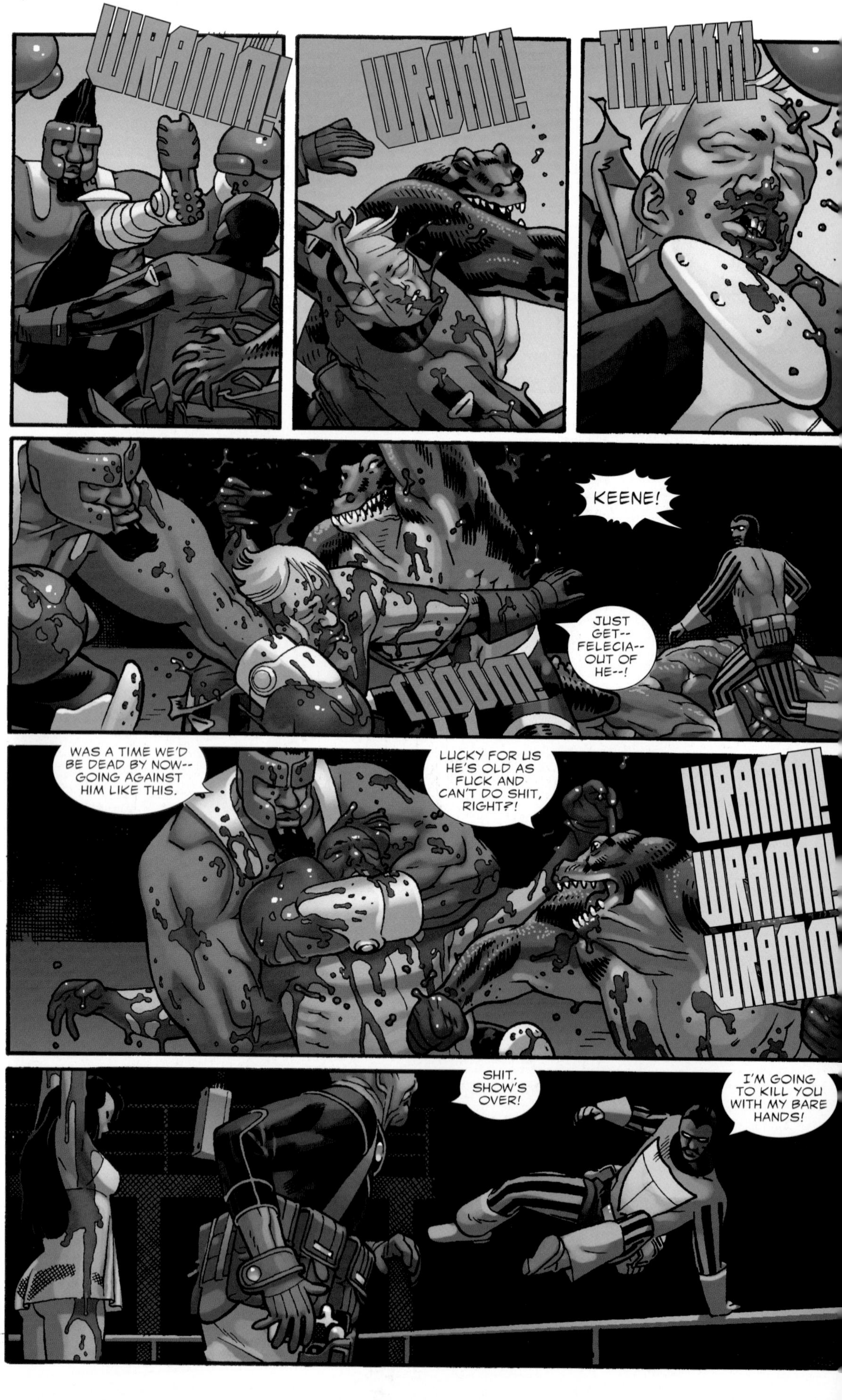
WRAMM!
WROKK!
THROKK!
KEENE!
JUST GET-- FELECIA-- OUT OF HE--!
CHOOM!
WAS A TIME WE'D BE DEAD BY NOW-- GOING AGAINST HIM LIKE THIS.
LUCKY FOR US HE'S OLD AS FUCK AND CAN'T DO SHIT, RIGHT?!
WRAMM! WRAMM! WRAMM
SHIT. SHOW'S OVER!
I'M GOING TO KILL YOU WITH MY BARE HANDS!

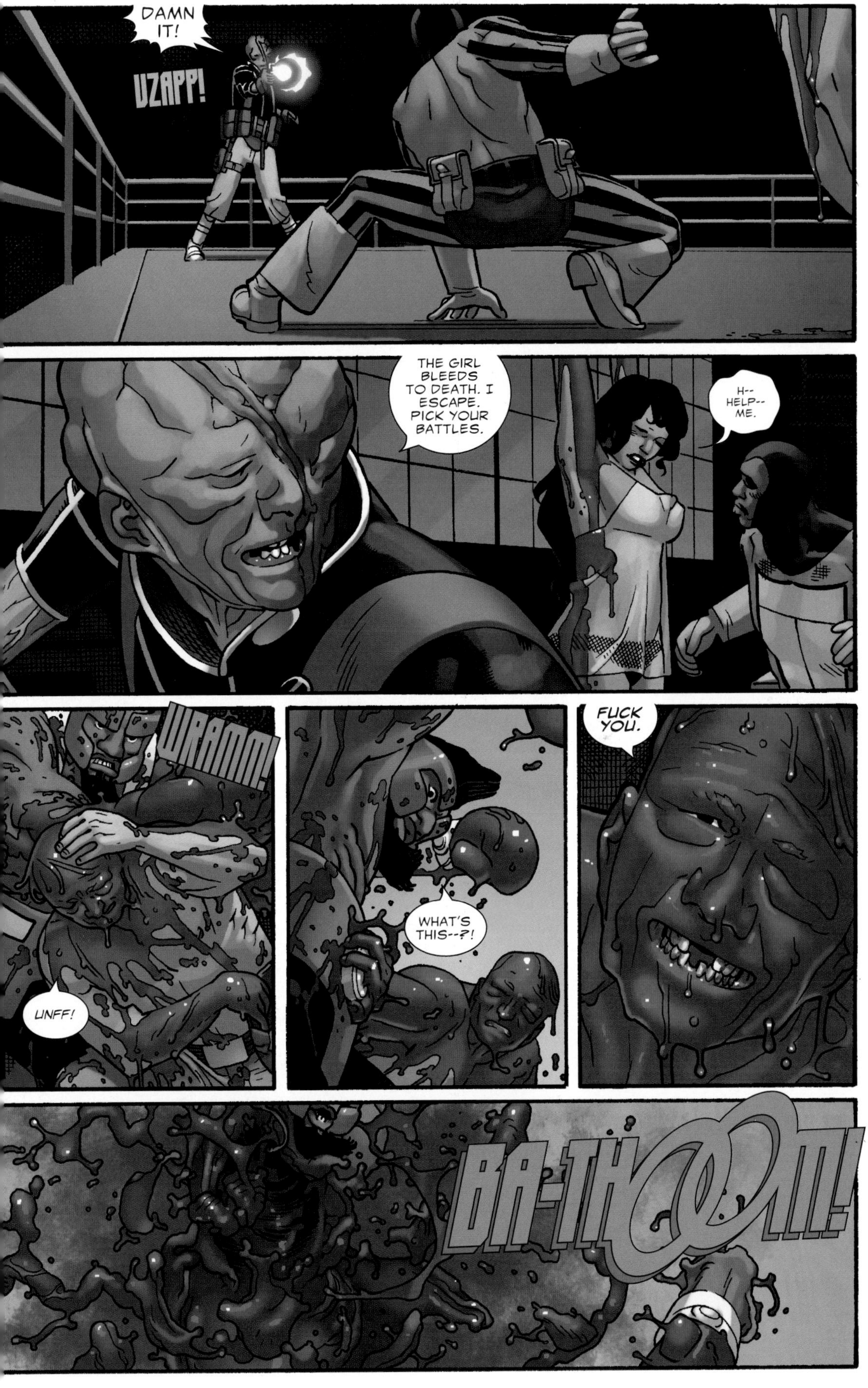
DAMN IT!
UZAPP!
THE GIRL BLEEDS TO DEATH. I ESCAPE. PICK YOUR BATTLES.
H-- HELP-- ME.
WRAMM!
UNFF!
WHAT'S THIS--?!
FUCK YOU.
BA-THOOM!

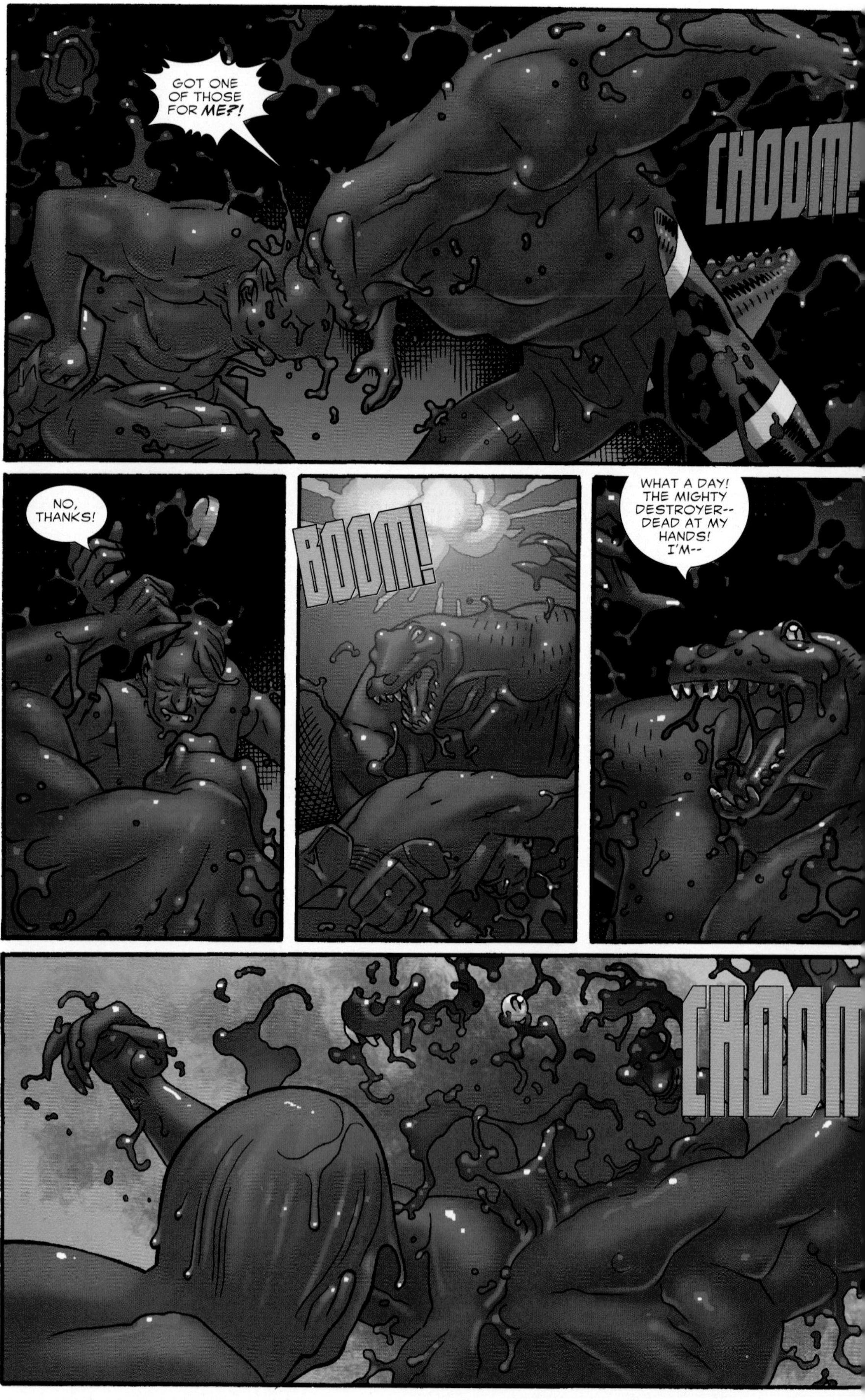
GOT ONE OF THOSE FOR *ME?!*
CHOOM!
NO, THANKS!
BOOM!
WHAT A DAY! THE MIGHTY DESTROYER--DEAD AT MY HANDS! I'M--
CHOOM

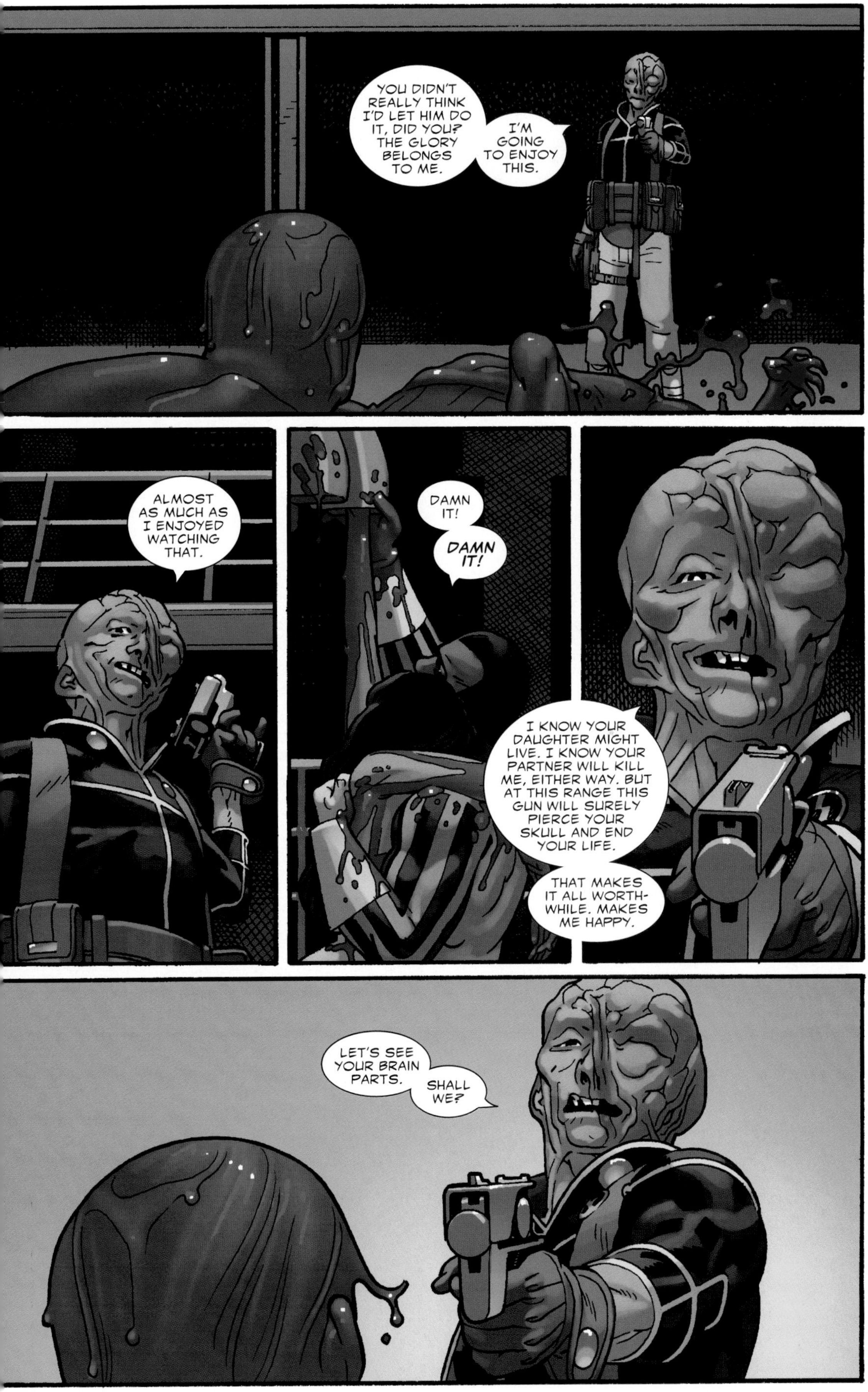
YOU DIDN'T REALLY THINK I'D LET HIM DO IT, DID YOU? THE GLORY BELONGS TO ME.
I'M GOING TO ENJOY THIS.
ALMOST AS MUCH AS I ENJOYED WATCHING THAT.
DAMN IT!
DAMN IT!
I KNOW YOUR DAUGHTER MIGHT LIVE. I KNOW YOUR PARTNER WILL KILL ME, EITHER WAY. BUT AT THIS RANGE THIS GUN WILL SURELY PIERCE YOUR SKULL AND END YOUR LIFE.
THAT MAKES IT ALL WORTH-WHILE. MAKES ME HAPPY.
LET'S SEE YOUR BRAIN PARTS.
SHALL WE?

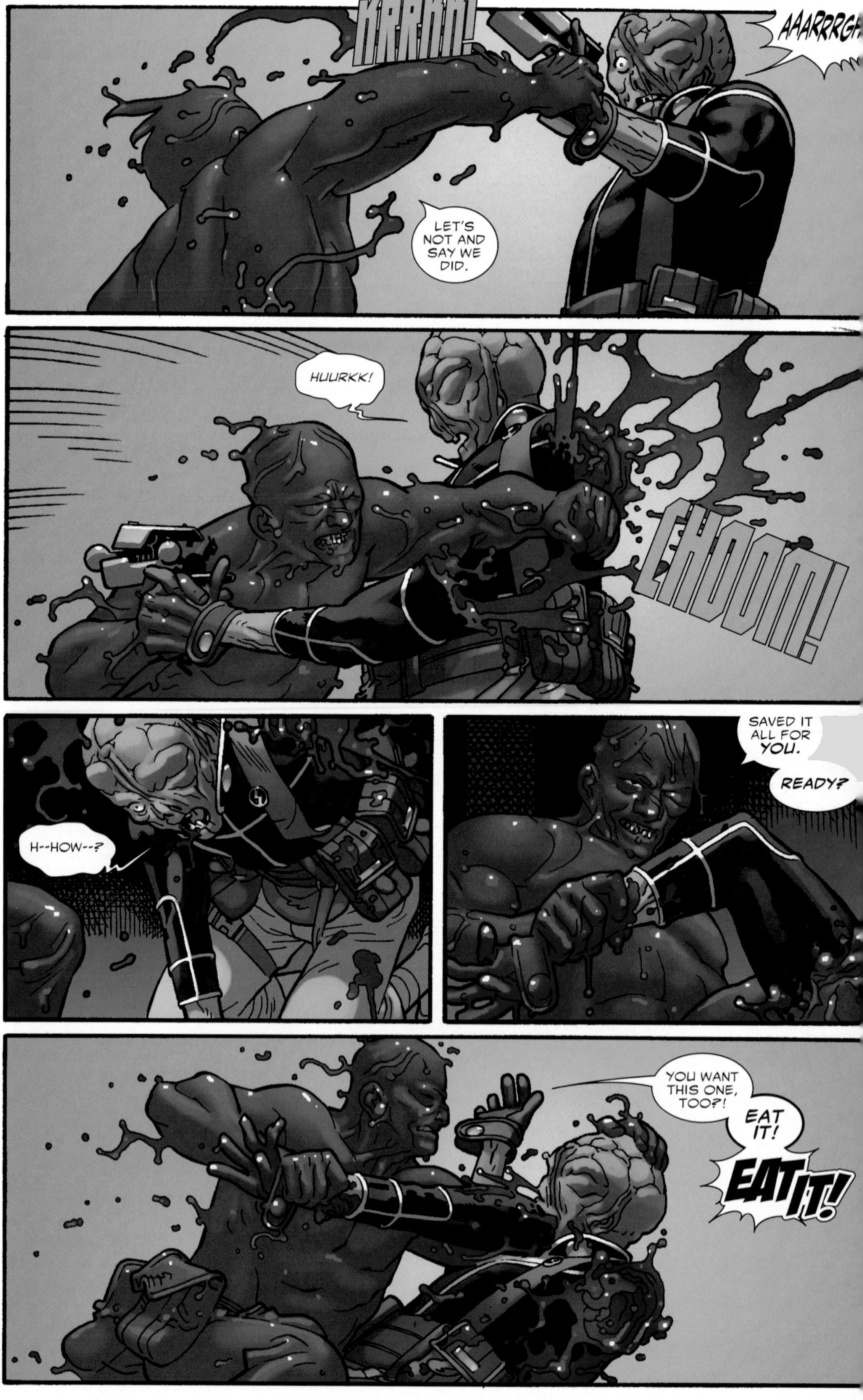
KRRKK!
AAARRRGH
LET'S NOT AND SAY WE DID.
HUURKK!
CHOOM!
H--HOW--?
SAVED IT ALL FOR YOU.
READY?
YOU WANT THIS ONE, TOO?!
EAT IT!
EAT IT!

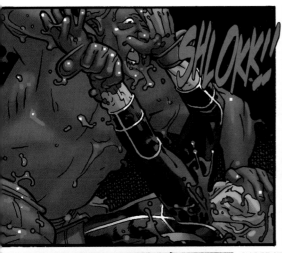

SHLOKK!

UNPH!

SHKKK!

SUBJECT IS IN HAND-- REPEAT--SUBJECT IS IN HAND! WE'RE IN NEED OF *IMMEDIATE* MEDICAL ASSISTANCE!

GET HERE *NOW!*

KROOM!

GLGLPH.

KROOM!

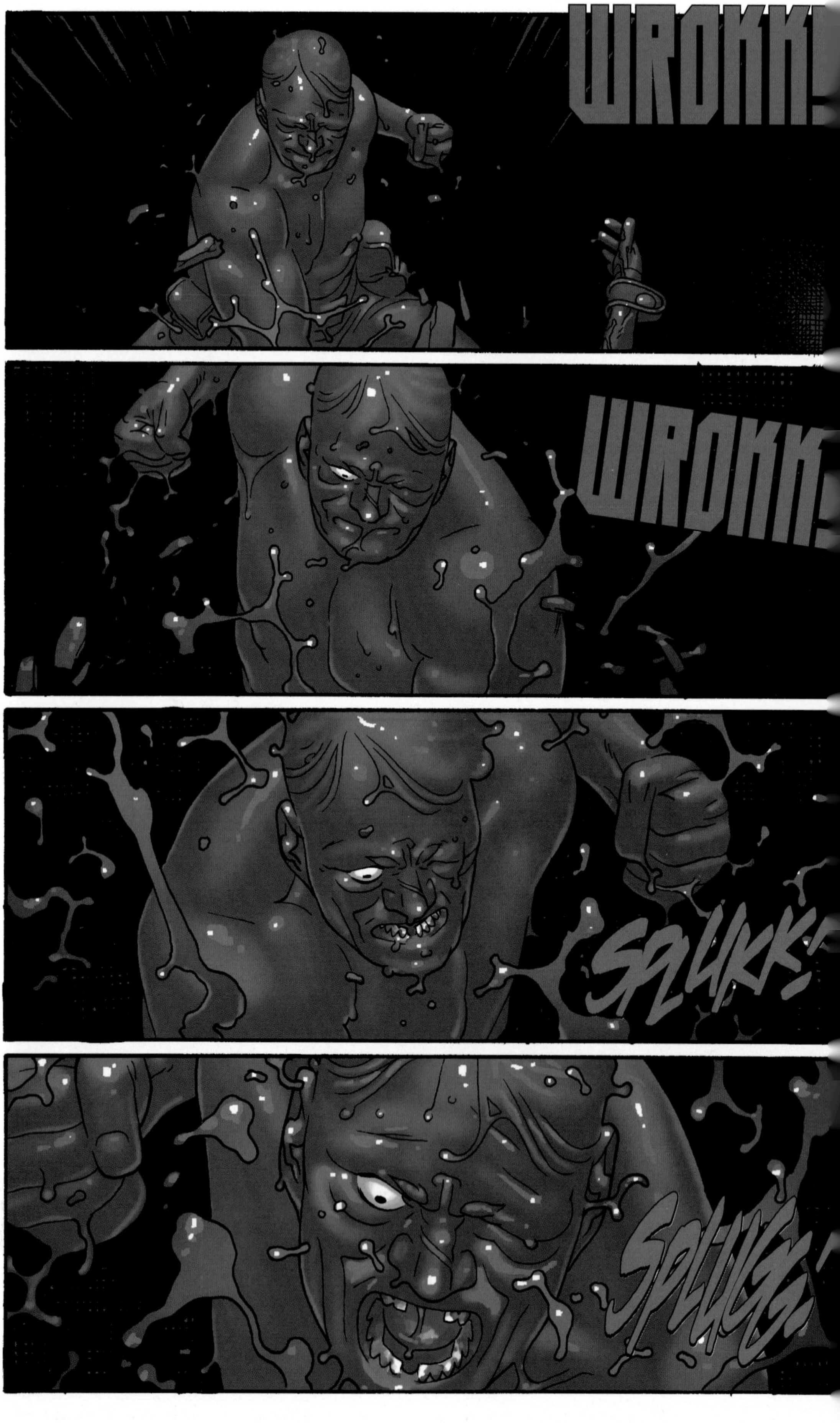
WROKK!
WROKK!
SPLUKK!
SPLUGG!

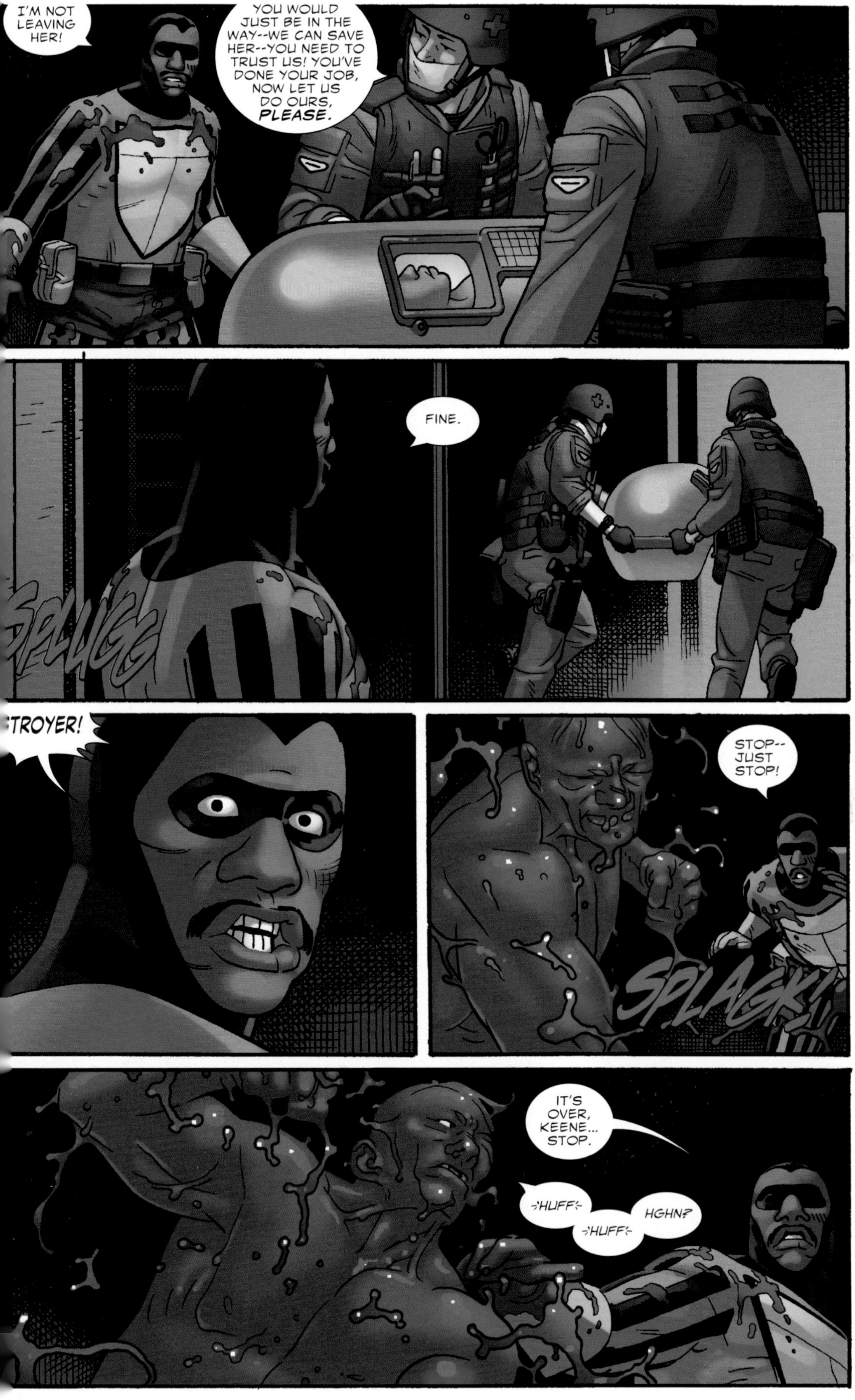
I'M NOT LEAVING HER!
YOU WOULD JUST BE IN THE WAY--WE CAN SAVE HER--YOU NEED TO TRUST US! YOU'VE DONE YOUR JOB, NOW LET US DO OURS, PLEASE.
FINE.
SPLUGG
TROYER!
STOP-- JUST STOP!
SPLAGK!
IT'S OVER, KEENE... STOP.
HUFF
HUFF
HGHN?

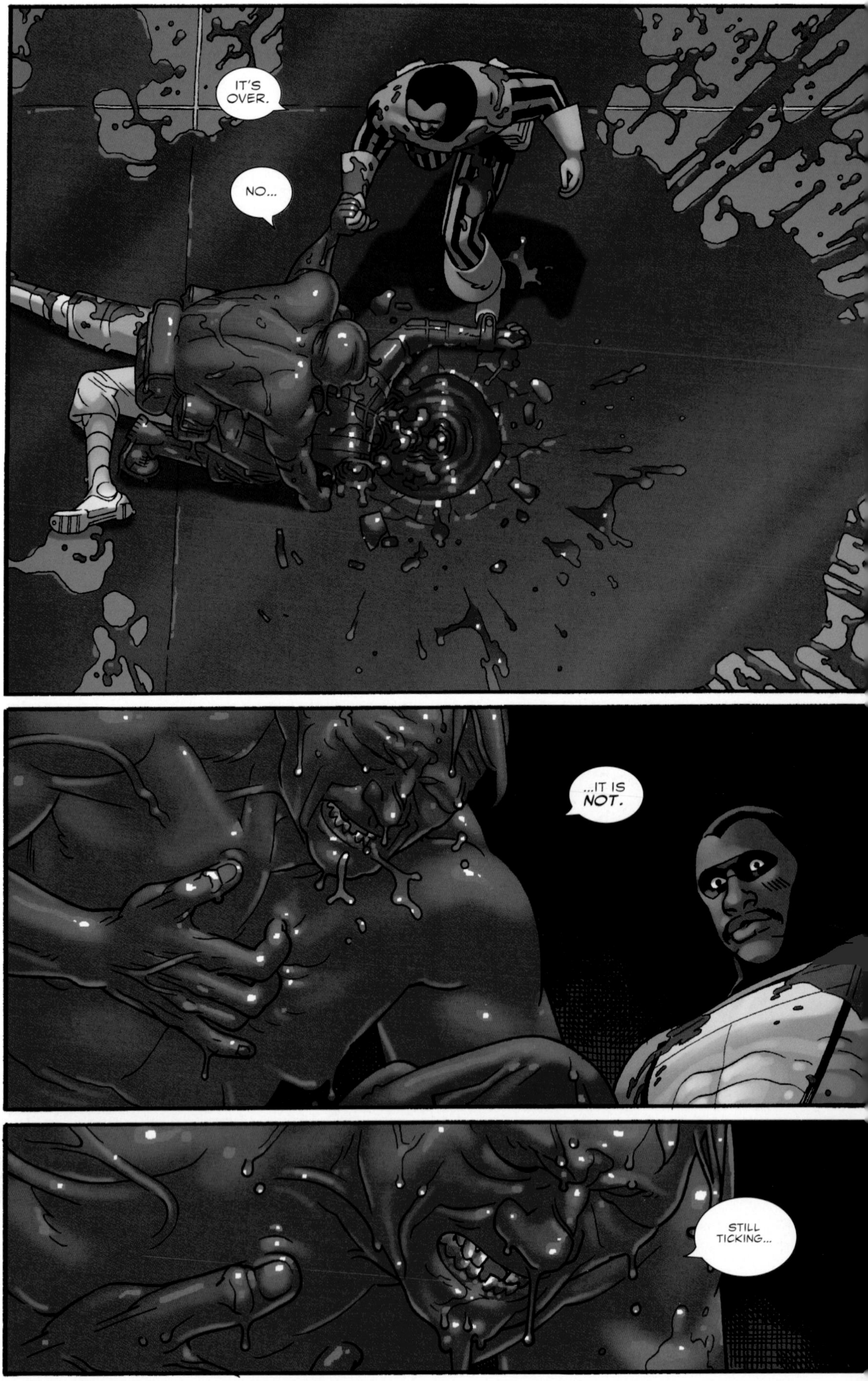
IT'S OVER.
NO...
...IT IS NOT.
STILL TICKING...

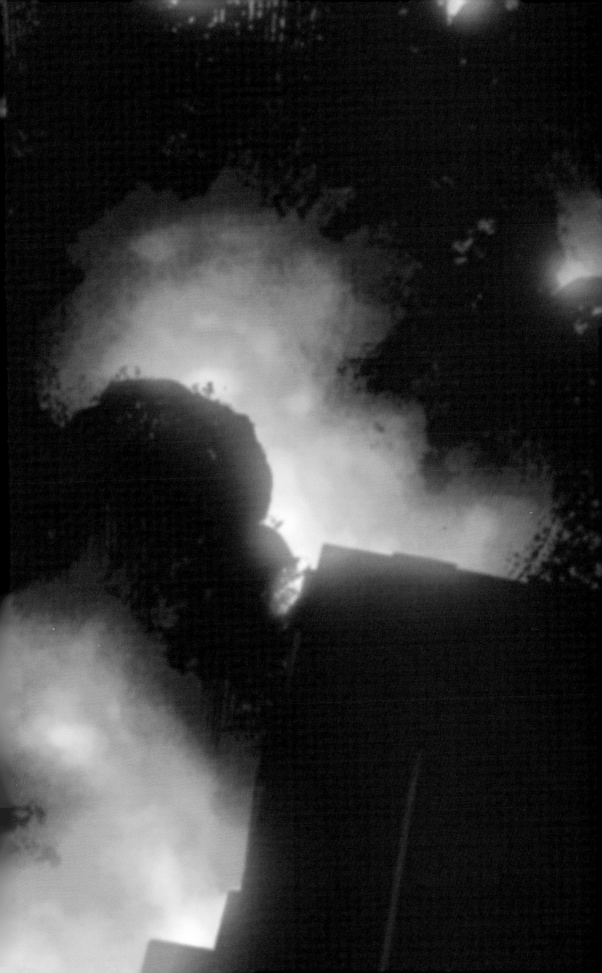

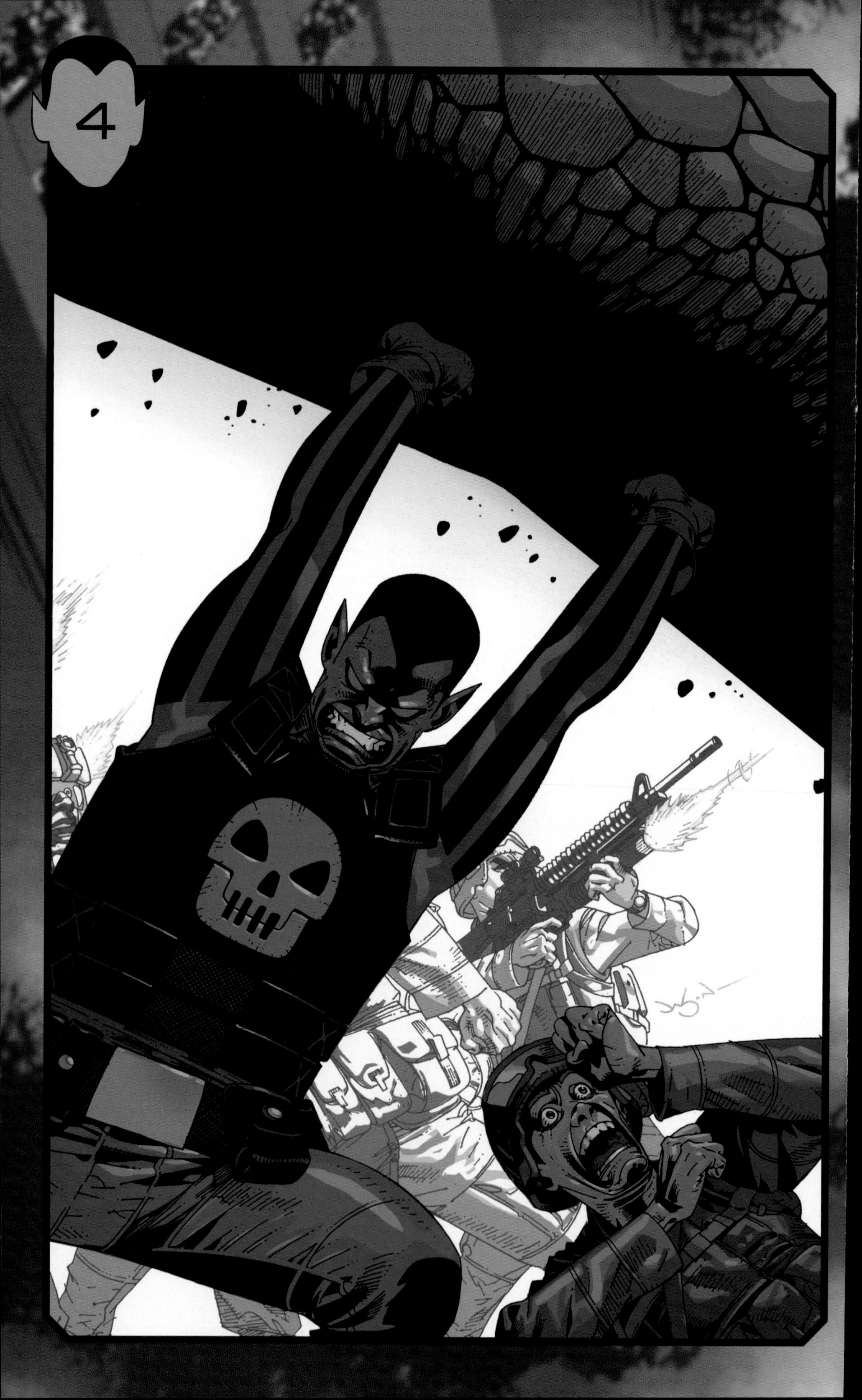
4

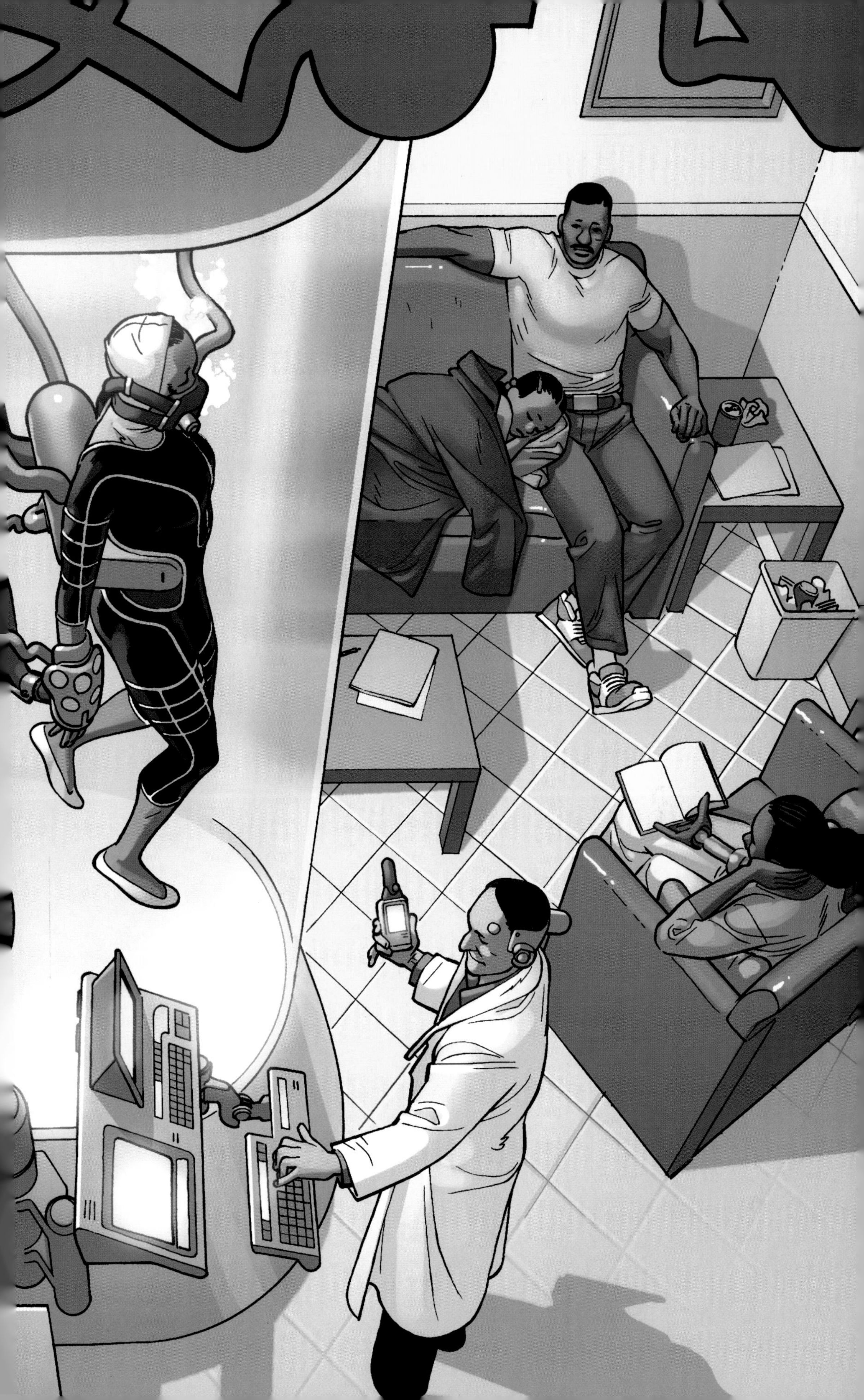

SHE'S GOING TO BE OKAY.

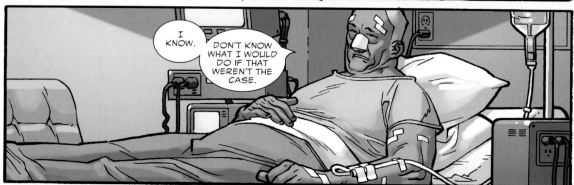

I KNOW.

DON'T KNOW WHAT I WOULD DO IF THAT WEREN'T THE CASE.

AFTER WHAT YOU DID TO SCAR, THERE'S NOTHING LEFT TO DO.

JESUS, MAN.

I WAS ANGRY.

I PICKED UP ON THAT. ANYWAY, SINCE YOU'RE IN HERE. I THOUGHT YOU MIGHT NEED CHEERING UP SO I GOT YOU A PRESENT.

WHAT IS THIS?

DETAILED OUTLINE OF *HORDE'S* CENTRAL HEADQUARTERS. THAT'S RIGHT, KEENE... WE *FOUND* THEM.

WE CAN TAKE THOSE BASTARDS DOWN ONCE AND FOR--

WHAT ARE YOU DOING?!

I MAY NOT HEAL AS FAST AS I USED TO--BUT I STILL BOUNCE BACK QUICKLY. I'M NOT ONE HUNDRED PERCENT--BUT IT'S *ENOUGH.*

LET'S *GO.*

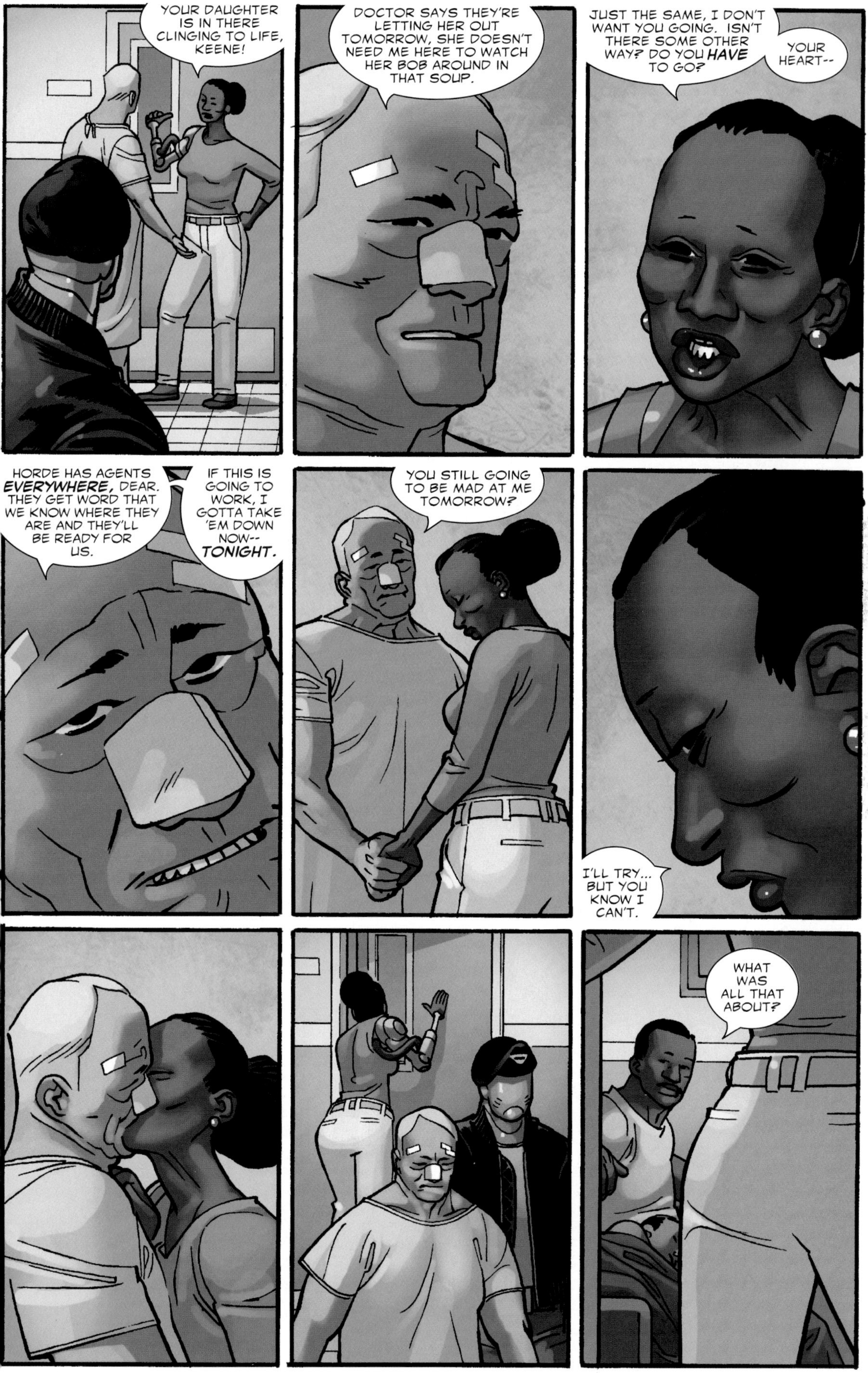
YOUR DAUGHTER IS IN THERE CLINGING TO LIFE, KEENE!
DOCTOR SAYS THEY'RE LETTING HER OUT TOMORROW, SHE DOESN'T NEED ME HERE TO WATCH HER BOB AROUND IN THAT SOUP.
JUST THE SAME, I DON'T WANT YOU GOING. ISN'T THERE SOME OTHER WAY? DO YOU HAVE TO GO?
YOUR HEART--
HORDE HAS AGENTS EVERYWHERE, DEAR. THEY GET WORD THAT WE KNOW WHERE THEY ARE AND THEY'LL BE READY FOR US.
IF THIS IS GOING TO WORK, I GOTTA TAKE 'EM DOWN NOW-- TONIGHT.
YOU STILL GOING TO BE MAD AT ME TOMORROW?
I'LL TRY... BUT YOU KNOW I CAN'T.
WHAT WAS ALL THAT ABOUT?

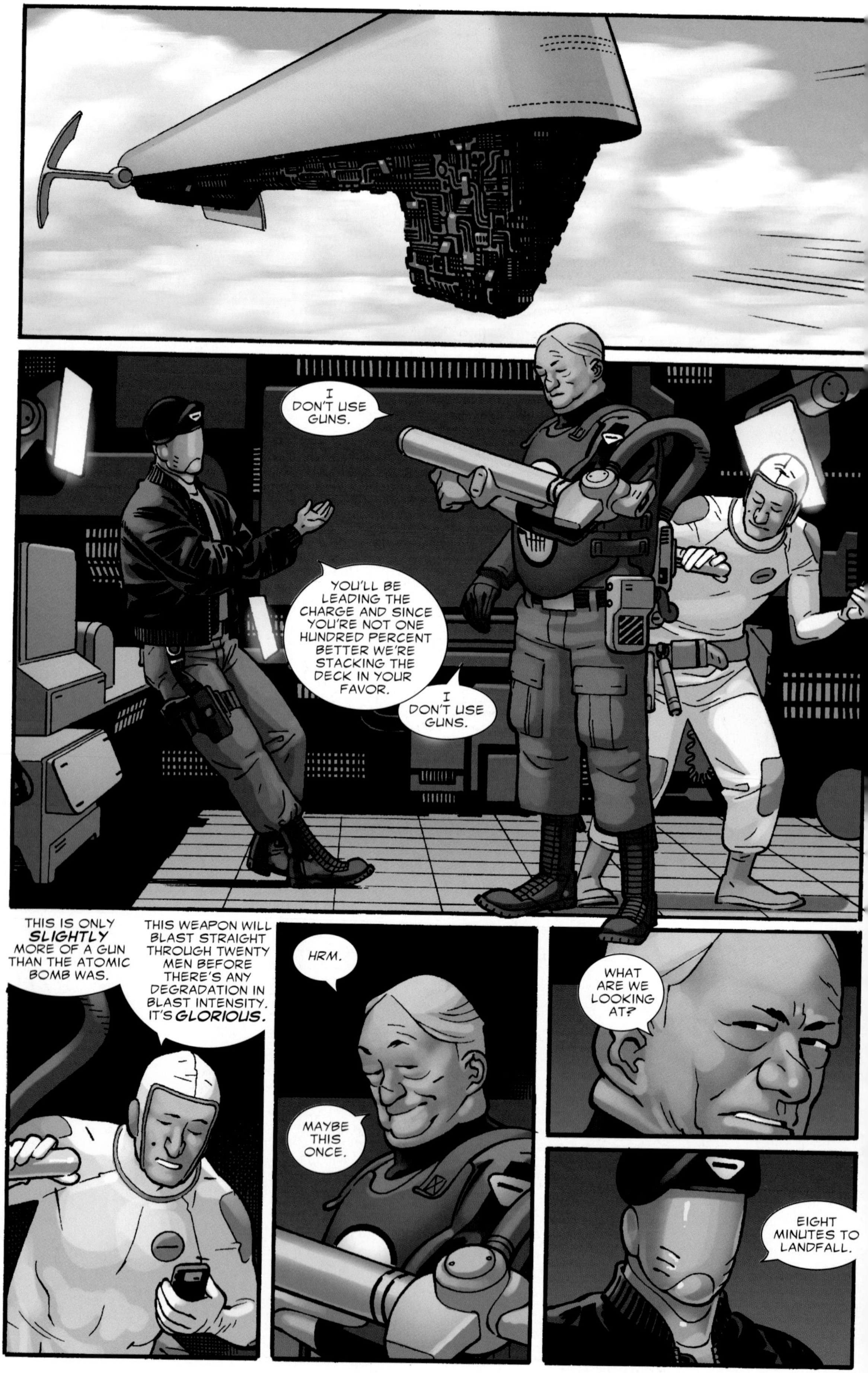
I DON'T USE GUNS.
YOU'LL BE LEADING THE CHARGE AND SINCE YOU'RE NOT ONE HUNDRED PERCENT BETTER WE'RE STACKING THE DECK IN YOUR FAVOR.
I DON'T USE GUNS.
THIS IS ONLY *SLIGHTLY* MORE OF A GUN THAN THE ATOMIC BOMB WAS.
THIS WEAPON WILL BLAST STRAIGHT THROUGH TWENTY MEN BEFORE THERE'S ANY DEGRADATION IN BLAST INTENSITY. IT'S *GLORIOUS.*
HRM.
MAYBE THIS ONCE.
WHAT ARE WE LOOKING AT?
EIGHT MINUTES TO LANDFALL.

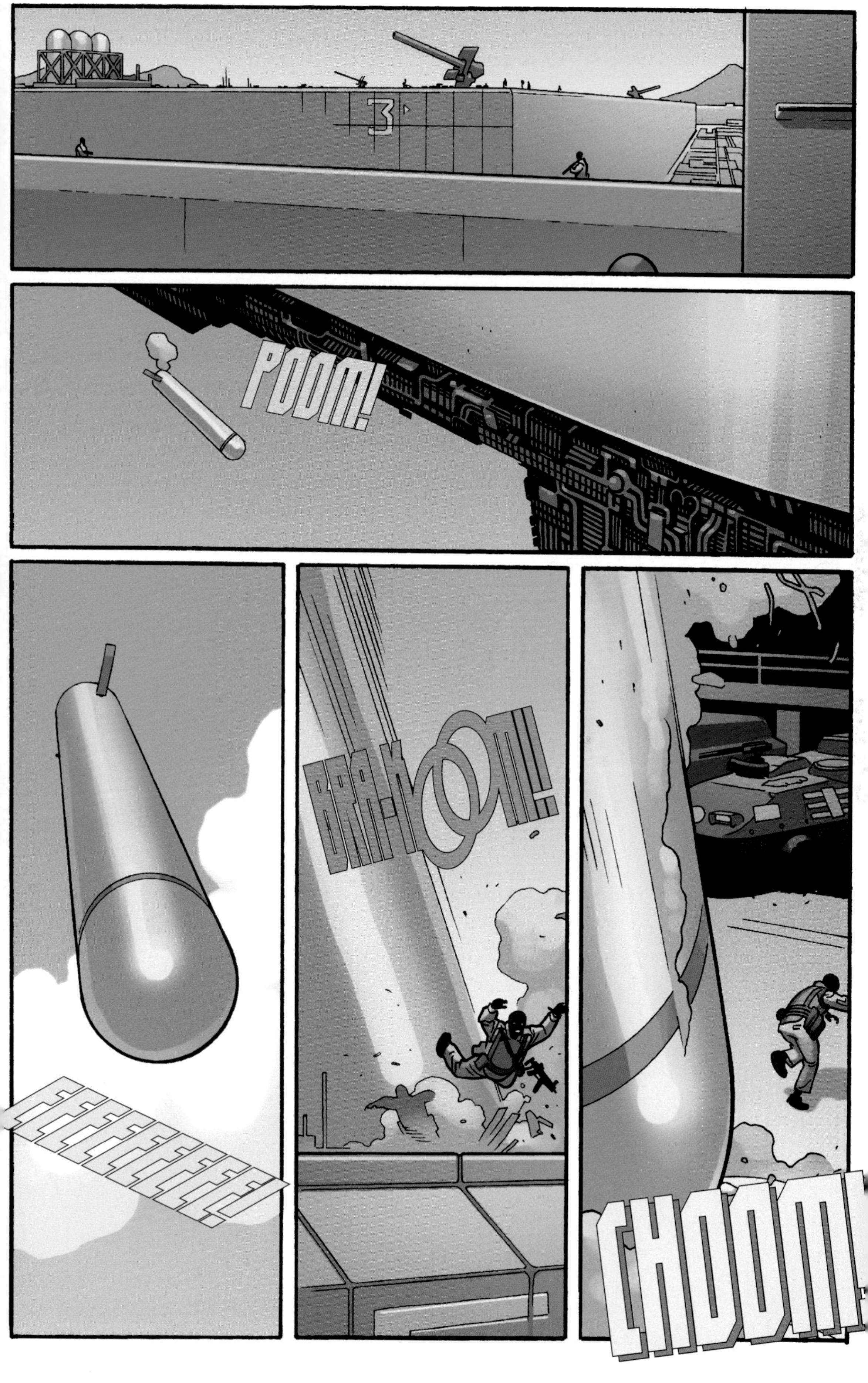
POOM!
EEEEEEEEE!
BRA-KOOM!!
CHOOM!

HM.

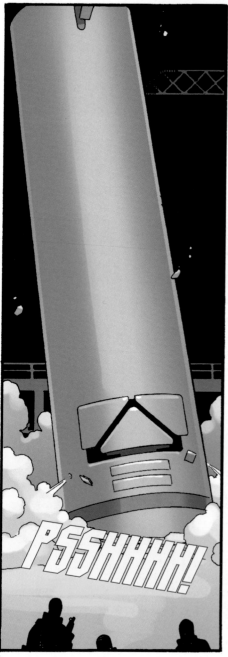

PSSHHHH!

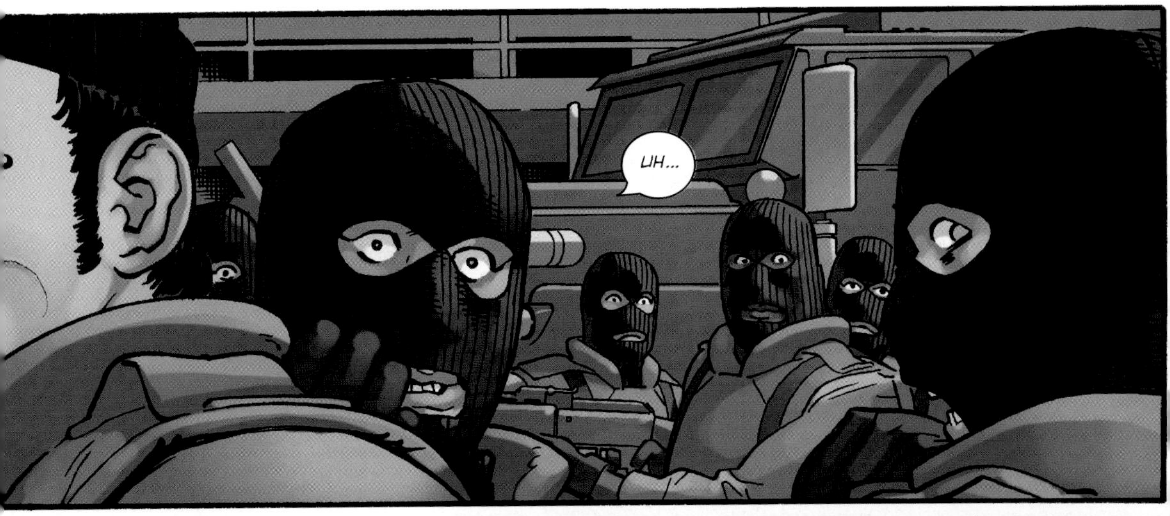
UH...

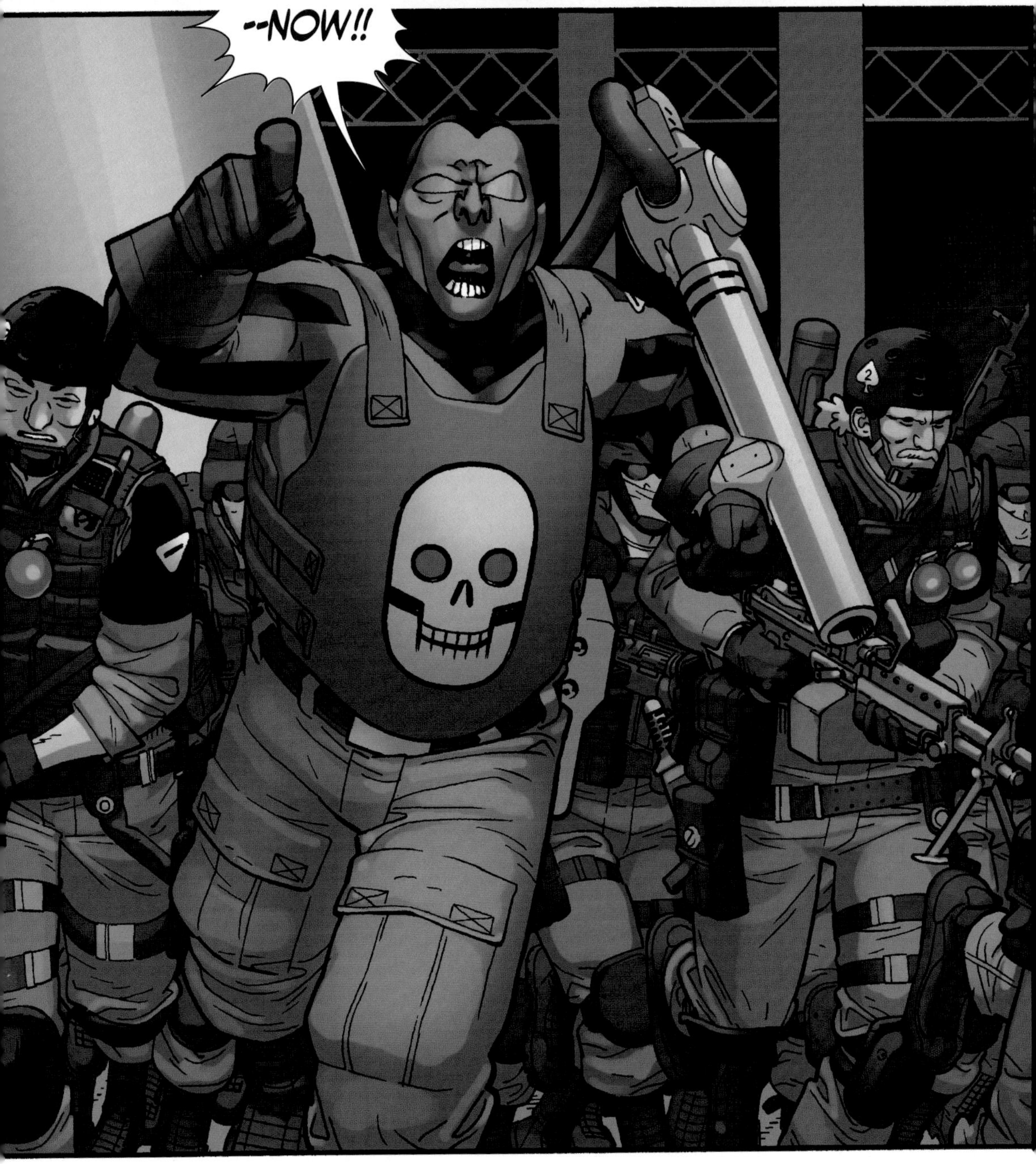
--NOW!!

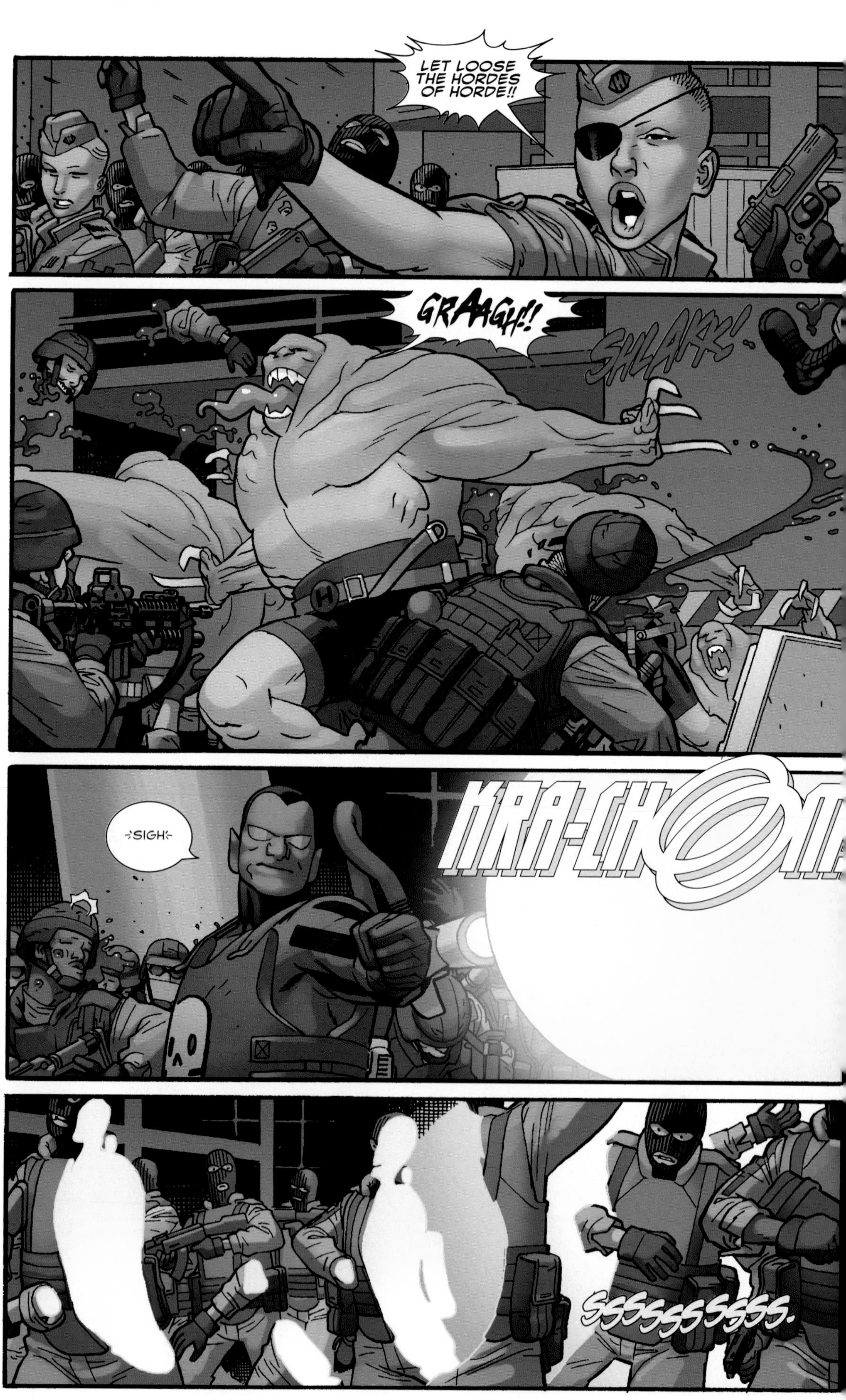
LET LOOSE THE HORDES OF HORDE!!
GRAAGH!!
SHLAKK!
-SIGH-
KRA-KOOM
SSSSSSSSSS.

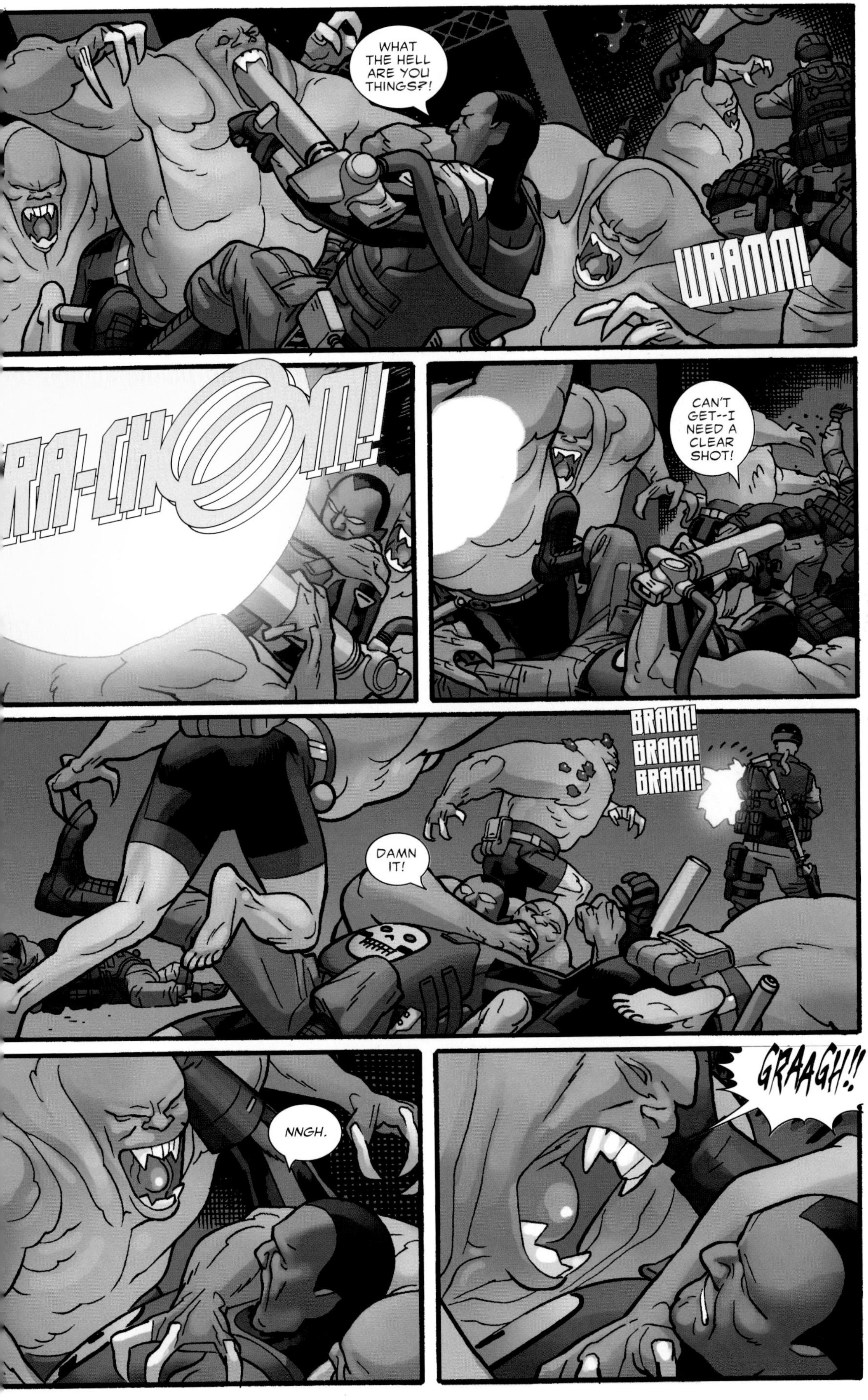
WHAT THE HELL ARE YOU THINGS?!
WRAMM!
RA-CHOOM!
CAN'T GET--I NEED A CLEAR SHOT!
BRAKK! BRAKK! BRAKK!
DAMN IT!
NNGH.
GRAAGH!!

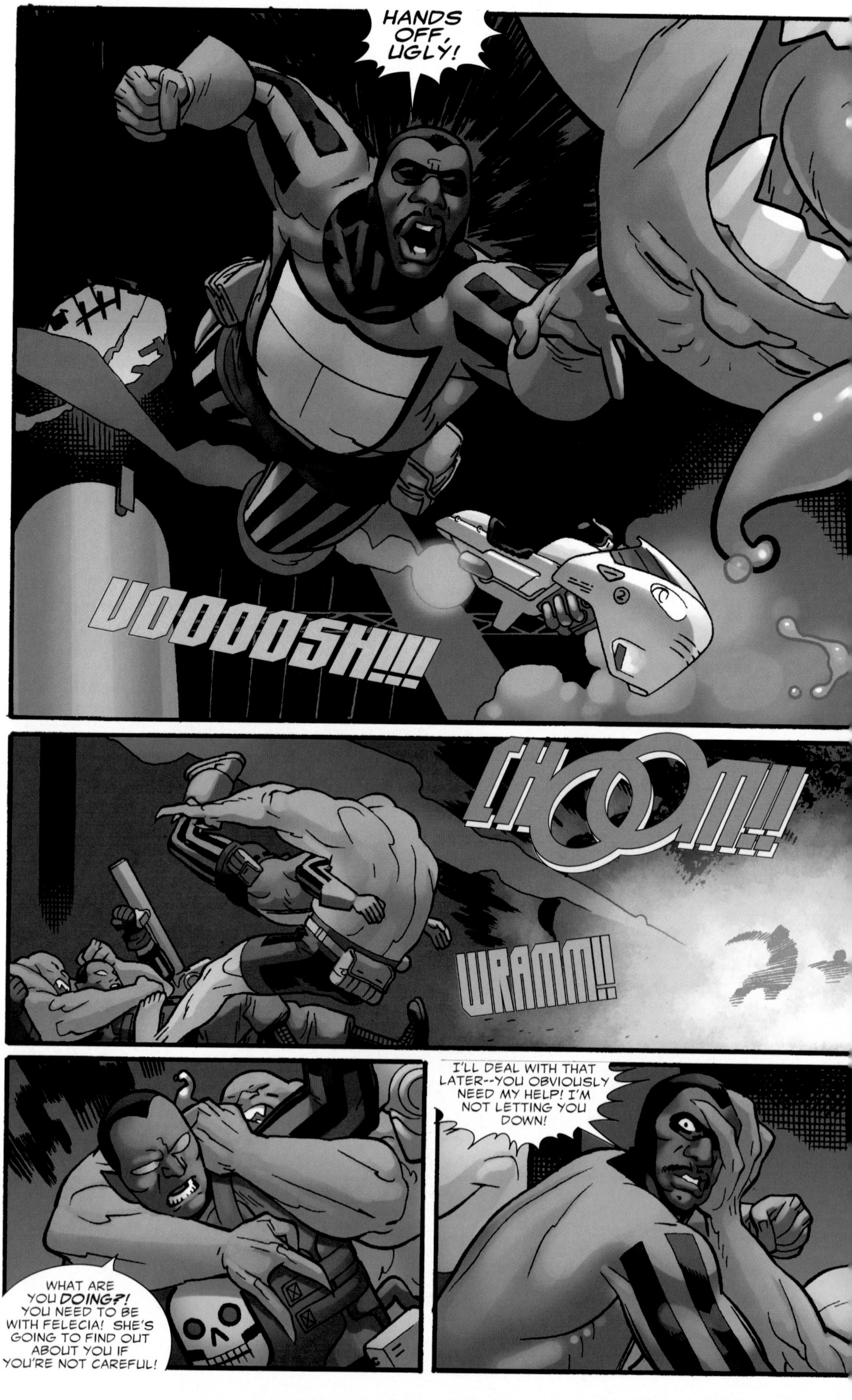
HANDS OFF, UGLY!
VOOOOOSH!!!
CHOOM!!
WRAMM!!
WHAT ARE YOU *DOING?!* YOU NEED TO BE WITH FELECIA! SHE'S GOING TO FIND OUT ABOUT YOU IF YOU'RE NOT CAREFUL!
I'LL DEAL WITH THAT LATER--YOU OBVIOUSLY NEED MY HELP! I'M NOT LETTING YOU DOWN!

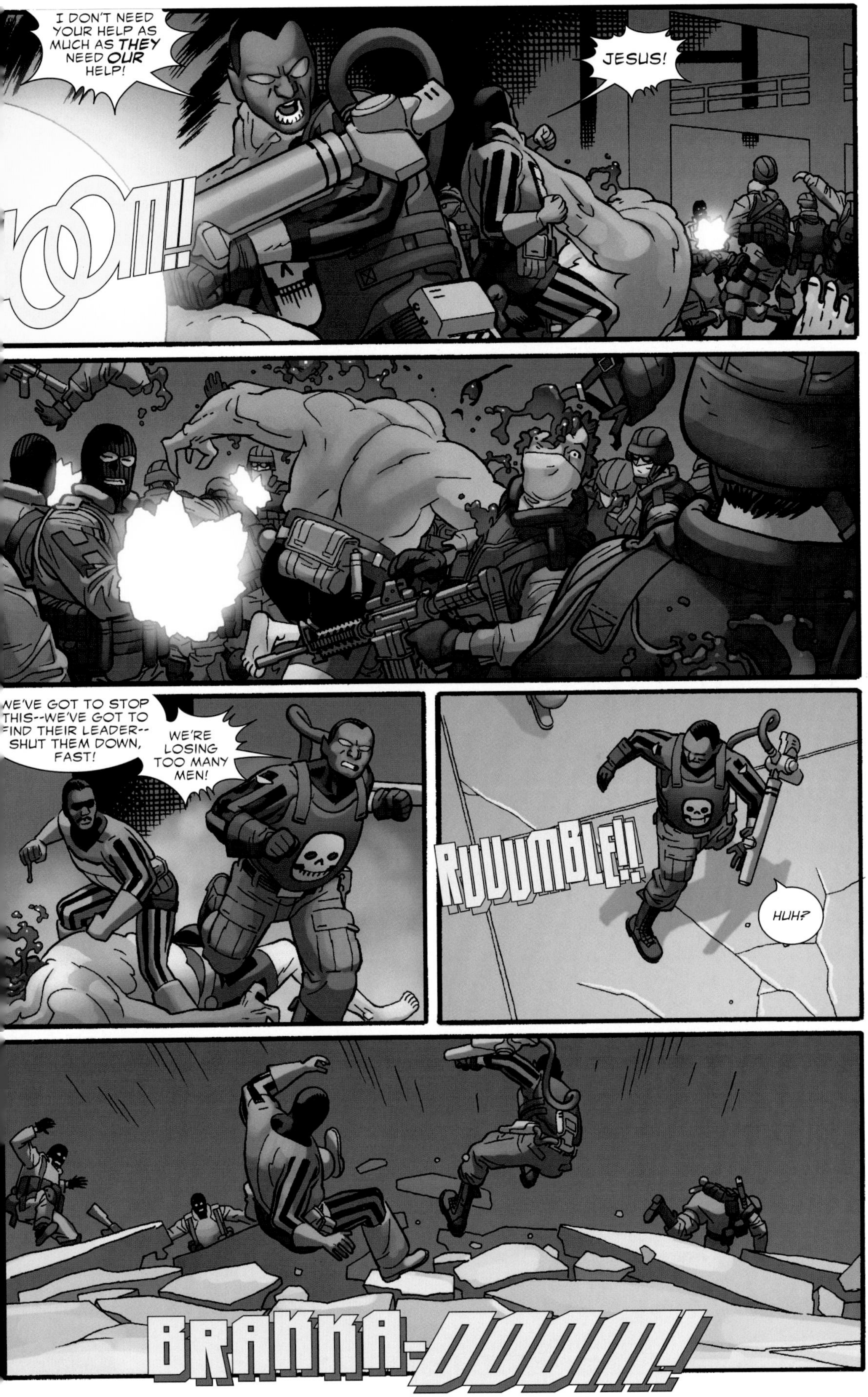
I DON'T NEED YOUR HELP AS MUCH AS THEY NEED OUR HELP!
JESUS!
VOOM!!
WE'VE GOT TO STOP THIS--WE'VE GOT TO FIND THEIR LEADER--SHUT THEM DOWN, FAST!
WE'RE LOSING TOO MANY MEN!
RUUUMBLE!!
HUH?
BRAKKA-DOOM!

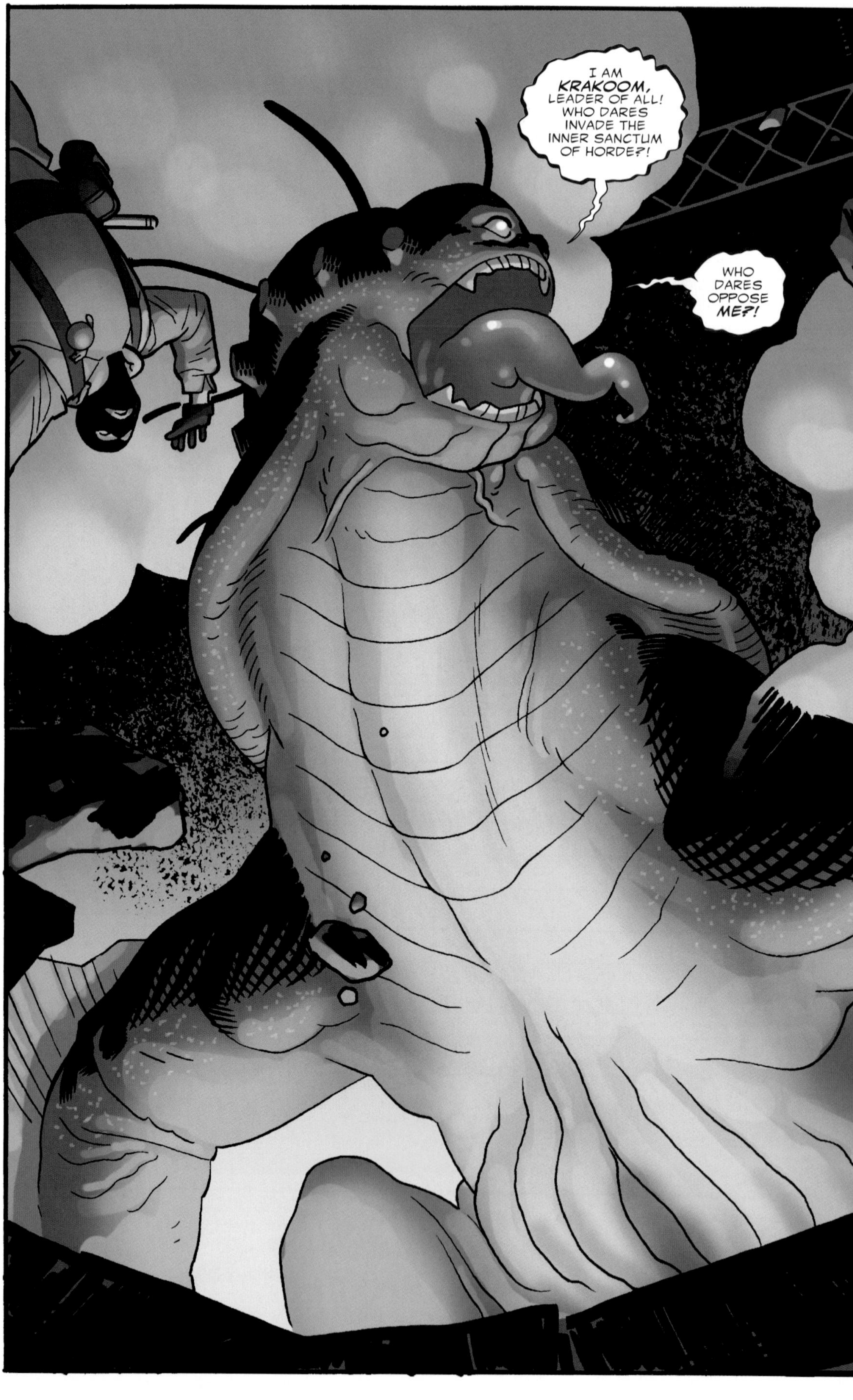
I AM KRAKOOM, LEADER OF ALL! WHO DARES INVADE THE INNER SANCTUM OF HORDE?!
WHO DARES OPPOSE ME?!

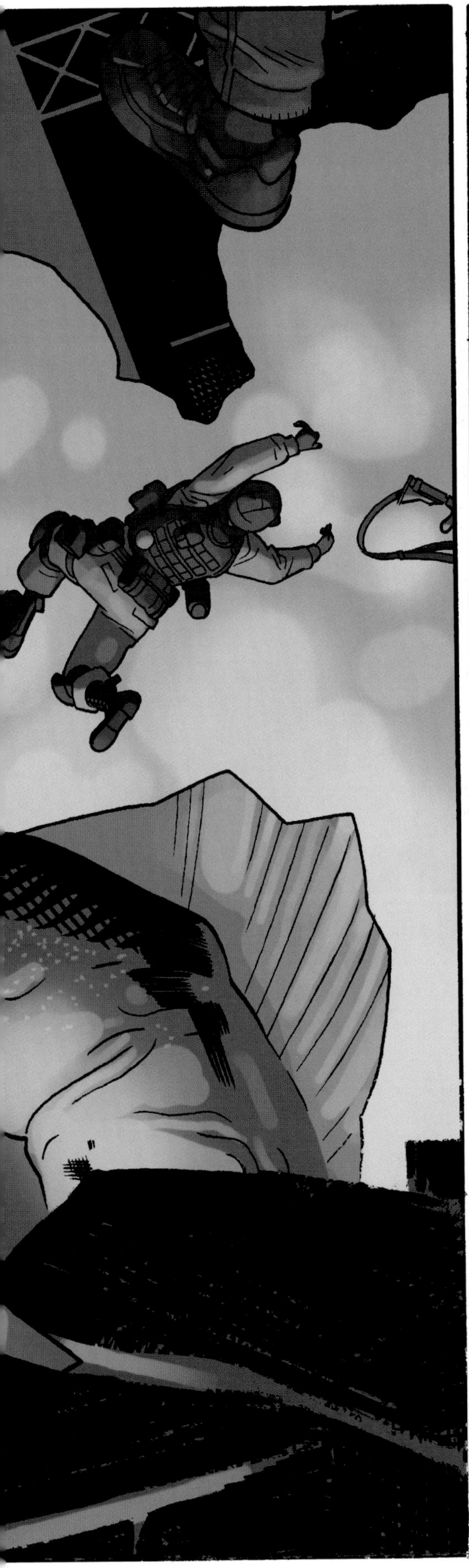

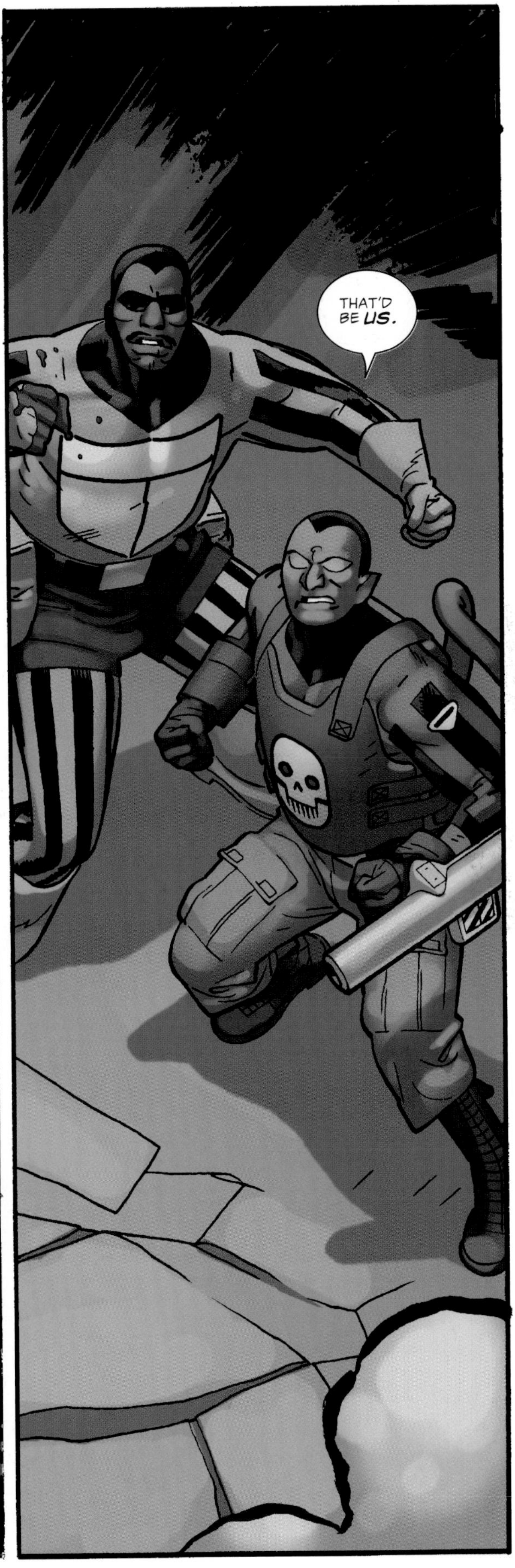
THAT'D BE US.

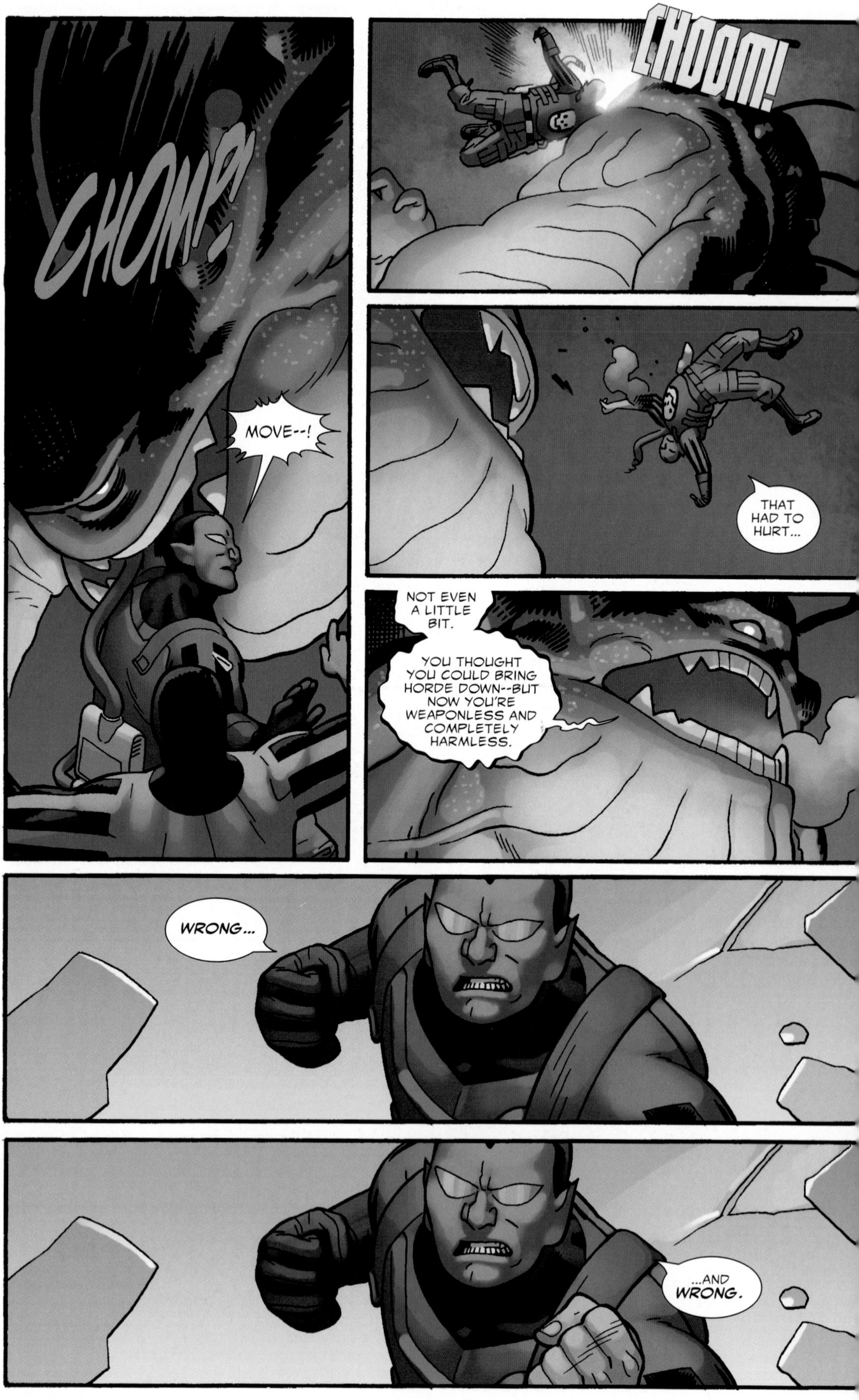
CHOMP!
CHOOM!
MOVE--!
THAT HAD TO HURT...
NOT EVEN A LITTLE BIT.
YOU THOUGHT YOU COULD BRING HORDE DOWN--BUT NOW YOU'RE WEAPONLESS AND COMPLETELY HARMLESS.
WRONG...
...AND WRONG.

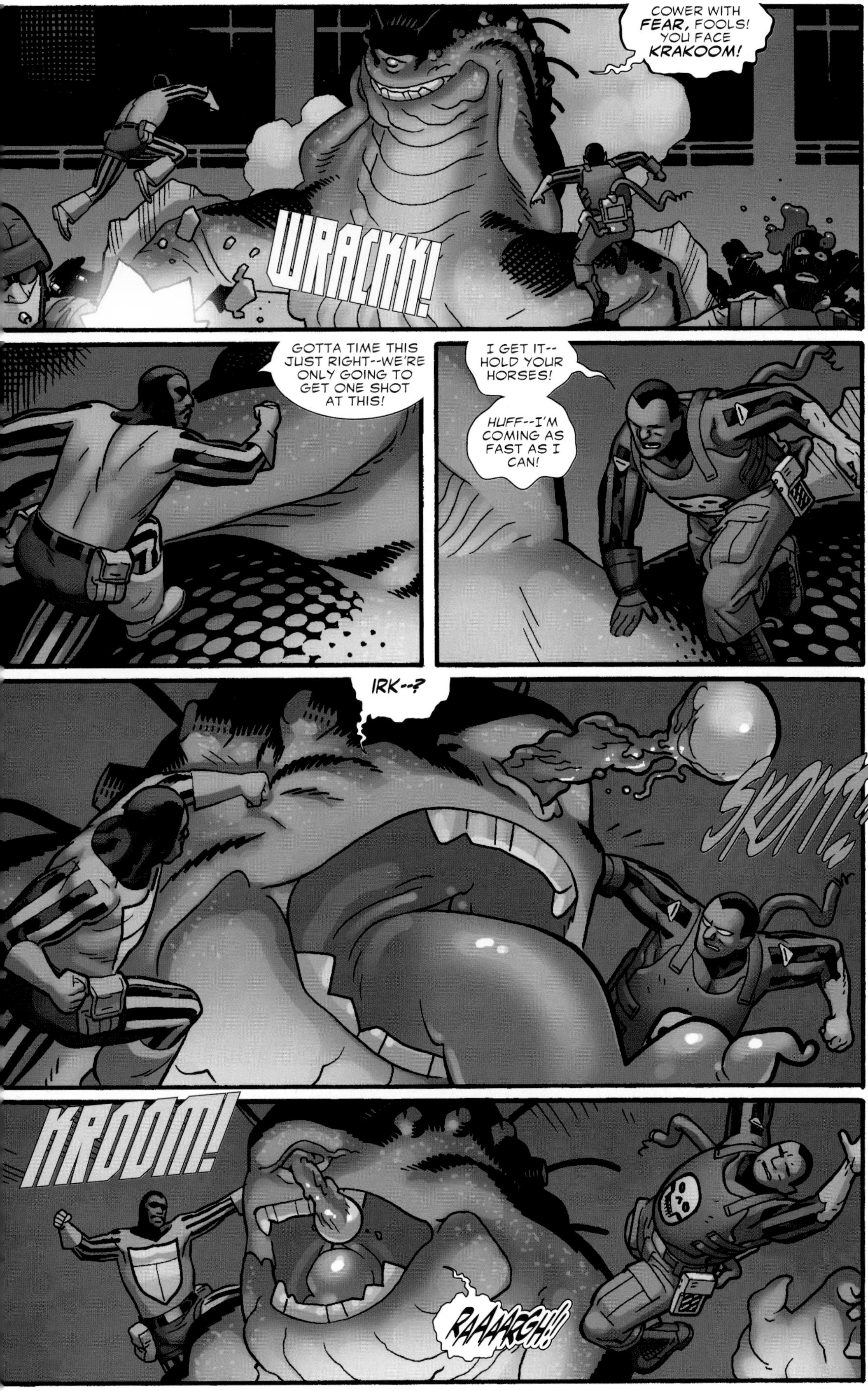
COWER WITH FEAR, FOOLS! YOU FACE KRAKOOM!
WRACKK!
GOTTA TIME THIS JUST RIGHT--WE'RE ONLY GOING TO GET ONE SHOT AT THIS!
I GET IT--HOLD YOUR HORSES!
HUFF--I'M COMING AS FAST AS I CAN!
IRK--?
SKUTT!!
KROOM!
RAAAARGH!!

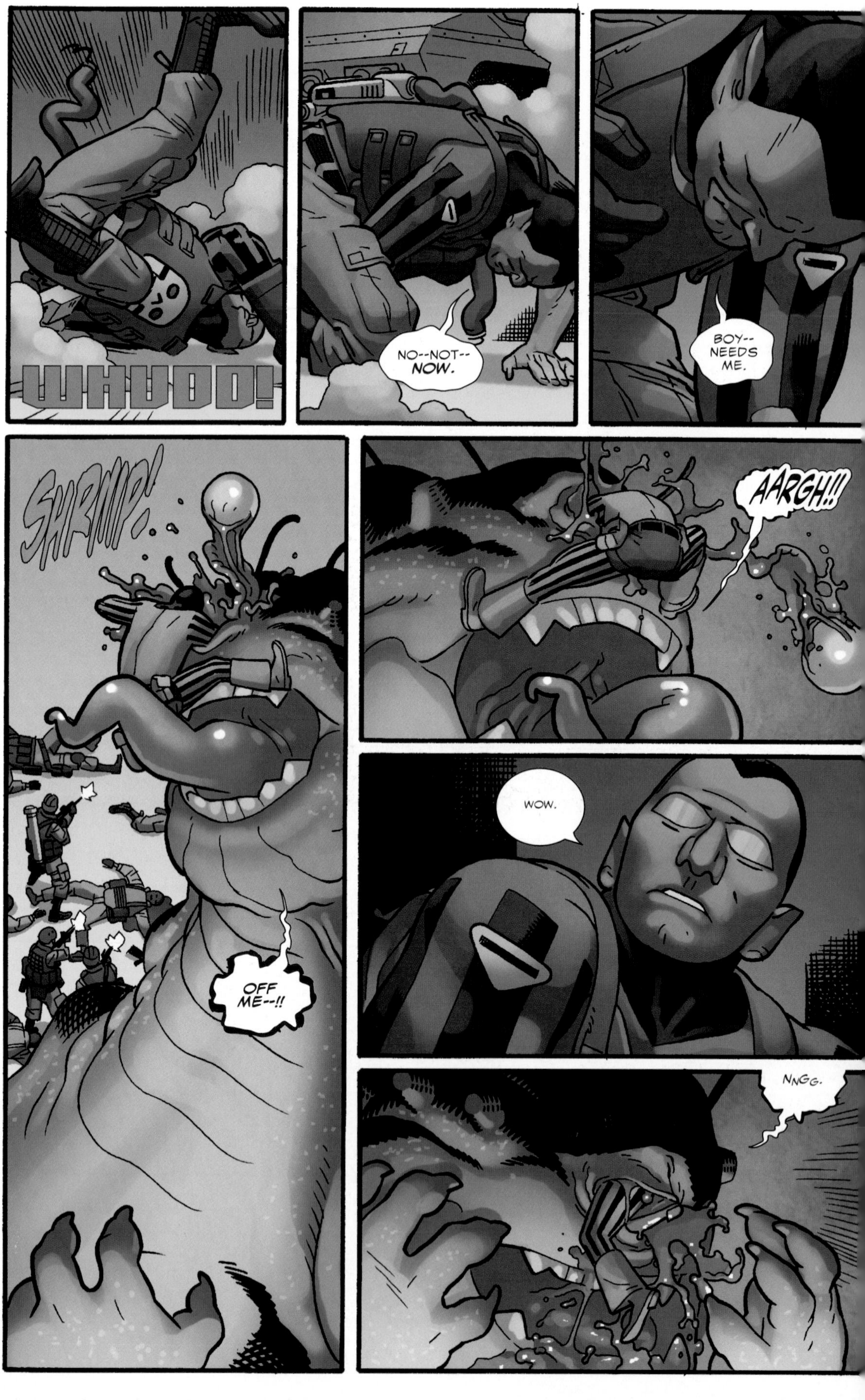
WHUDD!
NO--NOT--
NOW.
BOY--
NEEDS
ME.
SHRMP!
OFF
ME--!!
AARGH!!
WOW.
NNGG.

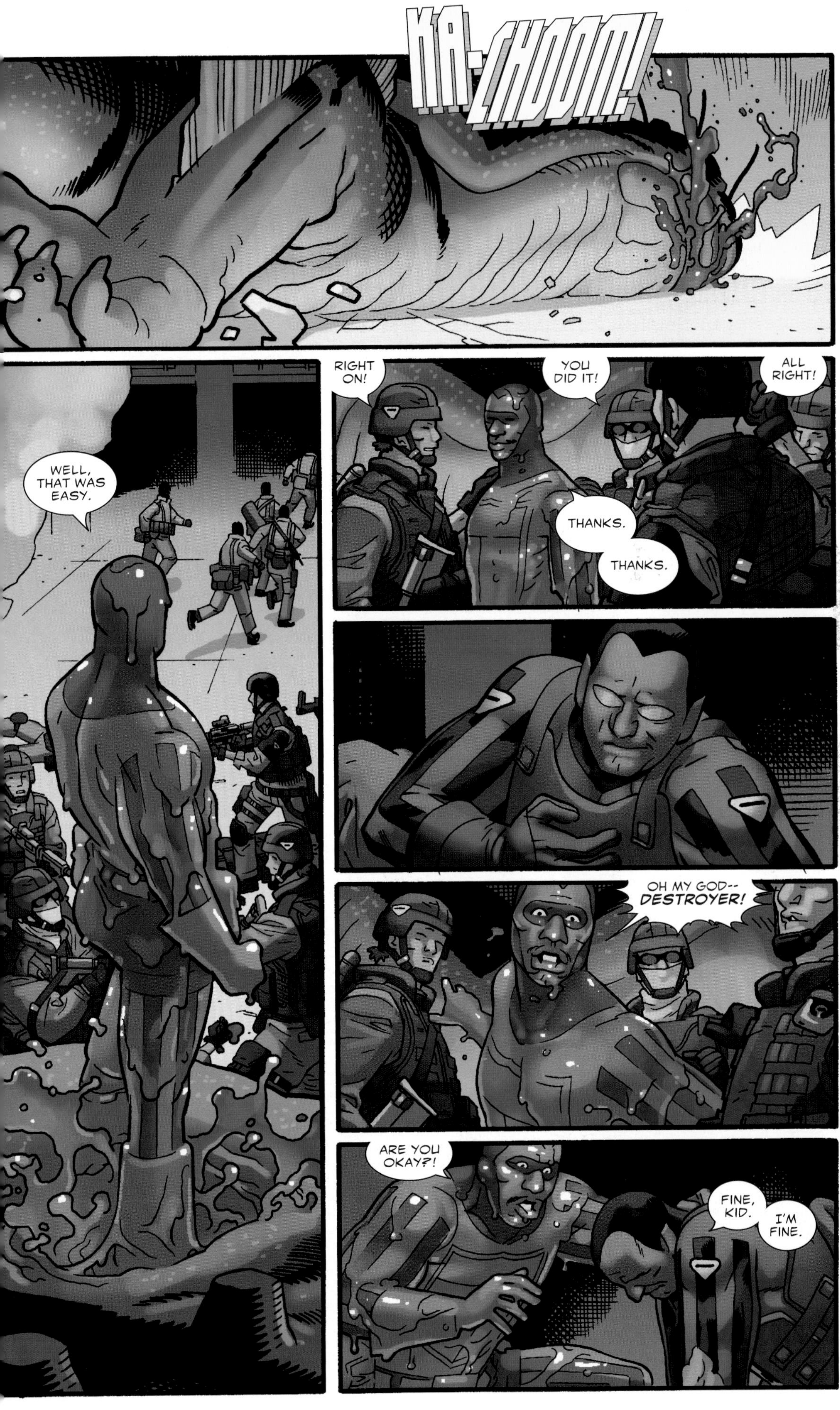
KA-CHOOM!
WELL, THAT WAS EASY.
RIGHT ON!
YOU DID IT!
ALL RIGHT!
THANKS.
THANKS.
OH MY GOD-- DESTROYER!
ARE YOU OKAY?!
FINE, KID.
I'M FINE.

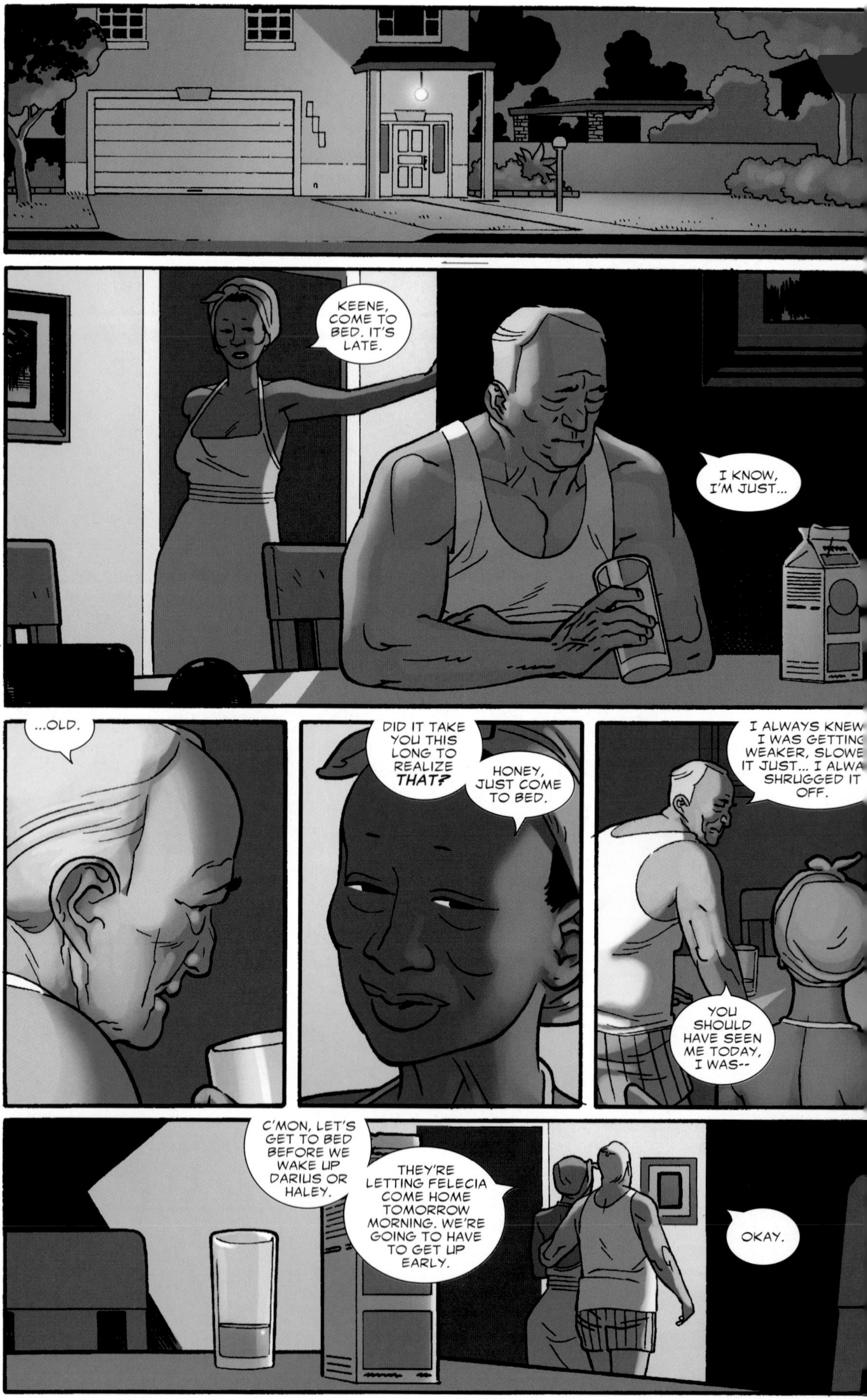
KEENE, COME TO BED. IT'S LATE.
I KNOW, I'M JUST...
...OLD.
DID IT TAKE YOU THIS LONG TO REALIZE *THAT?*
HONEY, JUST COME TO BED.
I ALWAYS KNEW I WAS GETTING WEAKER, SLOWE IT JUST... I ALWA SHRUGGED IT OFF.
YOU SHOULD HAVE SEEN ME TODAY, I WAS--
C'MON, LET'S GET TO BED BEFORE WE WAKE UP DARIUS OR HALEY.
THEY'RE LETTING FELECIA COME HOME TOMORROW MORNING. WE'RE GOING TO HAVE TO GET UP EARLY.
OKAY.

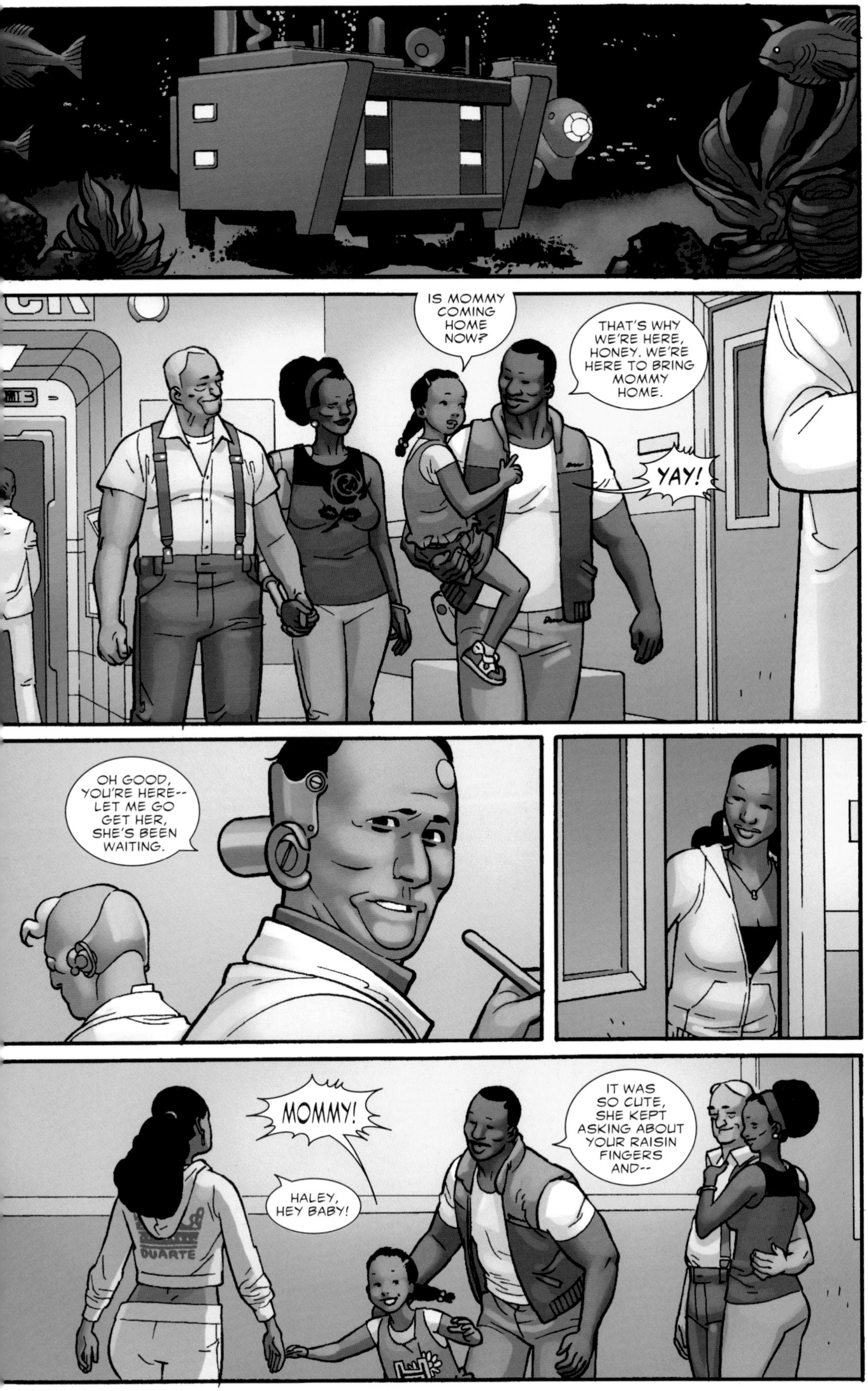

IS MOMMY COMING HOME NOW?
THAT'S WHY WE'RE HERE, HONEY. WE'RE HERE TO BRING MOMMY HOME.
YAY!
OH GOOD, YOU'RE HERE-- LET ME GO GET HER, SHE'S BEEN WAITING.
MOMMY!
HALEY, HEY BABY!
IT WAS SO CUTE, SHE KEPT ASKING ABOUT YOUR RAISIN FINGERS AND--
DUARTE

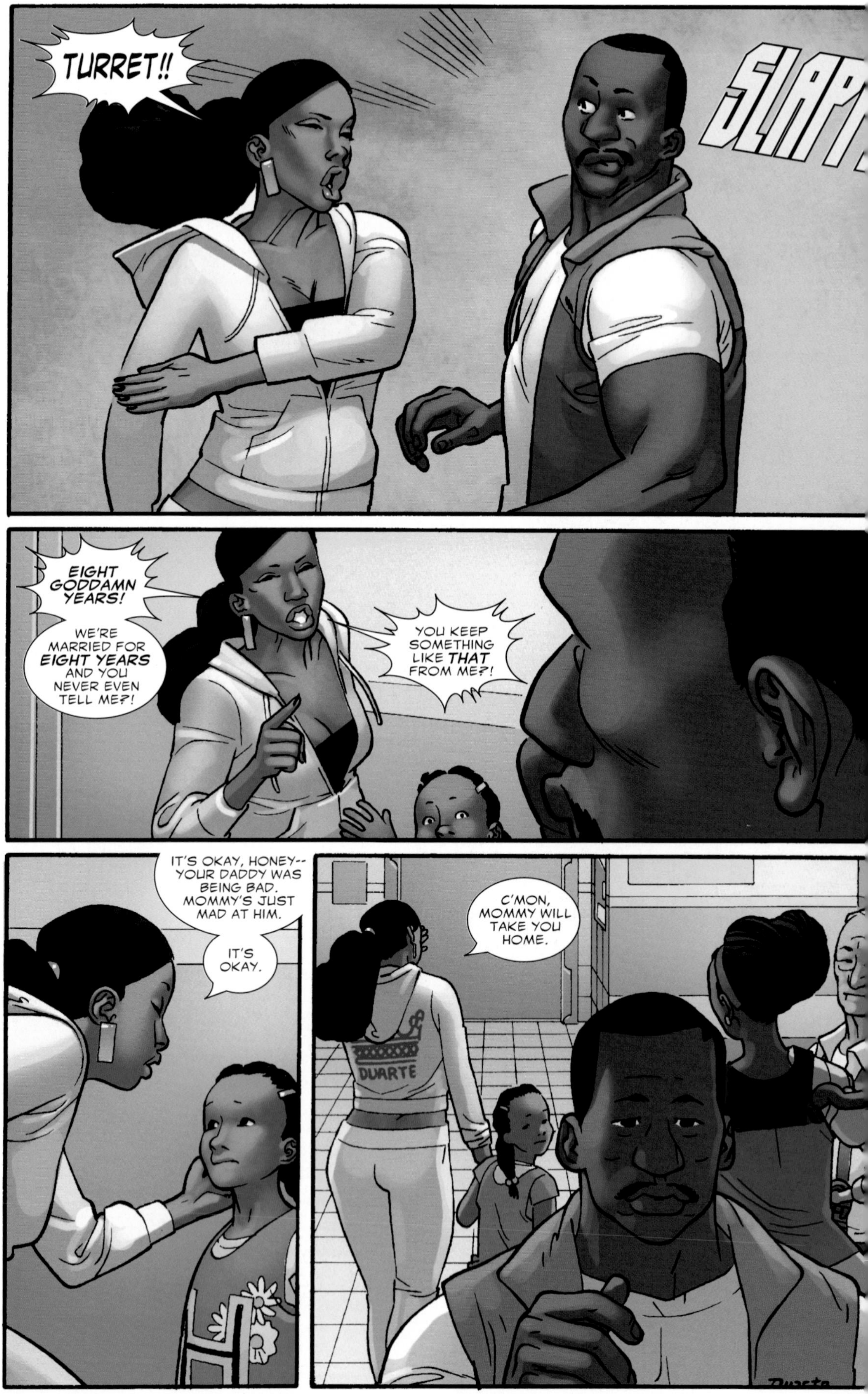
TURRET!!
SLAP
EIGHT GODDAMN YEARS!
WE'RE MARRIED FOR EIGHT YEARS AND YOU NEVER EVEN TELL ME?!
YOU KEEP SOMETHING LIKE THAT FROM ME?!
IT'S OKAY, HONEY-- YOUR DADDY WAS BEING BAD. MOMMY'S JUST MAD AT HIM.
IT'S OKAY.
C'MON, MOMMY WILL TAKE YOU HOME.
DUARTE

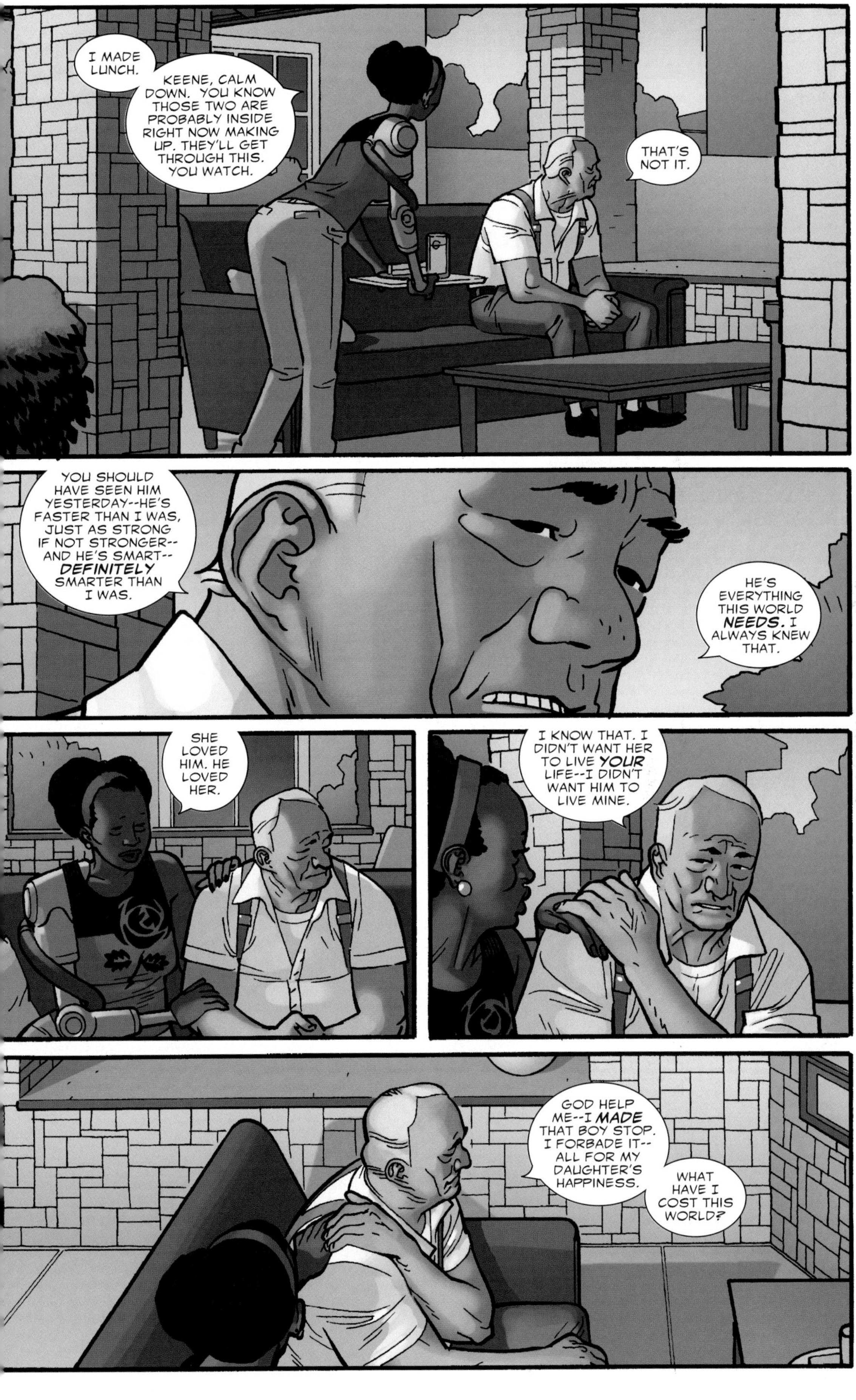
I MADE LUNCH.
KEENE, CALM DOWN. YOU KNOW THOSE TWO ARE PROBABLY INSIDE RIGHT NOW MAKING UP. THEY'LL GET THROUGH THIS. YOU WATCH.
THAT'S NOT IT.
YOU SHOULD HAVE SEEN HIM YESTERDAY--HE'S FASTER THAN I WAS, JUST AS STRONG IF NOT STRONGER--AND HE'S SMART--DEFINITELY SMARTER THAN I WAS.
HE'S EVERYTHING THIS WORLD NEEDS. I ALWAYS KNEW THAT.
SHE LOVED HIM. HE LOVED HER.
I KNOW THAT. I DIDN'T WANT HER TO LIVE YOUR LIFE--I DIDN'T WANT HIM TO LIVE MINE.
GOD HELP ME--I MADE THAT BOY STOP. I FORBADE IT--ALL FOR MY DAUGHTER'S HAPPINESS.
WHAT HAVE I COST THIS WORLD?

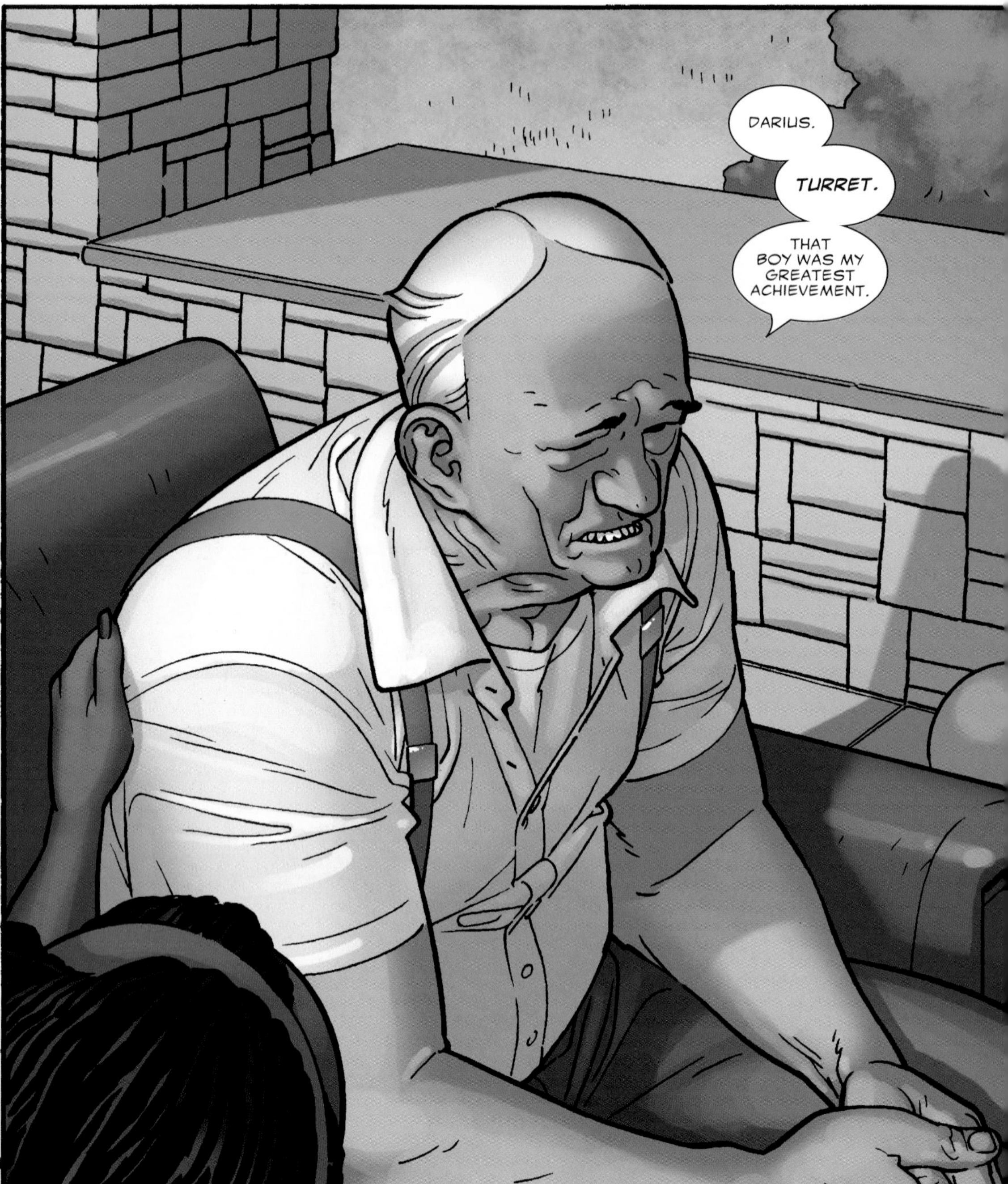
DARIUS.
TURRET.
THAT BOY WAS MY GREATEST ACHIEVEMENT.
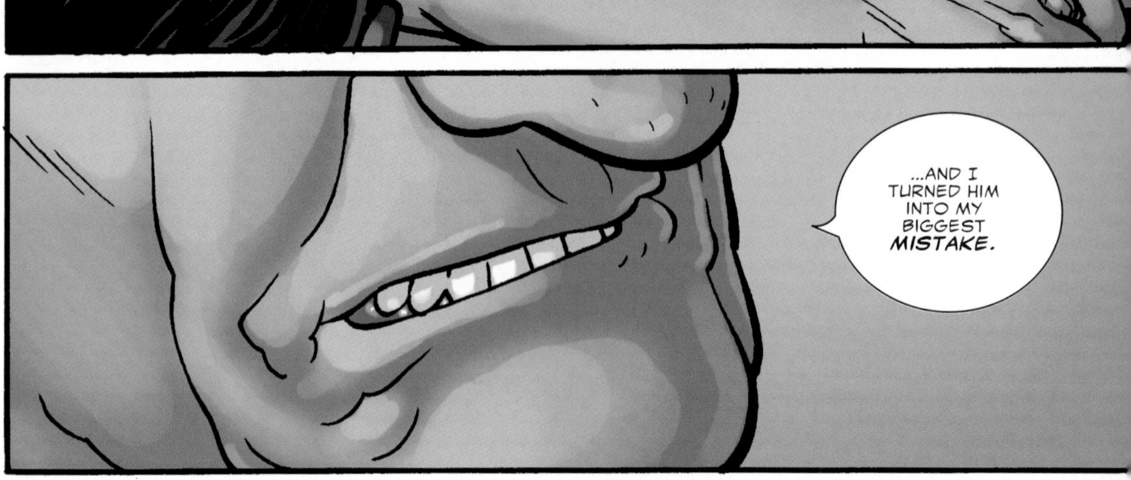
...AND I TURNED HIM INTO MY BIGGEST MISTAKE.

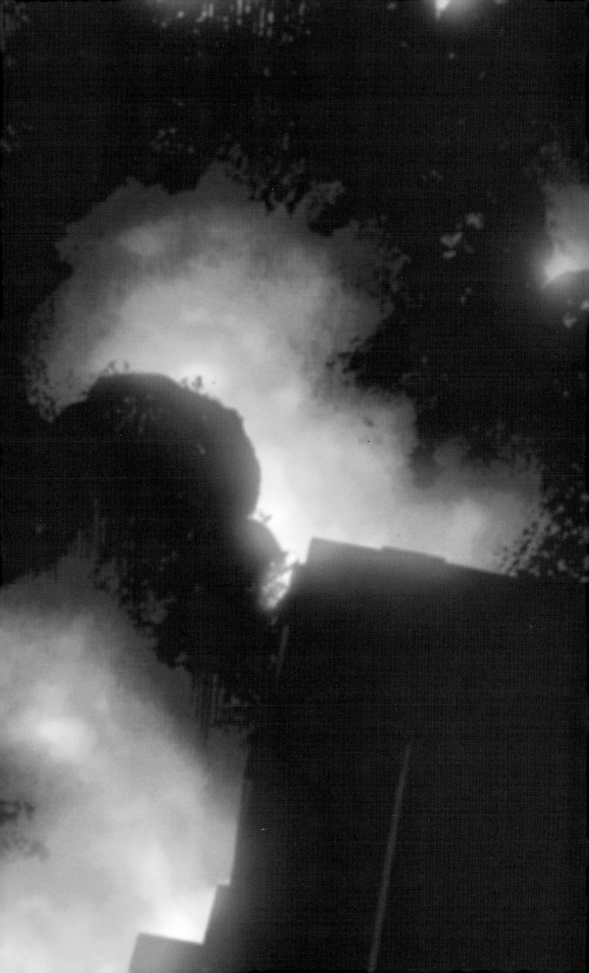

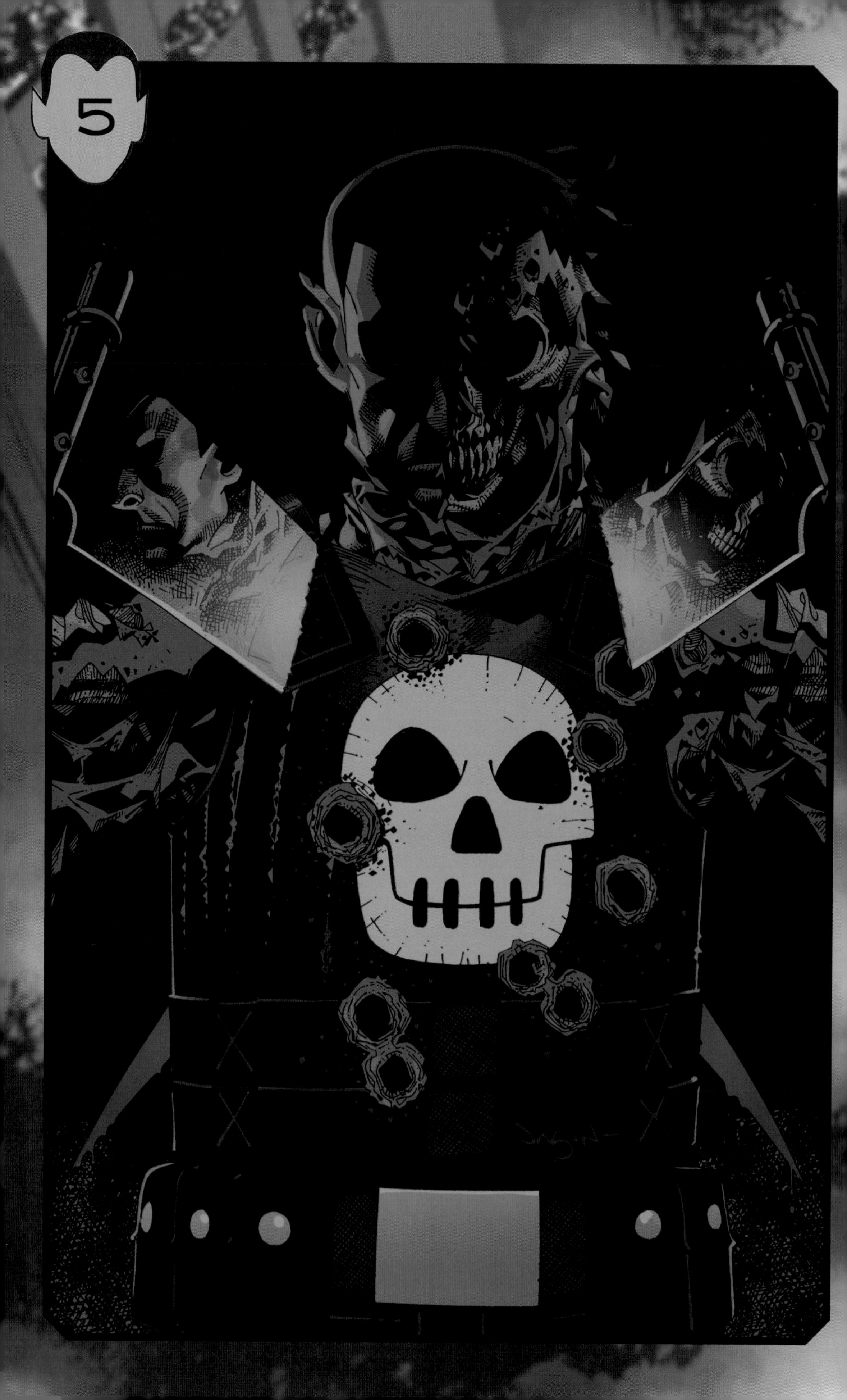
5

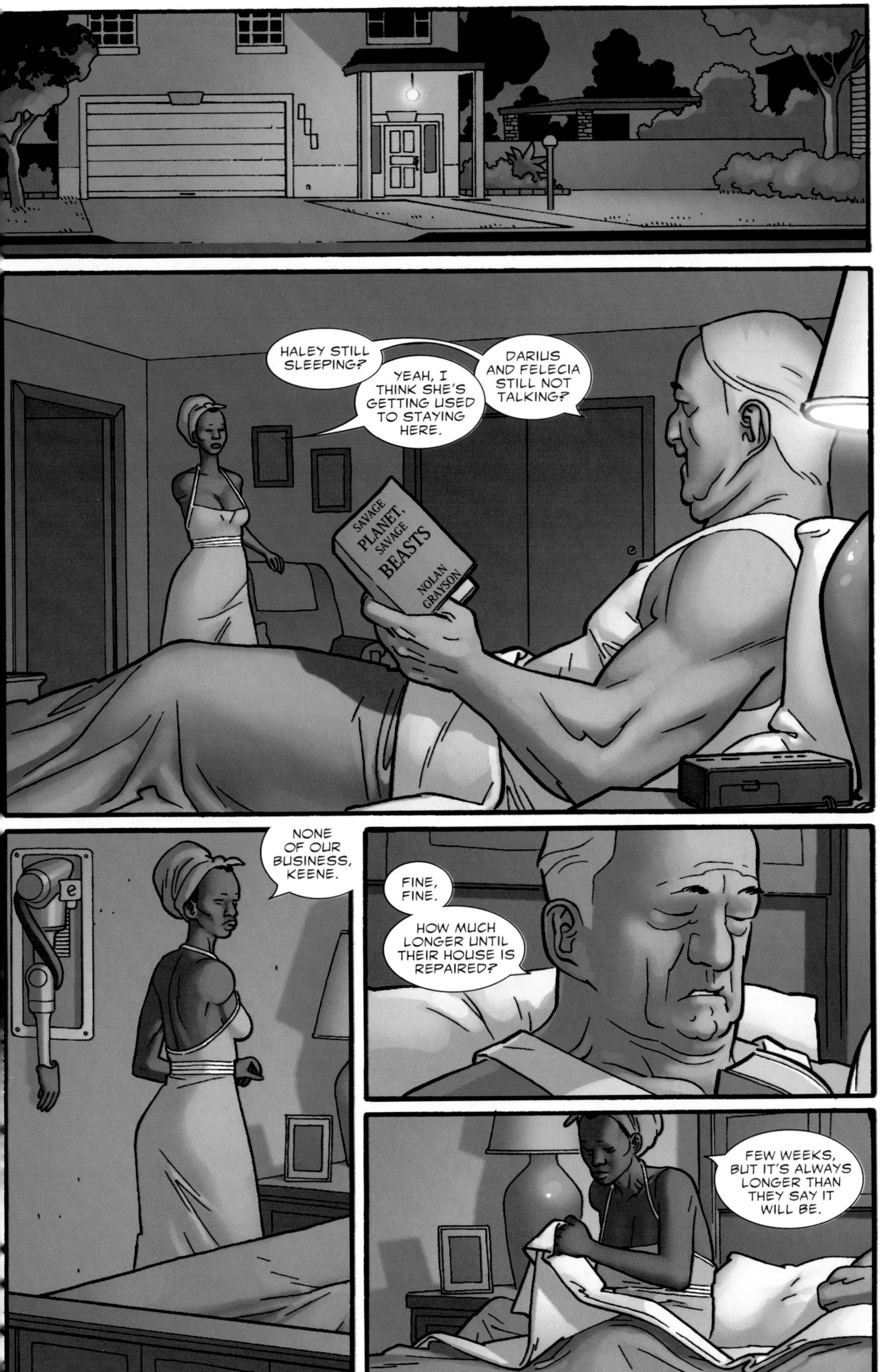
HALEY STILL SLEEPING?
YEAH, I THINK SHE'S GETTING USED TO STAYING HERE.
DARIUS AND FELECIA STILL NOT TALKING?
SAVAGE PLANET, SAVAGE BEASTS
NOLAN GRAYSON
NONE OF OUR BUSINESS, KEENE.
FINE, FINE.
HOW MUCH LONGER UNTIL THEIR HOUSE IS REPAIRED?
FEW WEEKS, BUT IT'S ALWAYS LONGER THAN THEY SAY IT WILL BE.

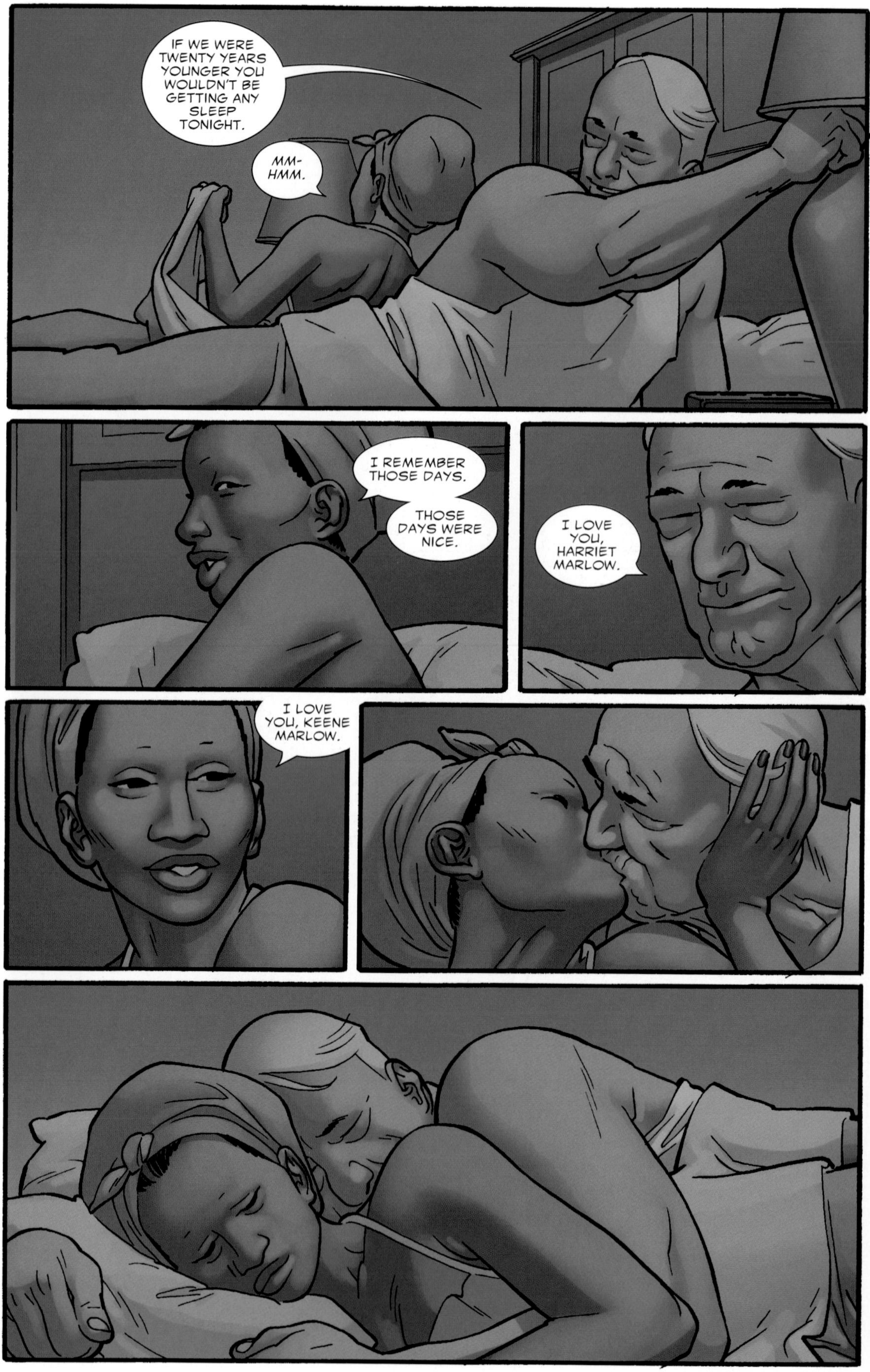
IF WE WERE TWENTY YEARS YOUNGER YOU WOULDN'T BE GETTING ANY SLEEP TONIGHT.
MM-HMM.
I REMEMBER THOSE DAYS.
THOSE DAYS WERE NICE.
I LOVE YOU, HARRIET MARLOW.
I LOVE YOU, KEENE MARLOW.

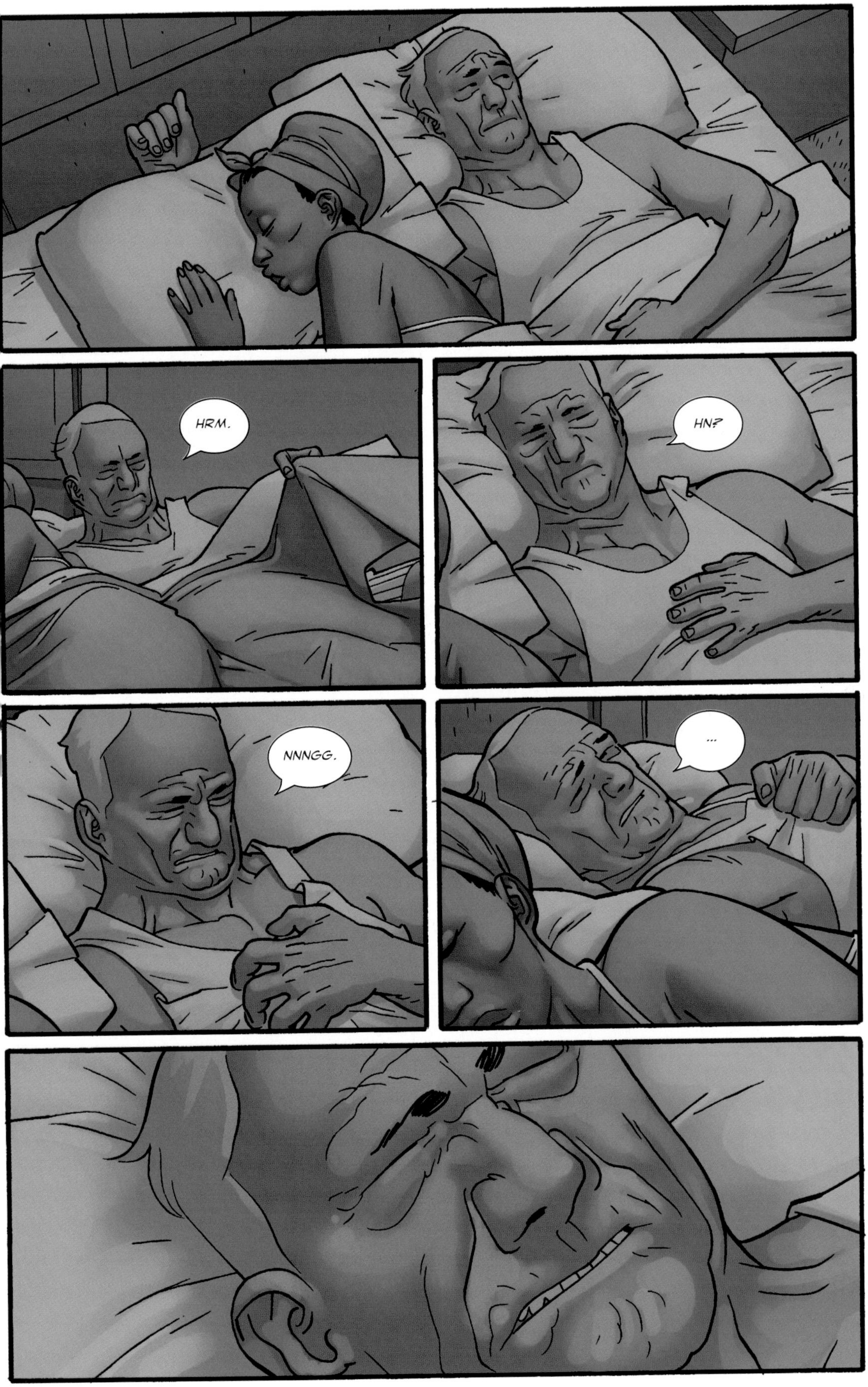
HRM.
HN?
NNNGG.
...

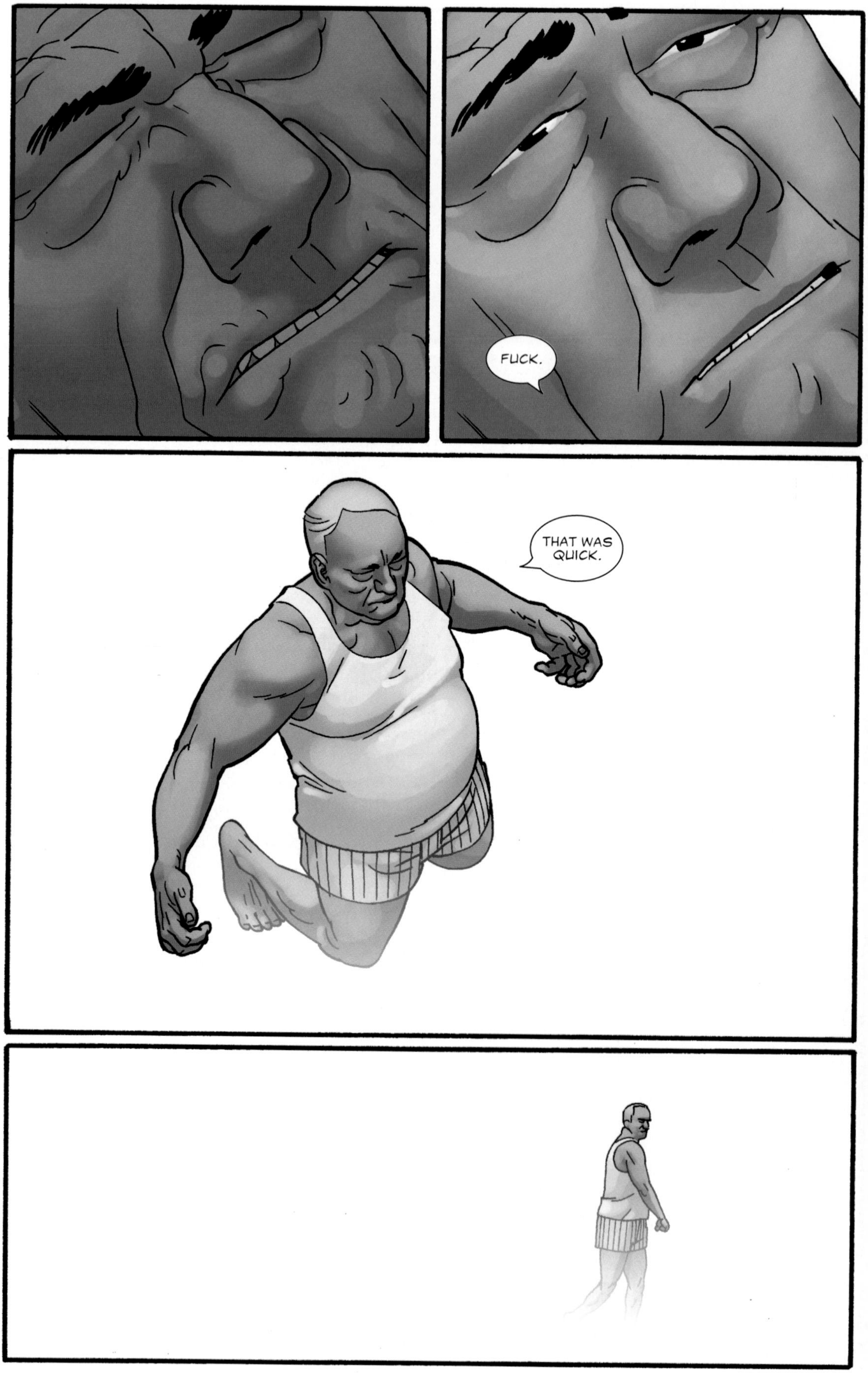
FUCK.
THAT WAS QUICK.

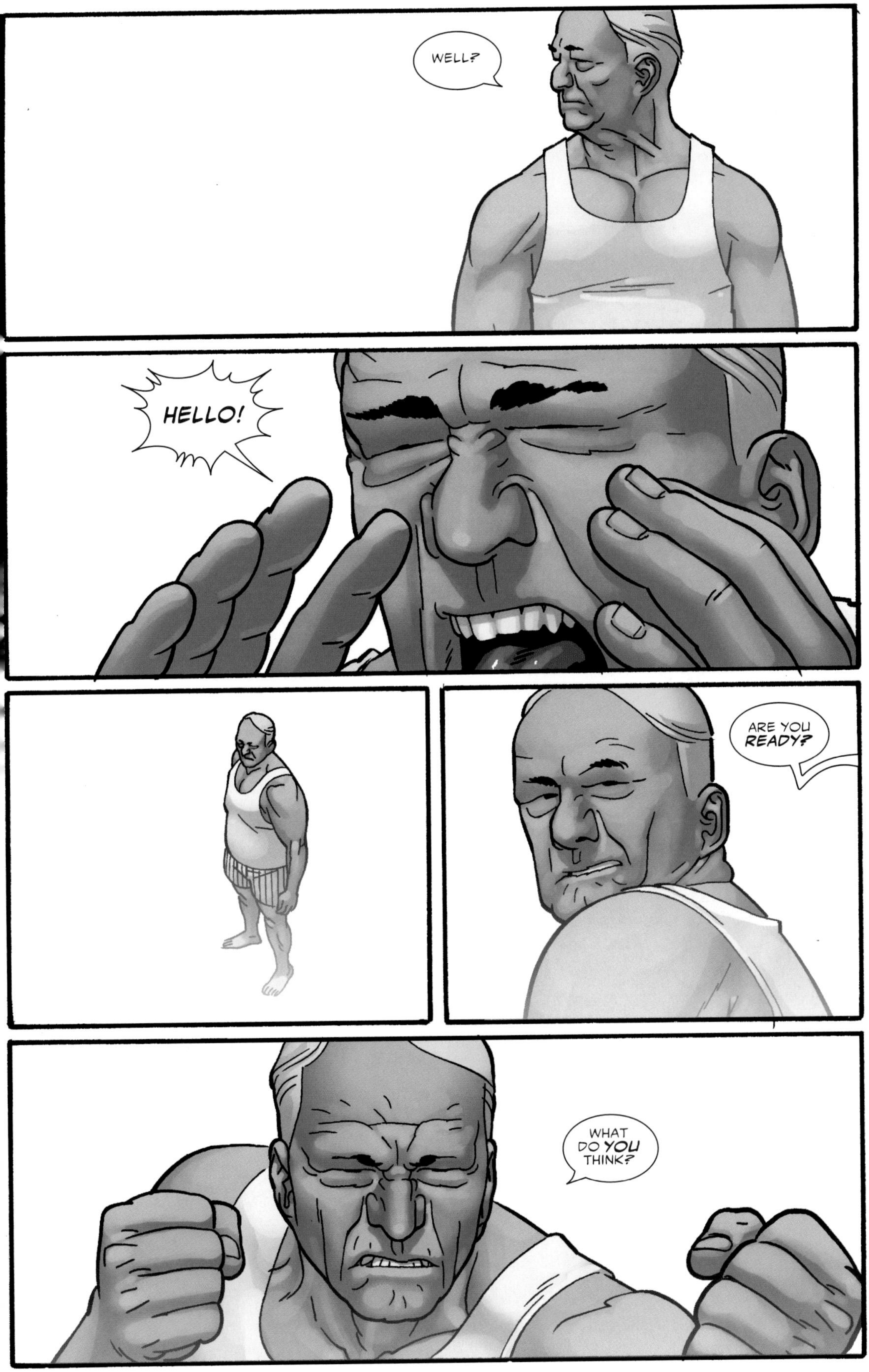
WELL?
HELLO!
ARE YOU READY?
WHAT DO YOU THINK?

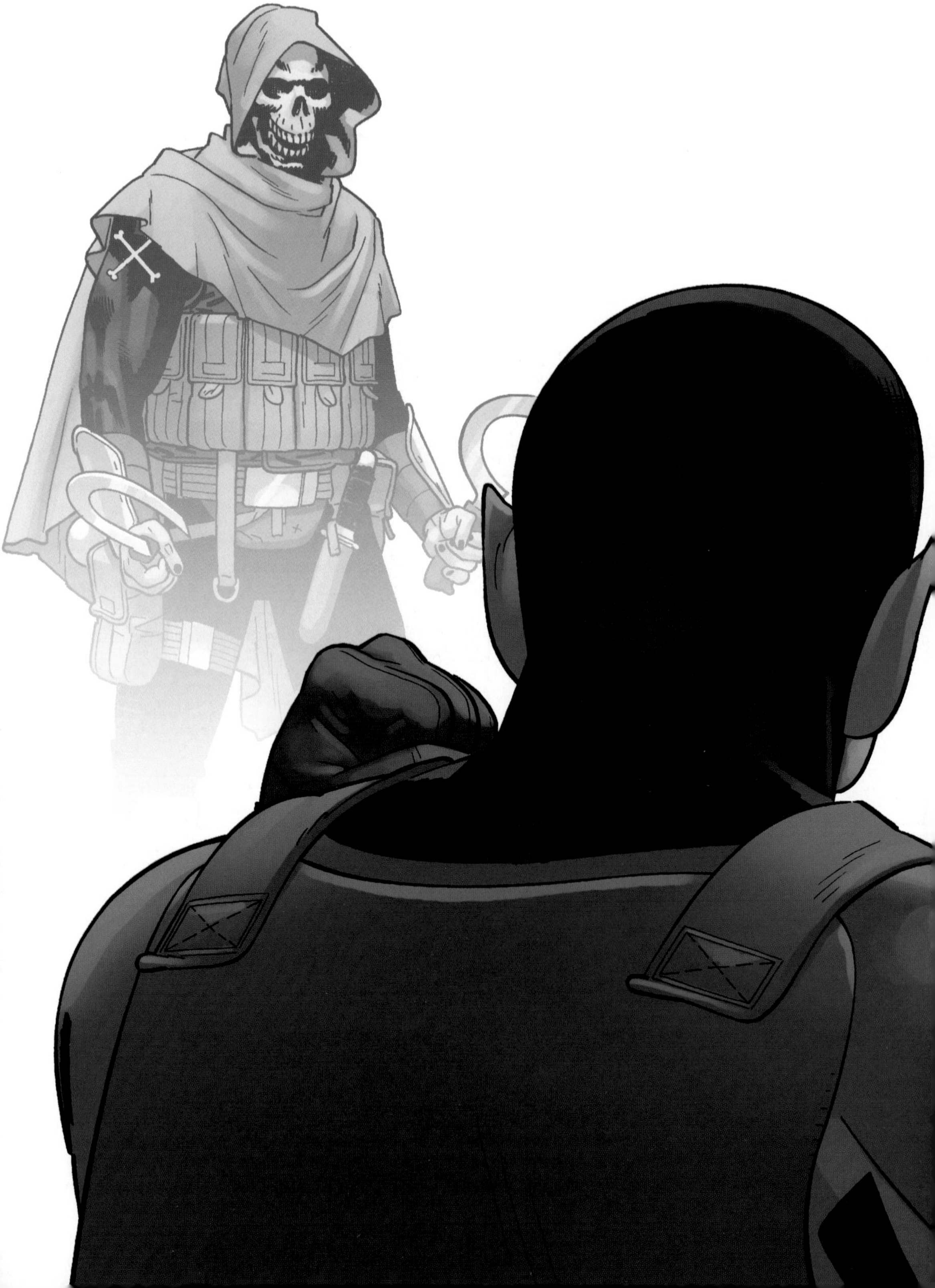

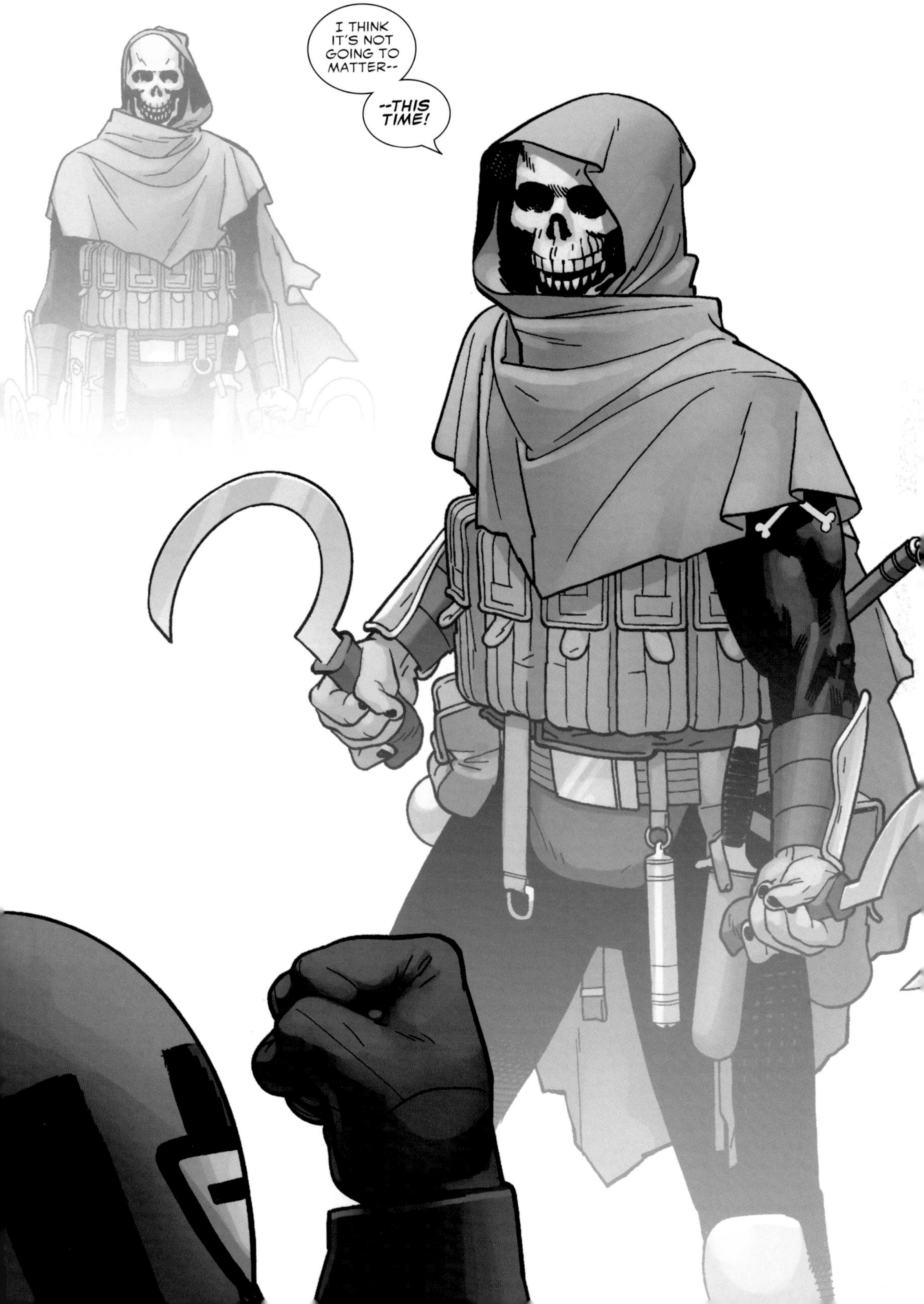
I THINK IT'S NOT GOING TO MATTER--
--THIS TIME!

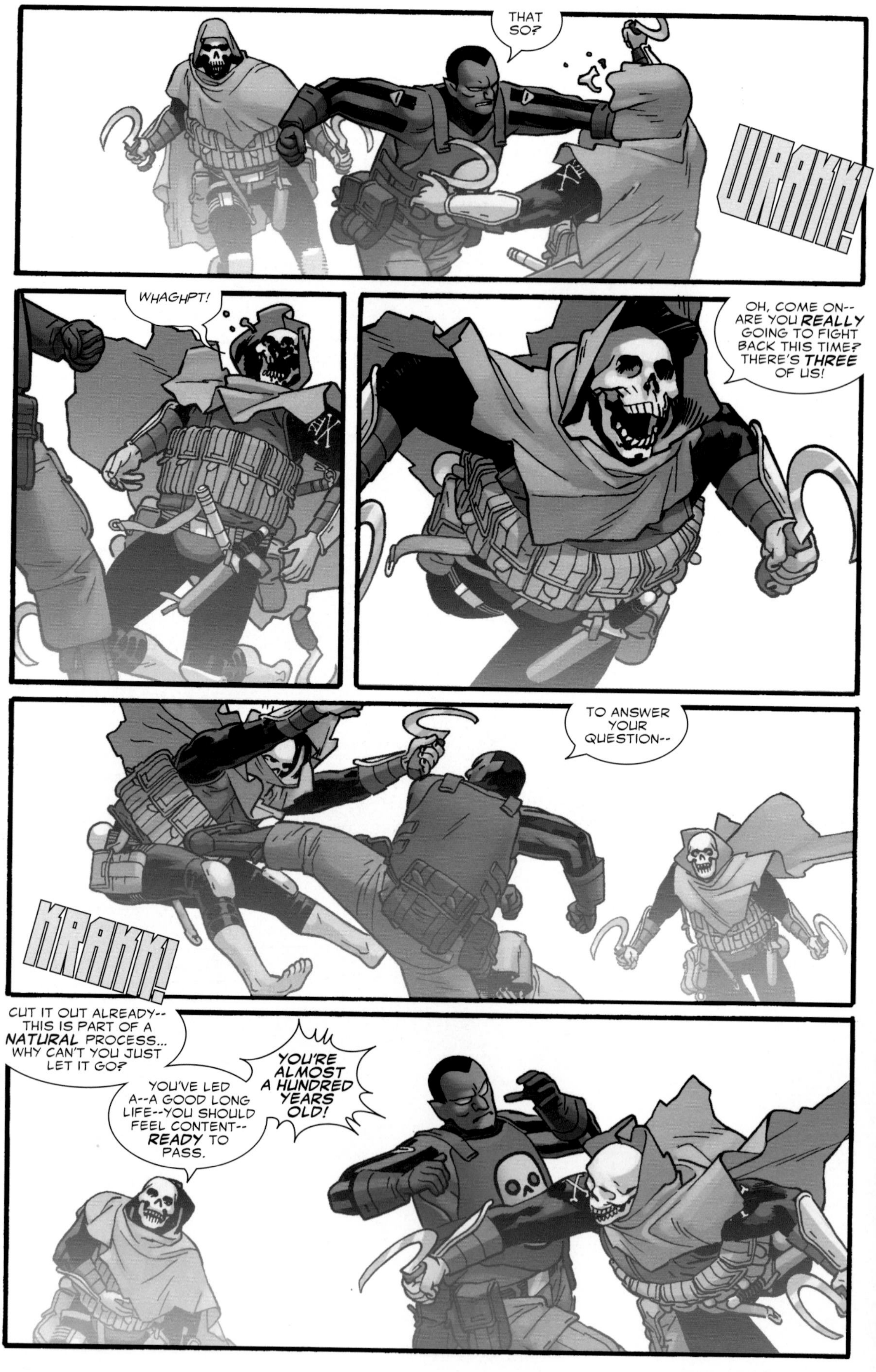
THAT SO?
WRAKK!
WHAGHPT!
OH, COME ON-- ARE YOU REALLY GOING TO FIGHT BACK THIS TIME? THERE'S THREE OF US!
TO ANSWER YOUR QUESTION--
KRAKK!
CUT IT OUT ALREADY-- THIS IS PART OF A NATURAL PROCESS... WHY CAN'T YOU JUST LET IT GO?
YOU'RE ALMOST A HUNDRED YEARS OLD!
YOU'VE LED A--A GOOD LONG LIFE--YOU SHOULD FEEL CONTENT-- READY TO PASS.

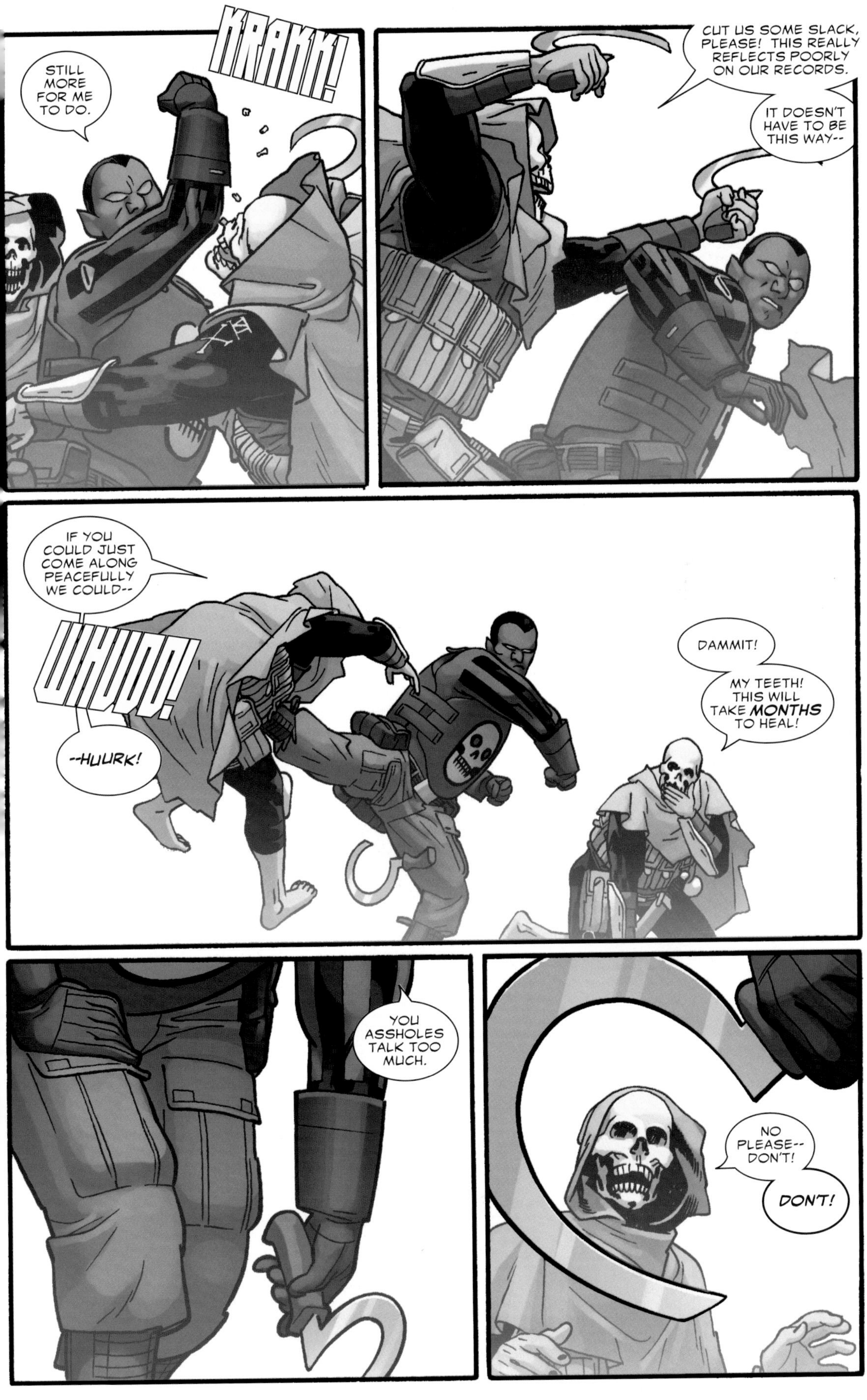
KRAKK!
STILL MORE FOR ME TO DO.
CUT US SOME SLACK, PLEASE! THIS REALLY REFLECTS POORLY ON OUR RECORDS.
IT DOESN'T HAVE TO BE THIS WAY--
IF YOU COULD JUST COME ALONG PEACEFULLY WE COULD--
WHUDD!
--HUURK!
DAMMIT!
MY TEETH! THIS WILL TAKE MONTHS TO HEAL!
YOU ASSHOLES TALK TOO MUCH.
NO PLEASE-- DON'T!
DON'T!

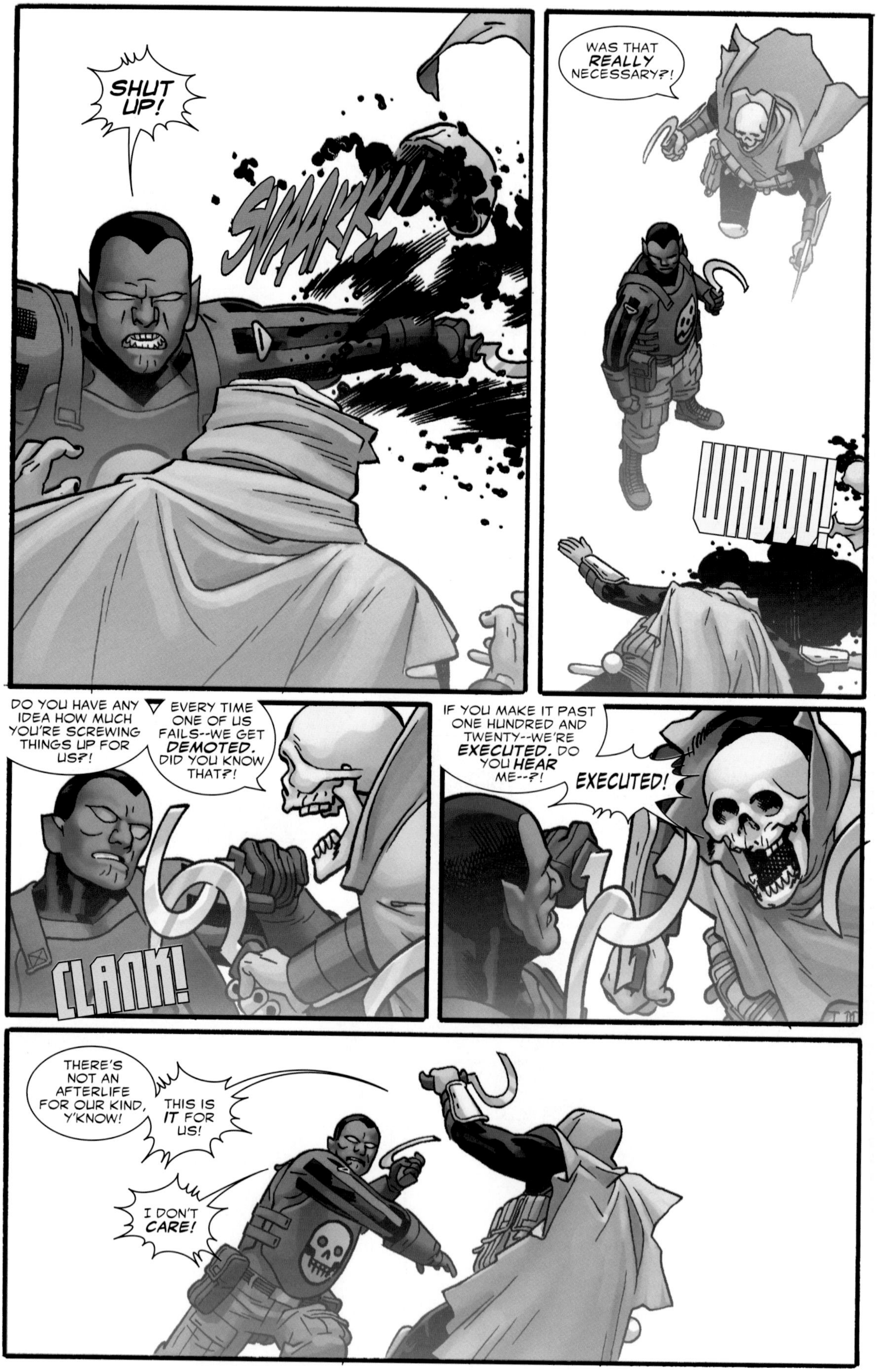

SHUT UP!
SNAKK!!...
WAS THAT REALLY NECESSARY?!
WHUDD!
DO YOU HAVE ANY IDEA HOW MUCH YOU'RE SCREWING THINGS UP FOR US?!
EVERY TIME ONE OF US FAILS--WE GET DEMOTED. DID YOU KNOW THAT?!
CLANK!
IF YOU MAKE IT PAST ONE HUNDRED AND TWENTY--WE'RE EXECUTED. DO YOU HEAR ME--?!
EXECUTED!
THERE'S NOT AN AFTERLIFE FOR OUR KIND, Y'KNOW!
THIS IS IT FOR US!
I DON'T CARE!

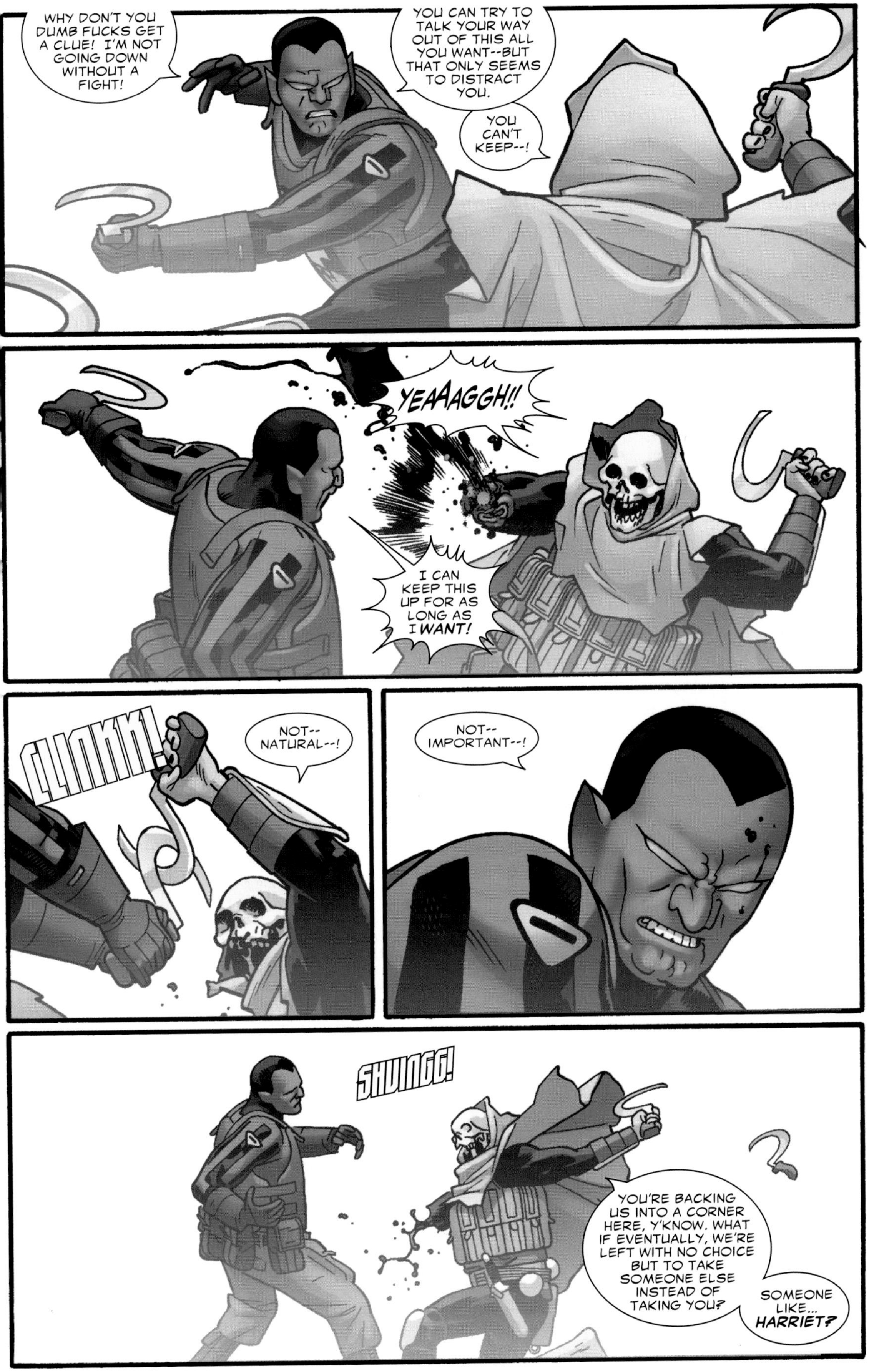
WHY DON'T YOU DUMB FUCKS GET A CLUE! I'M NOT GOING DOWN WITHOUT A FIGHT!
YOU CAN TRY TO TALK YOUR WAY OUT OF THIS ALL YOU WANT--BUT THAT ONLY SEEMS TO DISTRACT YOU.
YOU CAN'T KEEP--!
YEAAAGGH!!
I CAN KEEP THIS UP FOR AS LONG AS I *WANT!*
CLINKK!
NOT-- NATURAL--!
NOT-- IMPORTANT--!
SHVINGG!
YOU'RE BACKING US INTO A CORNER HERE, Y'KNOW. WHAT IF EVENTUALLY, WE'RE LEFT WITH NO CHOICE BUT TO TAKE SOMEONE ELSE INSTEAD OF TAKING YOU?
SOMEONE LIKE... **HARRIET?**

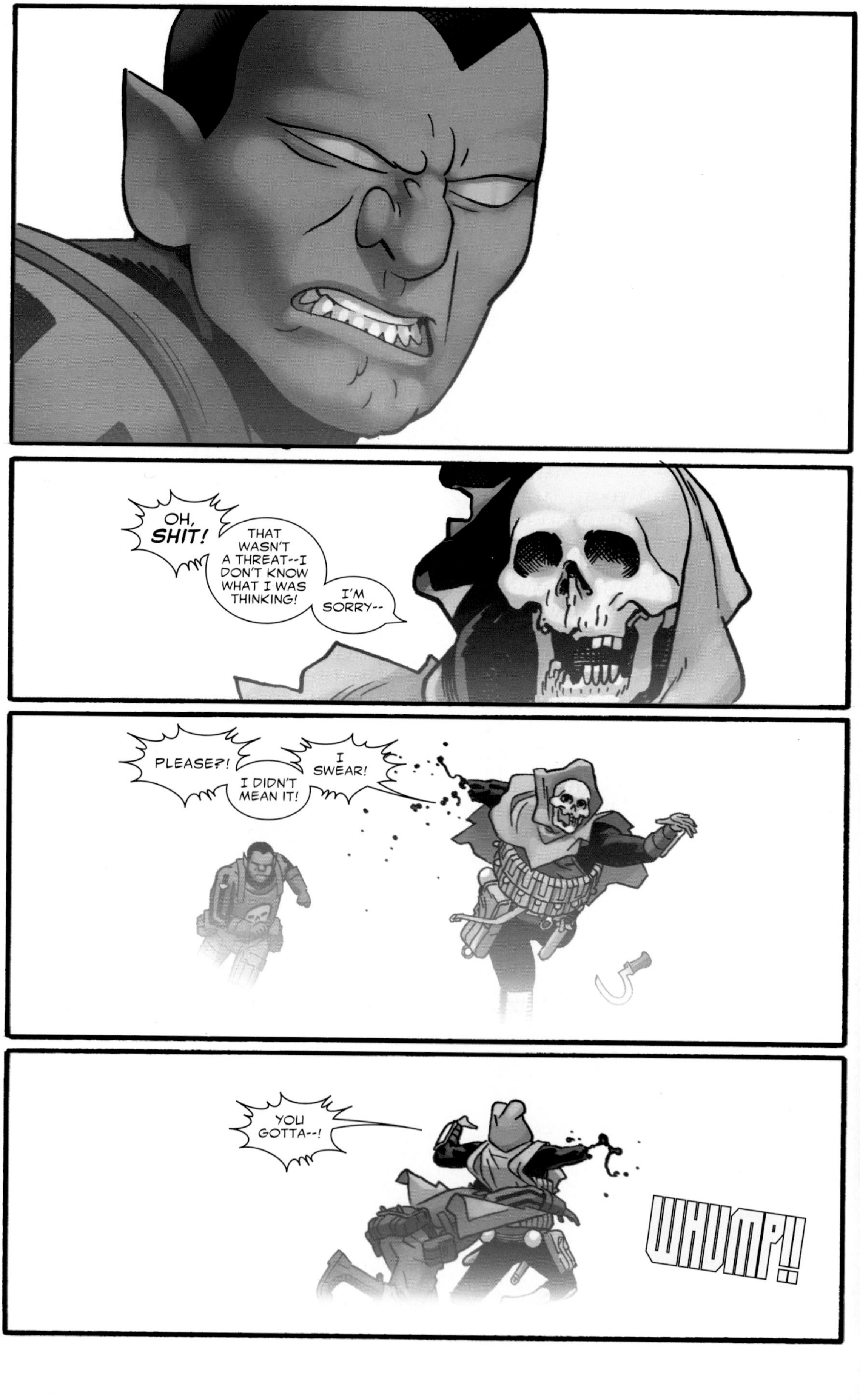
OH, SHIT!
THAT WASN'T A THREAT--I DON'T KNOW WHAT I WAS THINKING!
I'M SORRY--
PLEASE?!
I DIDN'T MEAN IT!
I SWEAR!
YOU GOTTA--!
WHUMP!!

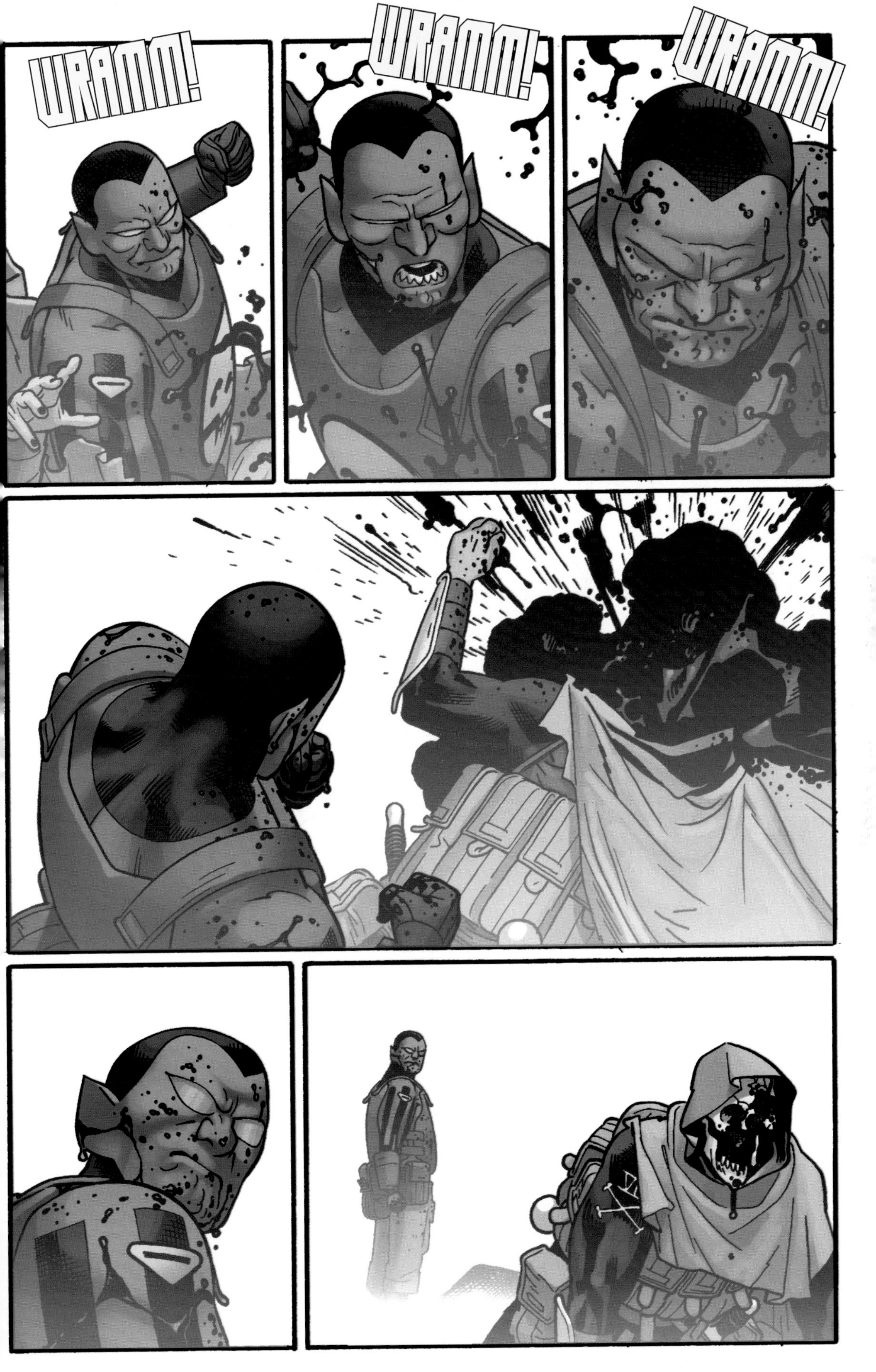
WRAMM!
WRAMM!
WRAMM!

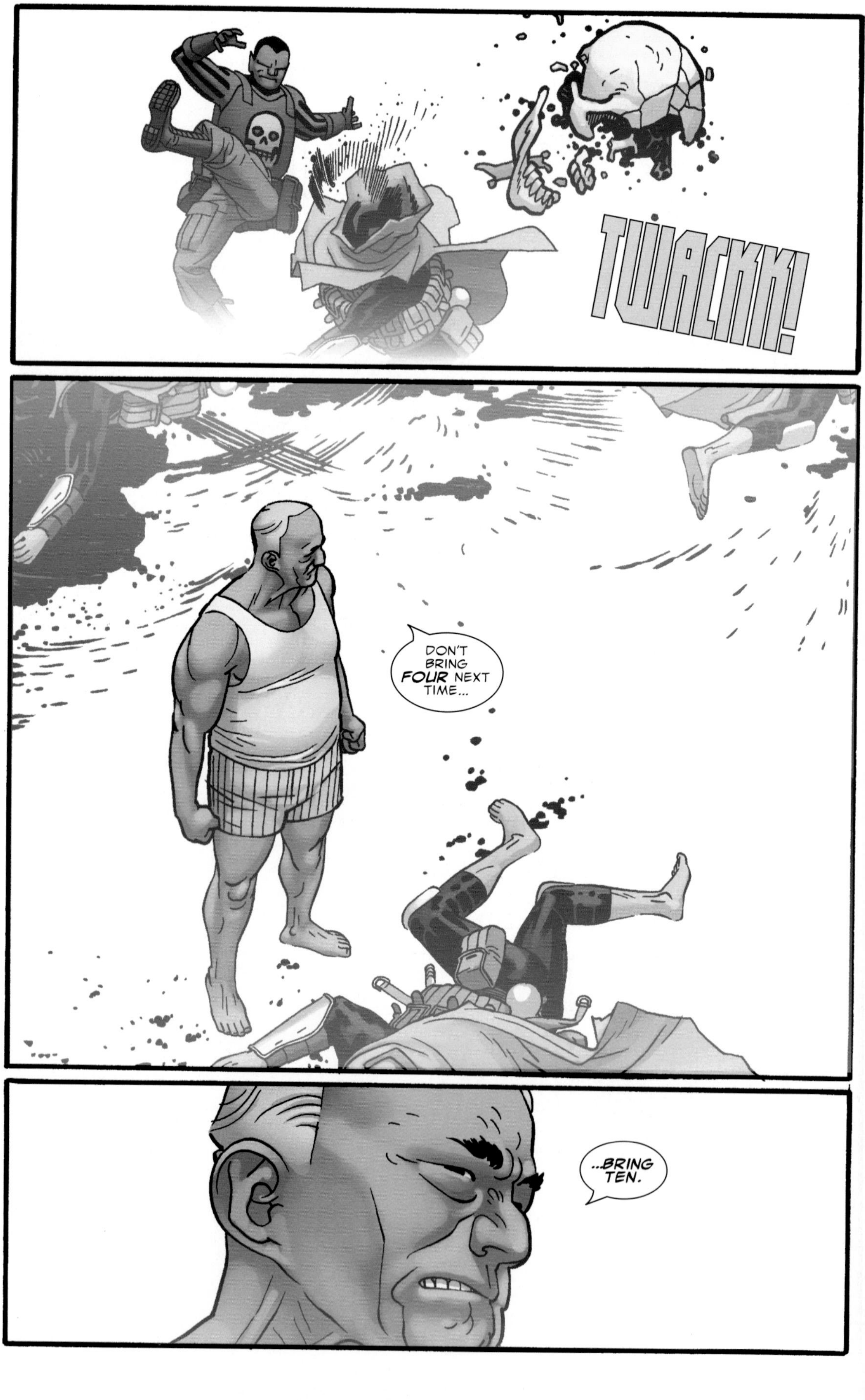
TWACKK!
DON'T BRING FOUR NEXT TIME...
...BRING TEN.

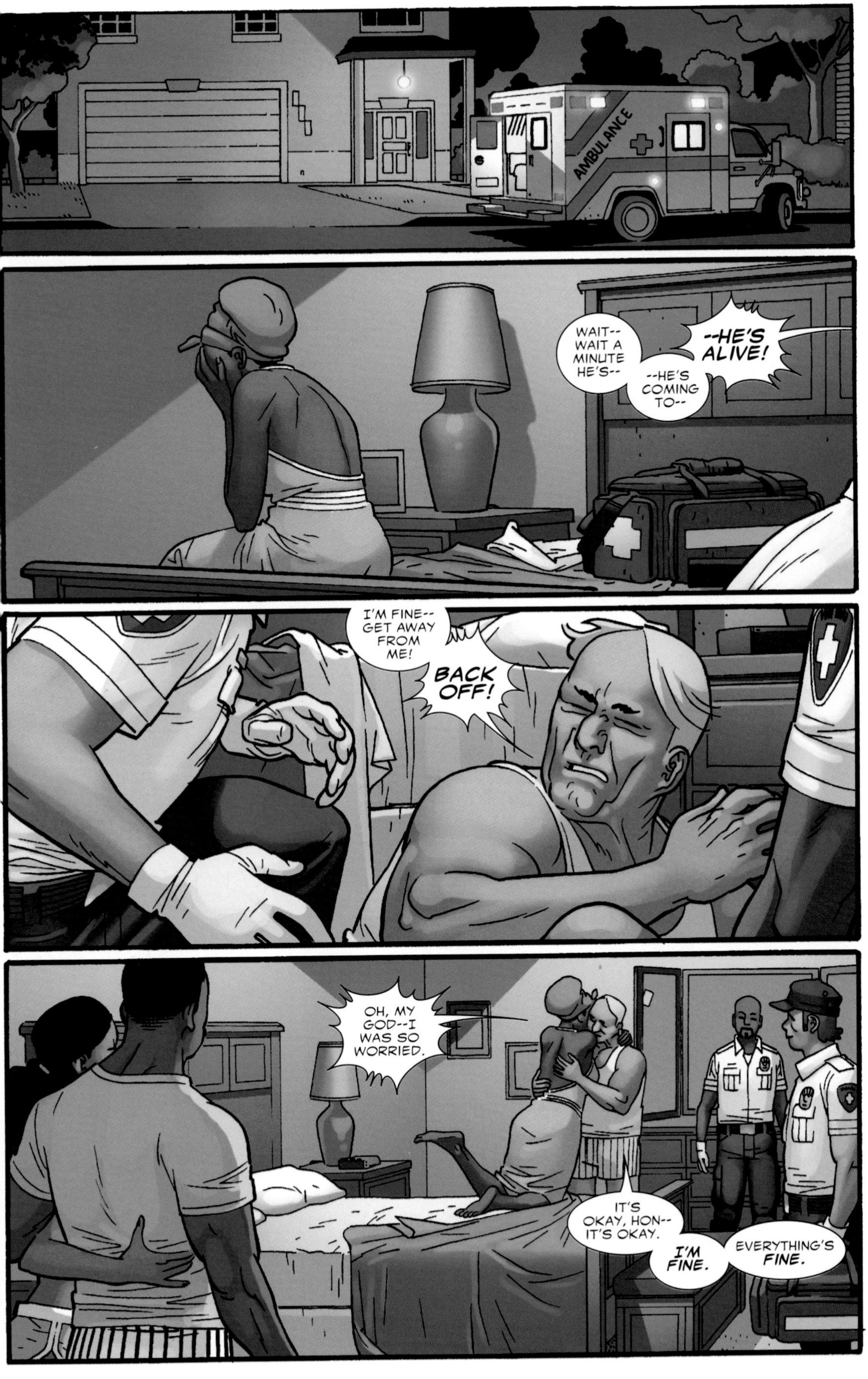
AMBULANCE
WAIT-- WAIT A MINUTE HE'S--
--HE'S COMING TO--
--HE'S ALIVE!
I'M FINE-- GET AWAY FROM ME!
BACK OFF!
OH, MY GOD--I WAS SO WORRIED.
IT'S OKAY, HON-- IT'S OKAY.
I'M FINE.
EVERYTHING'S FINE.

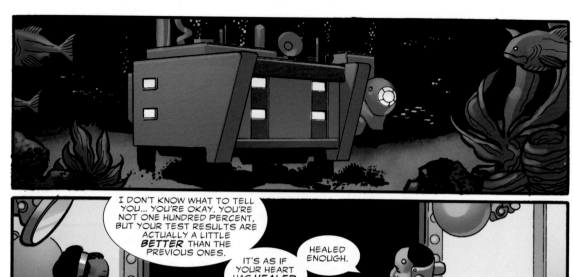

I DON'T KNOW WHAT TO TELL YOU... YOU'RE OKAY. YOU'RE NOT ONE HUNDRED PERCENT, BUT YOUR TEST RESULTS ARE ACTUALLY A LITTLE *BETTER* THAN THE PREVIOUS ONES.

IT'S AS IF YOUR HEART HAS *HEALED* JUST A BIT.

HEALED ENOUGH.

HM.

YOU'VE GOT ANOTHER CHANCE, DEAR.

I THINK YOU MAY HAVE A NEW SUPER-POWER.

I'VE NEVER SEEN ANYTHING LIKE THIS. SOMEONE YOUR AGE, AFTER *THREE* HEART ATTACKS...

ANOTHER CHANCE...

CHANCE TO MAKE THINGS RIGHT...

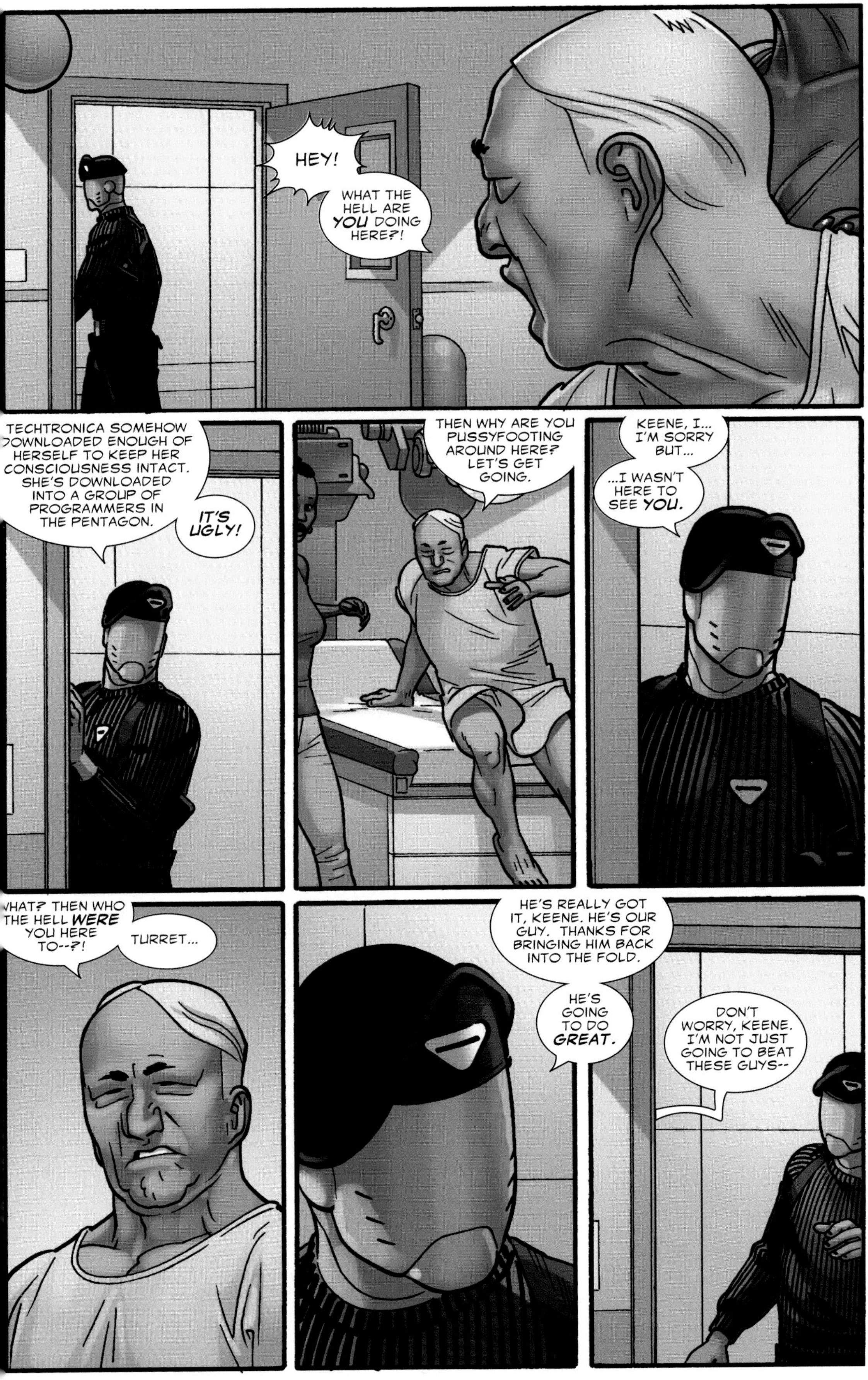
HEY!
WHAT THE HELL ARE YOU DOING HERE?!
TECHTRONICA SOMEHOW DOWNLOADED ENOUGH OF HERSELF TO KEEP HER CONSCIOUSNESS INTACT. SHE'S DOWNLOADED INTO A GROUP OF PROGRAMMERS IN THE PENTAGON.
IT'S UGLY!
THEN WHY ARE YOU PUSSYFOOTING AROUND HERE? LET'S GET GOING.
KEENE, I... I'M SORRY BUT...
...I WASN'T HERE TO SEE YOU.
WHAT? THEN WHO THE HELL WERE YOU HERE TO--?!
TURRET...
HE'S REALLY GOT IT, KEENE. HE'S OUR GUY. THANKS FOR BRINGING HIM BACK INTO THE FOLD.
HE'S GOING TO DO GREAT.
DON'T WORRY, KEENE. I'M NOT JUST GOING TO BEAT THESE GUYS--

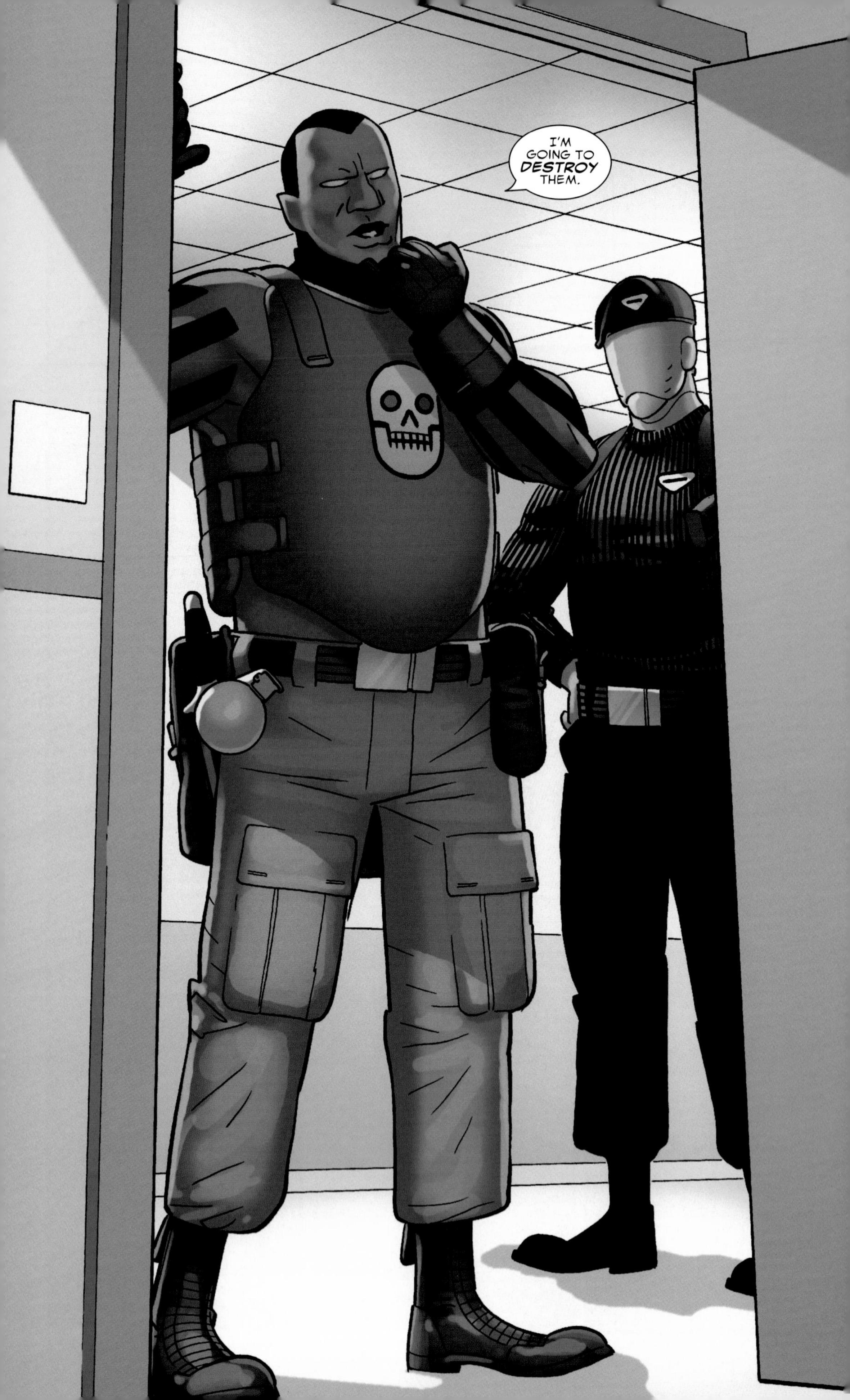
I'M GOING TO **DESTROY** THEM.

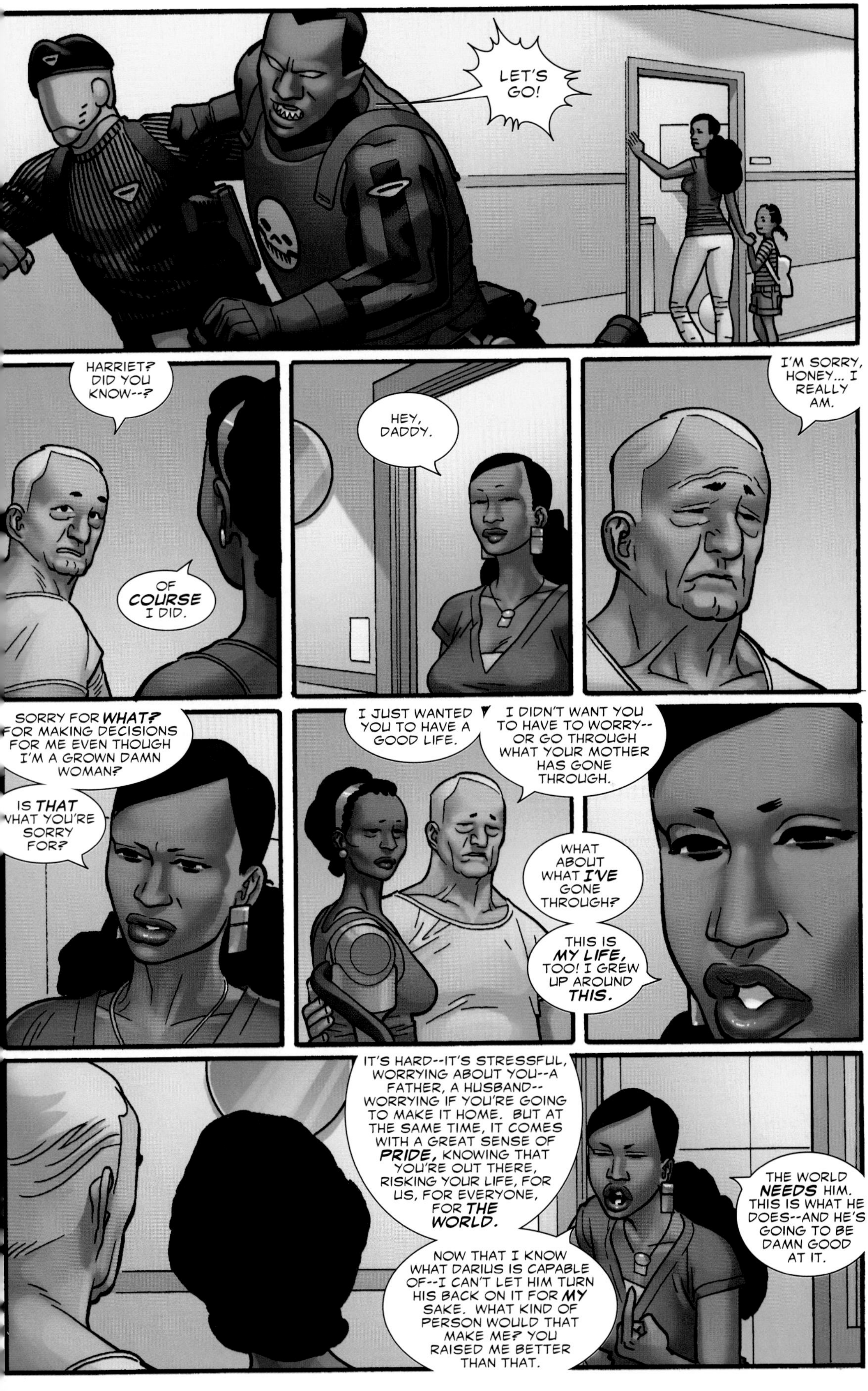
LET'S GO!
HARRIET? DID YOU KNOW--?
OF COURSE I DID.
HEY, DADDY.
I'M SORRY, HONEY... I REALLY AM.
SORRY FOR WHAT? FOR MAKING DECISIONS FOR ME EVEN THOUGH I'M A GROWN DAMN WOMAN?
IS THAT WHAT YOU'RE SORRY FOR?
I JUST WANTED YOU TO HAVE A GOOD LIFE.
I DIDN'T WANT YOU TO HAVE TO WORRY--OR GO THROUGH WHAT YOUR MOTHER HAS GONE THROUGH.
WHAT ABOUT WHAT I'VE GONE THROUGH?
THIS IS MY LIFE, TOO! I GREW UP AROUND THIS.
IT'S HARD--IT'S STRESSFUL, WORRYING ABOUT YOU--A FATHER, A HUSBAND--WORRYING IF YOU'RE GOING TO MAKE IT HOME. BUT AT THE SAME TIME, IT COMES WITH A GREAT SENSE OF PRIDE, KNOWING THAT YOU'RE OUT THERE, RISKING YOUR LIFE, FOR US, FOR EVERYONE, FOR THE WORLD.
NOW THAT I KNOW WHAT DARIUS IS CAPABLE OF--I CAN'T LET HIM TURN HIS BACK ON IT FOR MY SAKE. WHAT KIND OF PERSON WOULD THAT MAKE ME? YOU RAISED ME BETTER THAN THAT.
THE WORLD NEEDS HIM. THIS IS WHAT HE DOES--AND HE'S GOING TO BE DAMN GOOD AT IT.

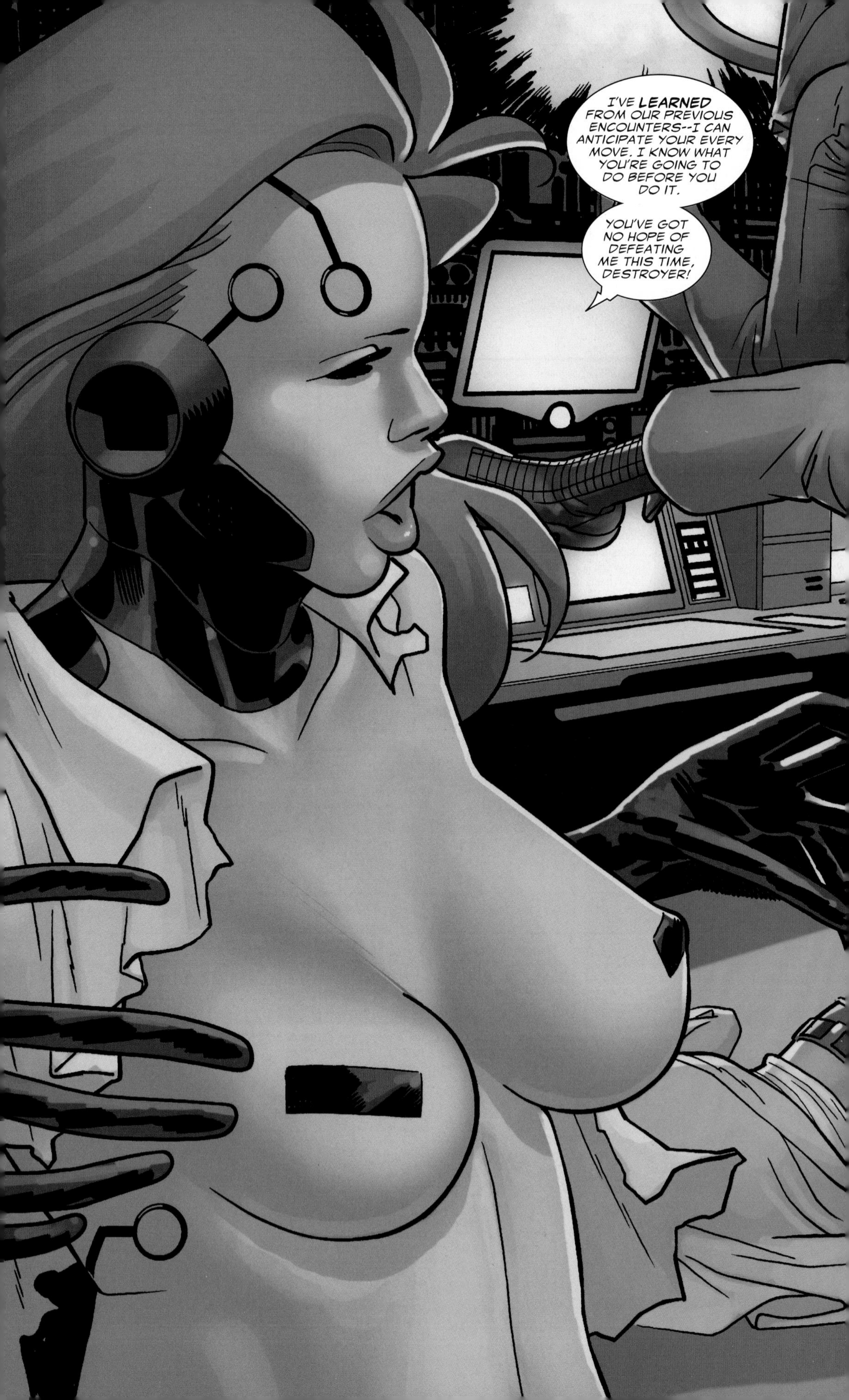
I'VE **LEARNED** FROM OUR PREVIOUS ENCOUNTERS--I CAN ANTICIPATE YOUR EVERY MOVE. I KNOW WHAT YOU'RE GOING TO DO BEFORE YOU DO IT.
YOU'VE GOT NO HOPE OF DEFEATING ME THIS TIME, DESTROYER!

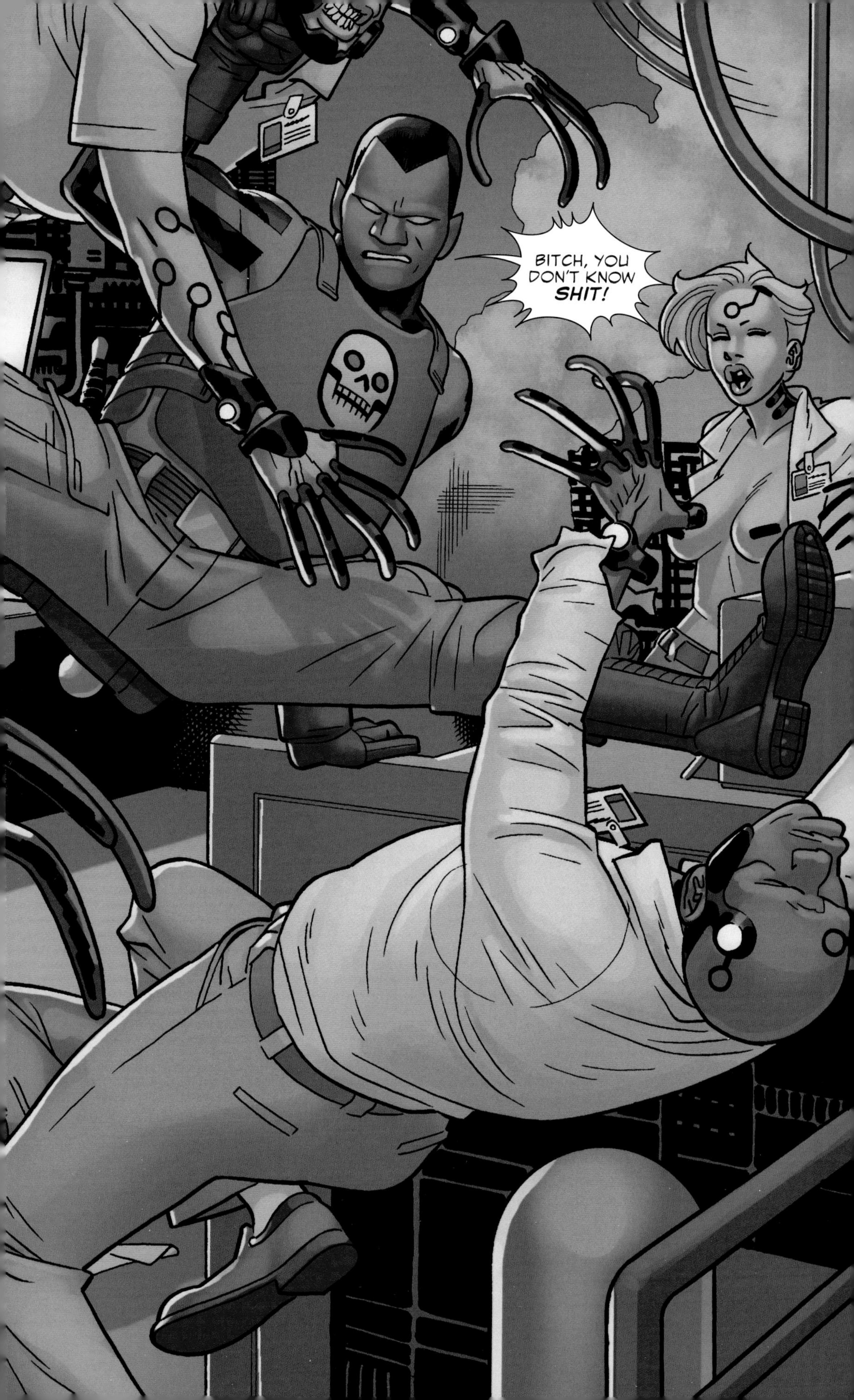
BITCH, YOU DON'T KNOW SHIT!

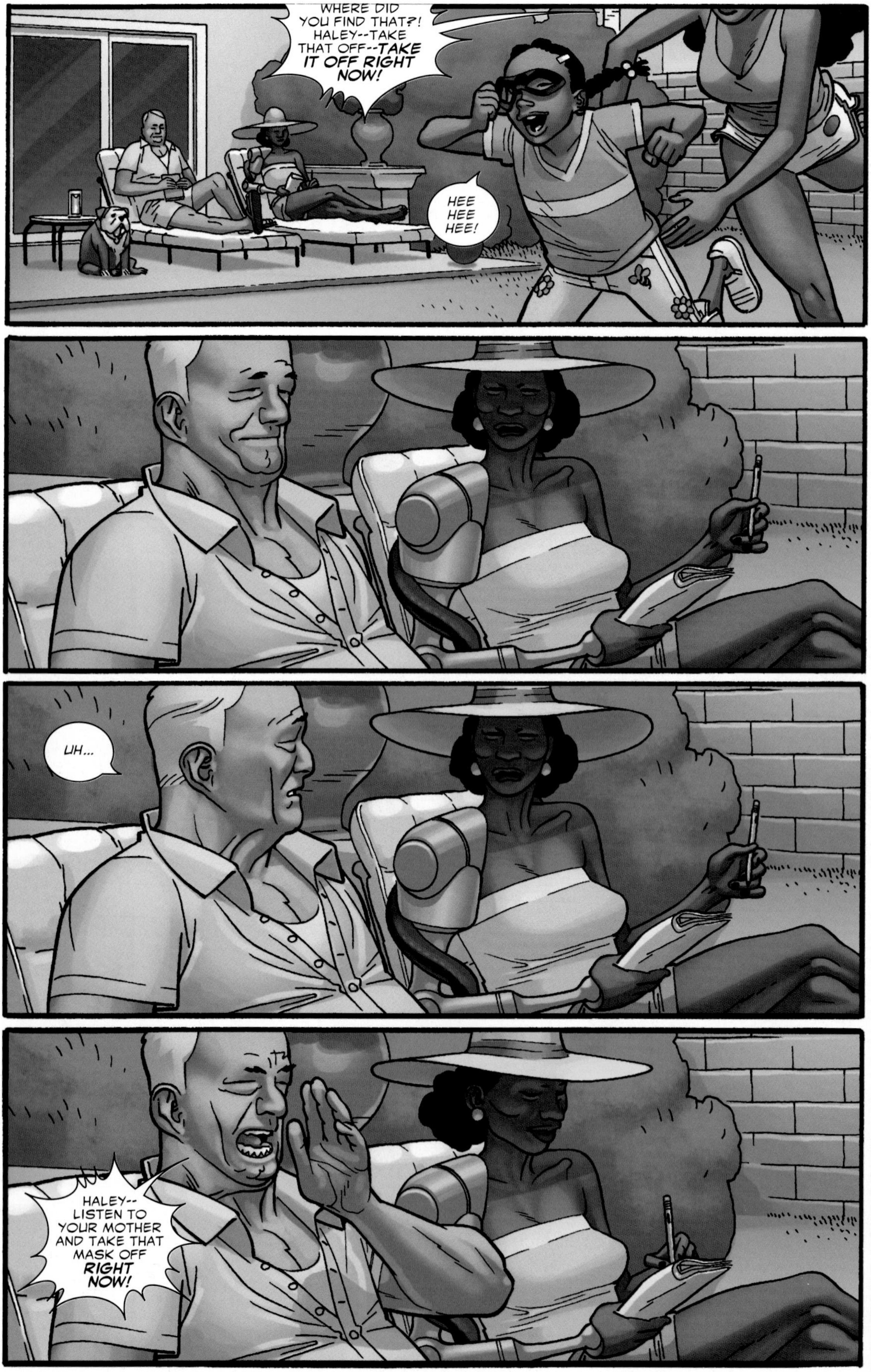

WHERE DID YOU FIND THAT?! HALEY--TAKE THAT OFF--TAKE IT OFF RIGHT NOW!
HEE HEE HEE!
UH...
HALEY-- LISTEN TO YOUR MOTHER AND TAKE THAT MASK OFF RIGHT NOW!